Bomber Crew Morale in WW2

Bomber Crew Morale in WW2

How Bomber Command's Airmen Faced Terrible Odds in the Second World War

Peter Croft

First published in Great Britain in 2025 by
Air World Books
An imprint of
Pen & Sword Books Ltd
Yorkshire - Philadelphia

Copyright © Peter Croft

ISBN: 978 1 03613 144 9

The right of the Peter Croft to be identified as author of this work has been asserted by him in accordance with the Copyright, Designs and Patents Act 1988.

A CIP catalogue record for this book is available from the British Library
All rights reserved.

All rights reserved. No part of this book may be reproduced, transmitted, downloaded, decompiled or reverse engineered in any form or by any means, electronic or mechanical including photocopying, recording or by any information storage and retrieval system, without permission from the Publisher in writing. No part of this book may be used or reproduced in any manner for the purpose of training artificial intelligence technologies or systems.

Typeset in INDIA by IMPEC eSolutions
Printed and bound in the UK by CPI Group (UK) Ltd, Croydon, CR0 4YY.

The Publisher's authorised representative in the EU for product safety is Authorised Rep Compliance Ltd., Ground Floor, 71 Lower Baggot Street, Dublin D02 P593, Ireland.
www.arccompliance.com

For a complete list of Pen & Sword titles please contact:

PEN & SWORD BOOKS LTD
47 Church Street, Barnsley, South Yorkshire, S70 2AS, UK.
E-mail: enquiries@pen-and-sword.co.uk
Website: www.pen-and-sword.co.uk

or

PEN AND SWORD BOOKS,
1950 Lawrence Road, Havertown, PA 19083, USA
E-mail: Uspen-and-sword@casematepublishers.com
Website: www.penandswordbooks.com

Contents

Glossary of Chapter Headings, as Defined in *A Dictionary of RAF Slang* by Eric Partridge — vii

List of Illustrations — ix

Initialisms and Abbreviations — xi

Senior Bomber Command and Air Ministry Personnel, Whose Memoranda and Minutes Affected the Lives of Aircrew — xiii

Acknowledgements — xv

Foreword — xvii

Introduction — xxi

Chapter 1	The Zeitgeist	1
Chapter 2	Volunteers	9
Chapter 3	A Bomber Type: Selection and Training	15
Chapter 4	The Crew	29
Chapter 5	The Squadron	40
Chapter 6	The Bomber Station	44
Chapter 7	Collecting a Gong: Incentives	59
Chapter 8	Ringmasters: Leadership	66
Chapter 9	Bags of Bull: Discipline	73
Chapter 10	Are You Happy in Your Work?: Humour and Argot	80
Chapter 11	Bus Drivers: The Tour	85
Chapter 12	There's No Future in It: Combat	99

Chapter 13	Newton Got Him: Occupational Hazards	115
Chapter 14	Bang On!: Bombing Results	135
Chapter 15	Sex-Appeal Bombing: Ethics	149
Chapter 16	Teased Out: Flying Stress	155
Chapter 17	Frozen on the Stick: Waverers	162
Chapter 18	Life With the Lions: Nine Months in the Life of 427 (RCAF) Squadron	172

Conclusion: A Matter of Life and Death	184
Endnotes	188
Bibliography	223
Index	233

Glossary of Chapter Headings, as Defined in *A Dictionary of RAF Slang* by Eric Partridge

Are you happy in your work? (Chapter 10): A catch-phrase addressed ironically or facetiously to a serviceman (or woman) performing some heavy or disagreeable or notoriously unsuitable task.

A type (Chapter 3): A person. e.g., 'He's a good type.'

Bags of (Chapter 9): Very much of; a great amount of. Especially in *bags of bull*, excessive spit-and-polish and/or parades, inspections and exasperating details and petty duties, and *bags of panic*, a pronounced state of nervousness or 'dithers'.

Bang on! (Chapter 14): All right! Correct! In Bomber Command: from a bomb dropped exactly on the target.

Bus driver (Chapter 11): A bomber pilot. He often travels the same route.

Collecting a gong (Chapter 7): To be awarded a decoration.

Frozen on the stick (Chapter 17): Paralysed with fear.

Newton got him (Chapter 13): He crashed. The force of gravity, always tending to bring a 'plane to earth. From Isaac Newton, the discoverer of the laws of gravity.

Ringmaster (Chapter 8): A squadron leader who actually leads a squadron in the air. From the circus, where the ringmaster superintends the performing animals.

Sex-appeal bombing (Chapter 15): The bombing of museums, schools, hospitals – indeed, of civilians in general.

Teased out (Chapter 16): Exhausted, or at least very tired; after a long duty on patrol or raid. Frayed nerves.

There's no future in it (Chapter 12): A catch-phrase that, among aircrews, is applied to a dangerous sortie, or attack. Sometimes means no more than that the work or undertaking is a thankless one.

List of Illustrations

1. Flight Sergeant Cadet J. Manton after his first flight, in an Oxford Trainer, at an OTU. (Courtesy of Imperial War Museum CH13877)
2. Halifax crews of 35 Squadron await transport to their aircraft at Linton-on-Ouse, Yorkshire. (Courtesy of Imperial War Museum D6034)
3. Bomber crews mount the flatbed of a dispersal truck to be transported to their aircraft for an operation. (Courtesy of Imperial War Museum D4751)
4. A Lancaster crew. (Courtesy of Imperial War Museum CH7487)
5. Aircrew relaxing in the Mess. (Courtesy of Imperial War Museum CH5654)
6. In the Sergeants' Mess. (Courtesy of Imperial War Museum CH7378)
7. On a Halifax bomber station. (Source: Alamy)
8. Hammersmith Palais de Danse, London, 1941. (Courtesy of Imperial War Museum D2975)
9. P/O. Wilkerson of No.35 Squadron with a WAAF officer at an all ranks dance at Linton-on-Ouse, Yorkshire. (Courtesy of Imperial War Museum D6057)
10. 'Scrubbed'. The last minute cancellation of an operation. (Courtesy of 50 and 61 Squadrons Association)
11. Sgt. G. Cameron, the pilot of Handley Page Halifax B Mark II, HR837 'NP-F' of No. 158 Squadron RAF, poses with two of his crew amidst the damage caused when it was hit by a falling bomb from another aircraft while raiding Cologne on the night of 28/29 June 1943. (Courtesy of Imperial War Museum CE84)
12. East Wretham, Norfolk. Two crew members examine the rear of their aircraft, a Lancaster of 115 Squadron, where the rear turret, complete with its unfortunate gunner, was sheared off by bombs dropped from an

aircraft above during a raid on Cologne on the night of 28/29 June 1943. (Courtesy of Imperial War Museum CE79)

13. Sergeant J.B. Mallett, Sergeant H.H. Turkentine and Sergeant R.H.P. Roberts, flight engineer, bomb-aimer and rear gunner respectively of a Lancaster of 57 Squadron at breakfast in the canteen at Scampton after an operation. (Courtesy of Imperial War Museum CH8806)
14. F/O. R.G. Hayes (left) and Flight Lieutenant J. Gordon, navigator and pilot respectively of a De Havilland Mosquito B Mark 1V of No. 105 Squadron RAF, listen intently during a briefing for a night raid on Berlin in the Operations Room at Marham, Norfolk. (Courtesy of Imperial War Museum CH18010)
15. A WAAF intelligence officer, Section Officer P. Duncalfe, questions the pilot, Warrant Officer H. Blunt (to her left), and crew of Avro Lancaster B Mark III, JB362 'EA-D' ("D" for "Donald") of No. 49 Squadron RAF. (Courtesy of Imperial War Museum CH18658)
16. Flight Lieutenant William Reid VC. (Courtesy of Imperial War Museum CHP794)
17. Flying Officer Michael Seamer Allen DFC. F/O. Allen was a Beaufighter navigator with 141 Squadron. (Courtesy of Imperial War Museum CH11449)
18. Wing Commander A.J. (Jim) Wright DFC. 61 Squadron and 630 Squadron navigator. (Courtesy of 50 and 61 Squadrons Association)
19. Flying Officer Pierre Richard DFC. F/O. Richard was a Mosquito navigator with 571 Squadron. (Courtesy of Stephen Richard)
20. George 'Johnny' Johnson MBE, DFM. Bomb aimer. Dambuster. (Courtesy of Sue Bartlam)
21. Wing Commander Dudley Burnside and his Wellington crew of 427 (RCAF) Squadron at Croft, Lincolnshire. (Courtesy of RAF Memorial Flight Club)
22. George Vandekerckhove DFC. (Courtesy of Canadian Warplane Heritage Museum)
23. Pilot Officer George Vandekerckhove DFC with his Halifax crew and ground crew. (Courtesy of Michel Becker, Aircrew Remembered)
24. Per Ardua ad Astra. Another op done. A Lancaster crew of 50 Squadron at RAF Swinderby. (Courtesy of 50 and 61 Squadrons Association)

Initialisms and Abbreviations

Initialisms

ACAS	Assistant Chief of Air Staff
ACM	Air Chief Marshal
AM	Air Marshal
AMP	Air Member for Personnel
AMSO	Air Member for Supply and Organisation
AMT	Air Member for Training
AOT	Air Officer Training
AVM	Air Vice Marshal
CAS	Chief of Air Staff
C-in-C	Commander-in-Chief
CO	Commanding Officer
DCAS	Deputy Chief of Air Staff
DFC	Distinguished Flying Cross
DFM	Distinguished Flying Medal
DGMS	Director General Medical Services
DGPS	Director General Procurement Support
DSO	Distinguished Service Order
EATS	Empire Air Training Scheme
FIDO	Fog Investigation and Dispersal Operation
FPRC	Flying Personnel Research Committee
HCU	Heavy Conversion Unit
LMF	Lacking Moral Fibre
MO	Medical Officer
NCO	Non-Commissioned Officer
OTU	Operational Training Unit

PFF	Pathfinder Force
RAF	Royal Air Force
RCAF	Royal Canadian Air Force
RFC	Royal Flying Corps
SASO	Senior Air Staff Officer
SOE	Special Operations Executive
VCAS	Vice Chief of Air Staff
WAAF	Women's Auxiliary Air Force

Abbreviations

a/c	Aircraft
e/a	Enemy aircraft
F/Lt.	Flight Lieutenant
F/O.	Flying Officer
I.G.	Inspector General of the RAF
M.U.	Mid-Upper Gunner
P/O.	Pilot Officer
S/L	Searchlight
TI	Target indicator
u/s	Useless
Wop/Ag.	Wireless Operator/Air Gunner
W/Cmdr.	Wing Commander
W/O.	Warrant Officer

Senior Bomber Command and Air Ministry Personnel, Whose Memoranda and Minutes Affected the Lives of Aircrew

Babington, Air Marshal Philip, Air Member for Personnel

Babington, John Tremayne, AOC Technical Training Command 1942, then C-in-C Flying Training Command from August 1944.

Baldwin, Air Marshal Jack, AOC 3 Group 1942

Balfour, H.H., Under Secretary of State for Air

Bennett, Air Vice Marshal Donald, AOC 8 Group (Pathfinders)

Bottomley, Air Chief Marshal Sir Norman, SASO Bomber Command HQ 1938-1940, AOC 5 Group November 1940, Deputy Chief of Air Staff 1941, ACAS (Operations) 1942, DCAS 1943, ACAS June 1943, C-in-C Bomber Command 1945

Bradley, J.S.T., AMSO

Breadner, Air Marshal Lloyd, RCAF

Bufton, Sydney, Director of Bombing Operations

Capel, Air Vice Marshal Arthur, Air Officer Training

Cochrane, Sir Ralph, AOC 3 Group 1942-1943 and 5 Group 1943-1945

Colyer, Air Vice Marshal Douglas, ACAS (Policy) 1944

Courtney, Air Chief Marshal Sir Christopher, AMSO

Curtis, Air Vice Marshal Wilfred, RCAF

Drummond, Air Marshal Sir Peter, AMT March 1945

Evill, Air Chief Marshal Sir Douglas, VCAS 1943-1946

Foster, Air Vice Marshal F. MacNeece, AOC 6 Group

Freeman, Air Chief Marshal Sir Wilfred, VCAS August and October 1942

Garrod, Air Marshal A.G.R., AMT from August 1942

Harris, Air Marshal Sir Arthur, C-in-C Bomber Command March 1942-1945

Joubert, Air Chief Marshal Sir Philip, Inspector General of the RAF from 1943

Ludlow-Hewitt, Air Chief Marshal Sir Edgar, Inspector General RAF from August 1942

Medhurst, Air Chief Marshal Sir Charles, VCAS 1942

Newall, Air Chief Marshal Sir Cyril, CAS 1937-1940

Oxland, Air Vice Marshal Robert, AOC 1 Group 1940-1943

Peirse, Air Chief Marshal Sir Richard, C-in-C Bomber Command 1940-January 1942

Portal, Marshal of the RAF Sir Charles, C-in-C Bomber Command, then CAS from 1940

Sandford, Folliott, Air Council, November 1944-1945

Satterly, Air Vice Marshal Harold, AOC 5 Group

Saundby, Air Marshal Sir Robert, SASO to Sir Arthur Harris

Sinclair, Sir Archibald, Secretary of State for Air 1940-1945

Slessor, Air Marshal Sir John, AOC 5 Group 1941

Sutton, Air Marshal Bertine, Commandant of the Staff College August 1942, then Air Member for Personnel 1943 to 1945

Symonds, Air Vice Marshal Sir Charles

Whittingham, H.E., DGMS Director General Medical Services February 1944

Williams, Air Marshal Thomas M., ACAS

Wood, Sir Kingsley, Secretary of State for Air 1938-1940

Acknowledgements

I expressed my gratitude to the following in 2000, when I completed my Masters degree. I repeat it here:

Linda Anderson, Language and Humanities Centre, University of Edinburgh, for the kind loan of a collection of letters which belonged to her uncle Sergeant Morrison. Fiona Carmichael and her staff of the Language and Humanities Centre, University of Edinburgh, for their assistance with my then rudimentary word processing skills.

The late Douglas Ratcliffe of the Bomber Command Association, who made it possible for me to contact a dozen members of the Association. I expressed my gratitude to the veterans themselves, who generously gave their time to complete my questionnaire in great detail. I write in the foreword to this work that I will not be using their words verbatim, which was my intention, before belatedly remembering that I had expressly informed them that their contributions were for the purposes of my dissertation only and not for publication. I intend to honour that promise. For his advice on this ethical dilemma I thank Alex, at the School of History, Classics and Archaeology, The University of Edinburgh. I was grateful to Professor Jeremy Crang and the late Dr. Paul Addison, my supervisors, who guided my dissertation in the right direction.

In relation to my recent research I wish to thank The British Library Board, All Rights Reserved. With thanks to the British Newspaper Archive for allowing the use of newspaper extracts. Thank you to the staff of the Reading Room at the Imperial War Museum and for their kind permission to use documents and photographs in this work. Particular thanks to Andrew Webb of the IWM for assistance with photographs. Thanks also to the Reading Room staff at The National Archives, the RAF Museum, Hendon and the National Library of Scotland.

I am grateful to Neil Wright for permission to include from my 2000 questionnaire the words of his father Wing Commander A.J. (Jim) Wright DFC and to Mike Connock, of 50 and 61 Squadrons Association, for permission to include the photograph of Wing Commander Wright. To Mike Connock thanks also for permission to use the photographs of 50 Squadron crews. I also thank the RAF Memorial Flight Club, Battle of Britain Memorial Flight, for permission to include the photograph of Group Captain Dudley Burnside DSO, OBE, DFC and his crew. Sue Bartlam, daughter of George 'Johnny' Johnson MBE, DFM, kindly gave permission for me to use the photograph of her father. Thanks to Ralph Snape of Aircrew Remembered, who passed on my request to Michel Becker, who, in turn, kindly gave permission to use the image of P/O. George Vandekerckhove and crew. Thanks to Malcolm Ramsay of the Canadian Warplane Heritage Museum for the image of George Vandekerckhove. Thanks to my good friend and erstwhile teaching colleague Stephen Richard for permission to use extracts from the audiotape of his father Pierre Richard DFC and for his father's photograph. My good friend Nick Brown, with whom I shared many experiences – some rewarding and some, shall we say, challenging – in our teaching careers, came to the rescue with his computer expertise, giving up his valuable time to help, for which I thank him. I thank William Austin for his computer assistance; his calm demeanour a vivid contrast to the panic displayed by Yours Truly when computer gremlins got to work.

John Grehan of Pen & Sword Books suggested that I write this book. I was far from sure that I wanted to revisit my old Masters dissertation but it was his prompting which spurred me on. I am grateful to him.

For your constant support and encouragement, and for the kind-hearted altruism which informs everything you do, thank you Janet.

Foreword

The genesis of this work is to be found in the degree course for which I studied. During the academic year 1999–2000 I was engaged in research for a Masters degree in Second World War Studies at the University of Edinburgh. My chosen subject was the war in the air and my Masters dissertation would eventually have the title *Morale in RAF Bomber Command Aircrew in Britain, 1939 – 1945*.

As part of my research I consulted the then secretary of the Bomber Command Association, Douglas Ratcliffe, who kindly sent questionnaires which I had compiled to twenty veterans of Bomber Command. Twelve responded. I had intended that their contributions would form the basis of this book, quoted verbatim. Unfortunately, I realised belatedly that I would be breaking a promise I made to them that their words were only intended for my dissertation and would not be published. They are no longer with us and I cannot ask their permission now. I regret depriving the reader of the first-hand insight into life in Bomber Command provided by the twelve. There is one exception: Wing Commander Jim Wright. His son Neil kindly gave permission for his father's words to be included. There was a certain uniformity in the responses to my questionnaire, on all aspects of life in Bomber Command, and I ask the reader to accept that Jim Wright's thoughts will serve to represent the thoughts of them all. Their service records are in the public domain and are therefore included below, in order to represent the many thousands of their fellow airmen. The twelve were:

Michael Allen DFC Michael Allen was a Beaufighter navigator, so his flying career deviated from the general pattern of heavy bomber crew experiences. His first posting was to 29 Squadron, Fighter Command, at West Malling, Kent in September 1941. Still with Fighter Command, he was transferred to 1455 Flight at Tangmere, West Sussex and then to 141 Squadron at Ford,

Sussex. Still with 141 Squadron, but now part of Bomber Command as a Bomber Support Development Unit, he returned to 141 Fighter Command, based at Wittering, Cambridgeshire.

His career with 141 Bomber Command took him to West Raynham, Foulsham and Swanton Morley, all in Norfolk, and then back to West Raynham. His operational record consisted of forty-nine defensive night patrols, fifty-six offensive night sorties, three anti-diver (V1) patrols and three air-sea rescue searches. His pilot throughout was Harry White, later to become Air Commodore H.E. White. Michael Allen recounted his experiences in the autobiography *Pursuit Through Darkened Skies*.

Group Captain Dudley Burnside DSO, OBE, DFC joined the RAF in 1935 and saw service on the North-West Frontier in India before taking command of 427 (RCAF) Squadron in 1942 as wing commander and 195 Squadron in 1943 as a group captain. He was stationed at Croft, Lincolnshire; Leeming, North Yorkshire and Wratting Common, Suffolk. He completed thirty-five operations.

Maxwell Chivers DFC served with 61 Squadron and was stationed at Syerston, Nottinghamshire and Wymeswold, Leicestershire. He flew on forty operations.

Frank Diamond served with 15 and 571 Squadrons at Mildenhall, Suffolk and Oakington, Cambridgeshire respectively. His operational record totals seventy-two.

Brian Edward Barton Harris DFC Brian Harris served as a navigator in XV and 627 Squadrons. His stations were Bourn, Cambridgeshire and Woodhall Spa, Lincolnshire. He completed 66 operations.

Harry LeMarchant served with 57, 630 and 97 (Pathfinder Force) Squadrons, being stationed respectively at Scampton, East Kirkby, and Coningsby, all in Lincolnshire. He completed thirty-three operations in 1942, 1943 and 1945.

Foreword xix

Reg Lewis's RAF service began on 17 February 1941. From 26 OTU Wing he went, as a navigator to 1657 Heavy Conversion Unit. He served with XV Squadron, 214 Squadron and 138 (Special Duties) Squadron, stationed respectively at Bourn, Cambridgeshire, Chedburgh, Suffolk and Tempsford, Bedfordshire. He completed a total of forty-five operations, including, while at Tempsford, conveyance of SOE agents and supplies to Europe. He evaded capture in France when his aircraft went down in 1944.

Charles Lofthouse served with 149 and 7 Squadrons. He was stationed at Mildenhall and Lakenheath, Suffolk and Oakington, Cambridgeshire. He completed forty-four operations.

Gordon Herbert Mellor served with 103 Squadron at Elsham Wolds, Lincolnshire. He had done seventeen operations when his plane was shot down near Maastricht. He evaded capture and made his way to Gibraltar via occupied Belgium and France, on to Spain and then home.

Douglas Newham served with 150 Squadron and 10 Squadron. He was stationed at Kirmington, Lincolnshire; Blida, Algeria; Melbourne, Yorkshire; Meiktila, Burma. He completed sixty-two operations as a navigator/bomb aimer.

Graham King Smith DFM was a pre-war pilot who served with 3 Squadron in 1937 at RAF Kenley, a suburb of Croydon; 115 Squadron at Marham, Norfolk from 1938 to November 1940; 37 Squadron at Shallufa, Egypt in 1941 and 97 (Pathfinder Force) Squadron at Bourn, Cambridgeshire in 1943. He completed 'over ninety' operations.

Wing Commander A.J. (Jim) Wright DFC served with 61 Squadron at Syerston from 10 September to 22 October 1943, then 630 squadron at East Kirkby from 17 December 1943 to 23 May 1944.

In addition, I had the privilege of meeting **Bill Reid VC**, to whom a questionnaire had been sent but was not returned to me completed. Mr. Reid later contacted me and invited me to his home in Crieff, where we ran through the questions informally. Naturally, as a holder of the Victoria Cross, Mr. Reid was interviewed many times and recollections from one of those interviews have been incorporated in this work. He served with 61 and 617 (Dambusters) Squadrons. It was with the former that he won the Victoria Cross (Dusseldorf, 3/4 November 1943) and with the latter that his aircraft was hit by 'friendly' bombs (Rilly-la-Montagne, 31 July 1944). He became a POW.

Mr. Reid, the only one of my respondents whom I met in person, was the same modest, unassuming man I had first seen in the episode on the bombing campaign in the 1973 landmark series *The World at War,* in which he related the events of the operation for which he was awarded the Victoria Cross. It was not a generation inclined to brag about experiences but I feel sure that my twelve respondents would have displayed the same phlegmatic disposition had I met them.

Many years after my studies I was privileged to meet **George 'Johnny' Johnson,** who was destined to become the last aircrew survivor of the Dambusters Raid. His recollections of training and the Dams Raid, and his thoughts on survival, given in conversation with me, feature briefly in this work. I visited Johnny, first at his home in Torquay and then in Bristol, where, on one occasion, he treated me to dinner. I can only say that dining with the last Dambuster, a true gentleman, was a memorable experience which will always stay with me.

The extraordinary exploits of all these ordinary men should not be forgotten. They provided the inspiration for this book and it is dedicated to them.

At current – rates a Medium or Heavy Bomber Pilot has roughly a 45% chance of surviving his first operational tour. Should he be called upon to do a second operational tour his chances of surviving the two are in the region of 20%.

…….only one crew in every five will in fact survive.

M.S. Laing, Most Secret Minute, Air Ministry, 13 November 1942

*

I am extremely anxious that statistical information relating to the 'chances of survival' of air crews in the various types of operational employment should be confined to the smallest possible number of people … the information can be so easily distorted, and is then so dangerous to morale, that all possible steps must be taken to safeguard it.

Sir Charles Portal, Chief of Air Staff, Most Secret Letter, 24 December 1942

Introduction

There exists a voluminous literature on the subject of the bombing offensive against Germany in the Second World War, addressing every aspect of the campaign. Much attention has been given to the morality of bombing civilians, to the effectiveness of the policy and to the grievous losses sustained by the aircrews. The man with the name most familiar to anyone with an interest in the subject, Sir Arthur Harris, gave his interpretation of events in his own memoir, as did others who experienced the sharp end of war and entered the pantheon of legendary air warriors, such as Guy Gibson and Leonard Cheshire. A plethora of other memoirs of the survivors is available, with graphic accounts of combat and reminiscences of camaraderie. Those men have now, with very few exceptions, gone, passed into history, participants and witnesses to events which shaped their young lives but events which to a young man now are as remote as the Crimean War was to the young men of Bomber Command.

A total of 125,000 aircrew served in RAF Bomber Command during the Second World War. They were all volunteers, highly-trained intelligent young men. 55,573 of them were killed. A 44% casualty rate for killed and 64% for wounded. 'That the majority of aircrew could not fail to be aware of the practical implications of the second figure [64%] only serves to make the first the more remarkable,' observed Dr. David Stafford-Clark, a Bomber Command medical officer.[1]

How did they climb into their aircraft night after night, when it was obvious to them that their chances of survival were so slim? How did they carry on? Well, of course, they had volunteered and were subject to the requirements of military life. Refusing to go on operations was not an option (although it did happen). Once aboard their 'kite', they had to dig deep into their reserves of courage. How was morale sustained in light of these appalling losses?

Introduction xxiii

*

Just five weeks after hostilities began Secretary of State for Air Sir Kingsley Wood assured the public that, 'The spirit and morale of the RAF are splendid. Officers and men are confident they can give a good account of themselves and take heavy toll of enemy. They are inspired by the knowledge that their job is to beat the enemy and to ensure once and for all that aggression and tyranny are ended.'[2] Fine words, but delving into the substance of morale presents difficulties. What is it?

Morale is a nebulous concept. It cannot be measured with accuracy. The Air Ministry had its own definition in 1940:

> Morale …… depends largely upon the individual's possession of those controlling forces which inhibit the free expression of the primitive instinctive tendencies ….. Its essence is to live up to an ideal, to face dangers and difficulties with confidence and tenacity of purpose and to be ready to sacrifice personal interests and safety in the course of duty. It can be fostered by the example of others in the group or unit. Its possession by the leaders will raise the standard of that of the others. Its absence will have a powerful contrary effect. It is more easily maintained in the presence of the leader, or when dangers can be faced in company of others. The greatest strain is placed upon morale when the individual is called upon to bear the strain alone.[3]

'….. Morale itself developed into one of the unique obsessions of the Second World War.'[4] Indeed, perusal of Air Ministry files gives the impression that everything was a 'threat to morale' and that the word itself was invoked at every opportunity to solve every problem or crisis. Morale means different things to different people. However, there are certain constants. The components which comprise good morale are: cheerfulness, belief in a cause, a sense of belonging, unselfishness and patriotism. To these intrinsic qualities can be added: leadership, efficient equipment, comfort, rest and medical care. Finally, perhaps most importantly, trust in the immediate group to which a soldier (or airman) belongs.[5]

How had the morale of Bomber Command fared in the five long years since Sir Kingsley Wood had made his statement? Sir Edgar Ludlow-Hewitt, who had been removed from the position of C-in-C Bomber Command in 1940 and had become one of the two Inspectors General of the RAF (Sir Philip Joubert was the other), came to the conclusion, in 1944, after visiting several stations that, petty complaints aside, morale in the Force was at a healthy level: ' ... with very few exceptions everybody is trying to take their fair share in winning the war.'[6] The Assistant Chief of Air Staff (Policy), Air Marshal Douglas Colyer, reported the Inspector General's findings to the Air Ministry, in a minute which included the following assessment by Ludlow-Hewitt:

> I believe that airmen and airwomen are fundamentally thoroughly sound. Where there is any rot, it is, in my opinion, much more likely to be due to bad organisation and indifferent leadership than to any intrinsic badness in the personnel themselves ……. The greatest danger to Service morale is the importation into the Service of the factory spirit with its suspicions, selfishness and distrust of authority …… Distrust between people is bred in an atmosphere of ignorance of each other. It disappears where there is the mutual understanding which comes of identity of interest.[7]

What were the factors which determined morale and led Ludlow-Hewitt to this conclusion? Two forces were at work: the extrinsic efforts of the Air Ministry to influence and control morale through policy directives and propaganda, and secondly, the intrinsic personal qualities of the aircrews themselves. The RAF Executive recognised its necessity, without actually having the ability to define it categorically. They did, however, place enormous importance on measures designed to sustain morale throughout all stages of an airman's active service. Discipline was the cornerstone of this policy; it was believed that strong, effective discipline created high morale.

Hew Strachan has commented, 'Remarkably little is said in theories of combat motivation about punishment and deterrence.'[8] 'Morale and discipline were so important that nothing too much could be done to achieve satisfactory standards,' was the view, in September 1943, of Vice Chief of Air Staff Sir

Douglas Evill.⁹ It is interesting to note how regularly the words 'discipline' and 'morale' occur in conjunction in Air Ministry files. The deterrent value of LMF (lacking moral fibre) (q.v.) as a means of controlling morale was recognised and became a key component of disciplinary policy.

More tangible extrinsic morale boosters were effective training, provision of reliable equipment and strong leadership. Coupled with these were the *intrinsic* qualities of the aircrews themselves. A strong sense of duty and patriotism guided them. They were drawn from a generation which displayed the qualities of stoicism, modesty, and resolve. They did not wear their emotions on their sleeves. Respect for authority and a sense of duty were imbued in them. When they 'crewed up', the individual efforts of each crew member became a matter of life and death to his colleagues. They relied on each other for their survival. No-one wished to 'let the side down' or be seen a coward. Many of them scared to death on every operation, they suppressed their fears and boarded their aircraft, fully aware each time that it could be the last time. Aircrew attitude to death was a realistic one. When a fellow airman was killed there would be collective sadness but life went on. If asked how they felt about their job, they would probably reply, with resigned fatalism, 'There's no future in it.'¹⁰

Bomber Command squadrons flew from the first day of the war to the last. Early daylight raids proved disastrous, forcing a switch to night bombing. From 1939 to early 1942 High Command and the crews were deluded into believing that they were successful in their efforts but the reality was that navigational difficulties resulted in wildly inaccurate bombing. Often the casualties suffered by the aircrews outnumbered those of the enemy beneath them.

Improvements in navigational radar technology, the arrival of the 'heavy' bombers – the Stirlings, Halifaxes and Lancasters – and a new Commander-in-Chief, Air Marshal Arthur Harris in early 1942, transformed the force. Harris was determined to alter the fortunes of his Command and resisted any attempt to weaken this ambition. In a letter to Secretary of State for Air Sir Archibald Sinclair he wrote, 'You will no doubt recall that the most persistent and vociferous exponent of the necessity to split up Bomber Command and send it anywhere and everywhere, except to Germany, is Dr. Goebbels.'¹¹ A gradual build-up of resources, successful 'concentration' raids and the development of an area bombing policy turned Bomber Command into an effective force, with staggering fire power. It came at a cost: the legions of dead aircrew and 9,000 aircraft destroyed.[12]

This work will be concerned exclusively with aircrew who served in Britain on medium or heavy bombers between 1939 and 1945 and who took the war to Germany and Italy, predominantly on night time operations. It should be made clear from the outset that the term *morale*, as applied to a collective body, was never in danger of collapse in Bomber Command. General morale in the Command *did not collapse*, nor was it ever close to collapse. However, there were periods when morale dipped and when it rose. This work will be concerned with the individual airman's response to morale imposed by the Executive and with his own efforts to live up to the standard expected of him as a member of a fighting force. By a study of the various factors which determined morale we may construct a model which gives some indication as to *how* it was sustained.

Chapter 1

The Zeitgeist

'In general, the considerations of civilian morale are more than ever before parallel with those of the soldier [or airman].'[1]

Aircrews had ample opportunity for contact with the wider community. All factors affecting morale in the population were of consequence to the morale of aircrews. Flagging support for the combatant can erode the will to continue, states Anthony Kellett, in his study of combat motivation.[2] The effects of government propaganda, of war news and of the entertainment media were felt by civilians and aircrew alike. Within the closed communities of bomber stations other factors came into play, such as interaction between comrades, conditions, discipline and leadership.

After the Battle of Britain the public focus shifted from RAF Fighter Command to the efforts of Bomber Command. The latter had been active from the very first day of the war but now it was the turn of the bomber crews to receive the adulation of the public. Flight Lieutenant Julian Badcock remembered that, 'In the Underground and elsewhere anyone in RAF uniform in those days was greeted with, "Drop one for me, Guv".'[3] Bomber Command fought its war *within* the population; it was highly visible. The admiration heaped upon the aircrews was a prime factor in encouraging thousands of volunteers to choose the RAF rather than the other services.[4] The crews were seen as gallant knights of the air, 'as dauntless dare-devils, thirsting for action, undeterred by odds.'[5] Countless tributes to their resolve, such as the following, appeared in print. 'What manner of men are those who nightly make these hazardous flights over enemy territory to smash up the production of Hitler's war machine …….. who, by their undaunted courage and self-sacrifice, are playing such a vital part in the defence of their country?'[6] More lyrically, and slightly jingoistic, a poem by Patience Strong

(Winifred May), reproduced in the *Daily Mirror* in 1940, reflected the public mood:

> On wings of fire they ride the storms of war in Heaven's height
> Striking at the enemy and putting them to flight
> Full into the face of death through flame and shot and shell
> Outnumbered but unmatched they fly into the jaws of hell
>
> Daring and courageous in the teeth of fearful odds
> They fight their way to glory with the valour of the gods
> With cool control and peerless skill and bravery sublime
> Helping Britain win the greatest battle of all times[7]

This romanticised perception was ridiculed by the aircrews themselves, as Dr. Stafford-Clark recalled: 'Their reaction to the popular conception of the Royal Air Force was one of amused contempt.'[8] There was no doubt, though, that:

> The RAF was the most admired by the general public as a brilliant set of individuals ……. Men in blue uniforms, it was said, could get lifts from cars and free cups of tea much more easily than 'brown jobs' [soldiers]. Members of the women's services ….. were said to grade escorts in an order of eligibility by which RAF officers rated tops, being classified in turn by rank and number of decorations; naval officers came second and 'brown jobs' a long way behind.[9]

Oliver Stewart, a veteran of the RFC who had become a contributor on air matters to *The Tatler*, with regular comments on the various Commands of the RAF, enthused:

> The men of the Bomber Command have been doing wonderful work. Those raids on Italy alone were triumphs of planning, navigation and technical and professional skill. Nothing like them had ever been attempted before or even thought possible. Sixteen hundred miles, with a crossing of the Alps into the bargain! ….. They are the men

who will turn the tide in our favour and who will set us firmly on the road to victory.[10]

Two years later an *Edinburgh Evening News* journalist heaped praise on the aircrews:

> Go for a trip in a bomber and the experience, however brief, will give you a new slant on the work of our airmen who wing their way through hostile skies. You will then comprehend with greater understanding and sympathy the meaning of the phrase, 'our crews experienced intense cold throughout the operation'...... Hot-headed dare-devilry may be all right in battle on the ground, but to keep cool, calm and collected in a small space calls for genuine heroism and dogged endurance. The RAF lads of Bomber Command have these qualities in goodly measure.......The RAF flying crews represent the flower of the nation's manhood.[11]

That may have been, but one young woman was less than enamoured of the 'Boys in Blue'. Miss G.P. of Salisbury complained:

> When boys join the RAF I don't know whether the uniform goes to their heads or what, but they all acquire the attitude that they are 'God's gift to women'. There must be nice men in the air but, candidly, I've only met one, and he is now a has-been. Their work, of course, takes them far afield, and their job is such a risky one that I think most of them believe in a short life and a gay one, and just take the girls out for their own convenience, and any decent girl resents that.[12]

For every Miss G.P. of Salisbury there were many more who welcomed news of any offensive action against Germany, and who were reassured by such headlines in the newspapers as: 'RAF assaults depress Berlin'[13], 'RAF fill sky in dawn raid'[14] and the charming caption 'Bomber Command "swot the Wops"', a report on raids to Turin and Milan in 1940.[15] They were not to know that in 1940 and 1941 many of these raids were ineffective and that the headlines were nothing more than propaganda. By 1943 there was verisimilitude in reports, with aircraft losses recorded, even though many reports still exaggerated the effectiveness of raids. 'Our bombers are "putting the Ruhr on the spot"'[16], 'Bomber Armadas out last night'[17], '4,000 bomb-tons hit Huns in 24 hours'[18]; and 'No wonder Germany's "big six" [Krupp, I.G. Farben and other giant industrial concerns] fear "Bomber" Harris.'[19]

The RAF was probably the most adroit of all the services in turning public approbation to its advantage. One Air Council minute recorded: 'Everybody must help in telling the story of the RAF and their minds should be attuned to that purpose. Propaganda has admittedly a nasty sound but what we aimed at was a true and modest statement of the deeds of the RAF.'[20] It was felt that 'there was a risk otherwise that the RAF might obtain less publicity than the other services which might well cause resentment among personnel and, in the long run, adversely affect morale.'[21]

A feature film, *The Lion Has Wings*, assisted in its production by the Air Ministry, was released in 1939 but was not regarded favourably, being seen as crude propaganda. A later film, *The Way to the Stars*, reflected the war weariness felt in 1945 and was sensitive in its treatment of human relationships. The film which made a real impact, though, was *Target for Tonight*, a box-office success in both Britain and the USA. The publication of the pamphlet *Bomber Command* coincided with the release of *Target for Tonight* in 1941. Both brought the exploits of the Command into sharper public focus. The pamphlet and film were successful because the *timing* was right. They appeared just when it was felt that *offensive* action was required after so long on the *defensive*. *Target for Tonight* 'was the first major film showing Britain taking the offensive against Germany rather than just stoically enduring enemy bombardment.'[22] As well as encouraging the aircrews already in action, *Target for Tonight* acted as a powerful incentive to volunteer, providing the double attractions of flying and hitting back at the enemy. The *Daily Mirror* film critic was impressed:

RAF Raid makes big film thrill.
A big thrill in store for picturegoers is the film of an RAF bombing raid over Germany, to be shown in London tomorrow. The film, 'Target for Tonight' shows the raid from start to finish – from the

take-off at a British aerodrome [Mildenhall] to the bomb-dropping amid fierce anti-aircraft fire, and back home again……..It is a wonderful piece of work, a tribute to the Crown Film Unit despite strong opposition from the Civil Service element in the Ministry of Information…… The enemy flak and searchlights go into action with terrifying realism………. The most exciting film produced since the war.[23]

If audiences had paused to consider the impossibility of obtaining film, in 1941, of British bombs hitting German factories with precision, they would have been able to deduce that it was fake footage, filmed in a British studio. But they were in no mood to question authenticity; they wanted to see Germans suffer, as *they* had made so many suffer and, at last, it appeared that the lion *did* have wings. There was nothing fake about the pilot featured in the film. Percy Charles 'Pick' Pickard flew 100 operations before he was killed on the raid which attempted to free French Resistance prisoners from Amiens Prison on 18 February 1944.

The playwright Terence Rattigan, himself an air gunner with Coastal Command, explored the emotional turmoil imposed on personal relationships by the strain of flying in his 1942 play *Flare Path,* the story of Bomber Command pilot Teddy Graham. In its eighteen and a half month run it was seen by half a million people, including Chief of Air Staff Sir Charles Portal and Eleanor Roosevelt.[24] The play was reworked into the 1945 film *The Way to the Stars,* which received warm praise from the critics. 'The first public performance of the film had a large number of Air Marshals [including Arthur Harris] and their wives in the audience…… It has been considered one of the most outstanding British films ever made.'[25] Whether either play or film had any effect on morale, the public's or the aircrews', is debatable but both were significant contributions to the understanding of what it was like to be a bomber crewman in the Second World War. Both captured the mood of the time perfectly. *The Way to the Stars* was: 'One of the few films which instantly bring back the atmosphere of the war for anyone who was involved.'[26] RAF mores shone through all its scenes.

The RAF set up its own film unit, explaining, 'There will be no need to go outside the service for personnel or "stars"……. Our first task is to make a proper film record of the RAF activities for historical purposes.'[27] Radio was also exploited to publicise the efforts of Britain's airmen. One early example, in October 1940, was the BBC Home Service programme *Bomber Over Berlin: An Impression of the Work of Bomber Command*.[28] Whilst emphasising the heroic, and downplaying the tragic, aspects of aerial warfare, broadcasts made by serving airmen did provide the public with evidence that something was being done to hit back.[29] A typical account was given by a pilot who recalled the early losses of Bomber Command and contrasted it with the changing nature of the air war. The friends he had lost in the early years 'had blazed the trail for Mr. Churchill's experiment by which collapse in Germany may be brought about.'[30] By this time – 1943 – there were no illusions about the glamorous aspect of aerial warfare, yet this pilot could tell his listeners, in carefully scripted words, 'A hazardous business? Not a bit of it. Rather an adventure.'[31]

The Air Ministry suffered the dilemma of what to reveal to the public. Secrecy had to be maintained whilst not appearing to deceive with false information.[32] When Arthur Harris was Commander-in-Chief of 5 Group in 1940, never one to mince words, he complained to Bomber Command Headquarters that, 'Much mischief has already been done by giving away valuable information to the enemy at the expense of our war effort and the lives of our crews in order to make snappy paragraphs for the gutter press.'[33] He contended that the morale of his crews would be adversely affected by these thoughtless actions of the press. The Air Ministry had, in fact, formulated a censorship policy early on, in which *selected* information was given to the public:

> The Air Council consider that it is of great importance to give publicity at the earliest possible moment to such information as can legitimately be released about important operations, both in order to sustain public morale in this country and to counter German propaganda at its source by making the truth widely known before the German version of the facts has been published.[34]

An Air Ministry minute written in 1941 deplored the fact that the terms 'large force' or 'small force' used in press and radio communiques were too vague and that, 'Several officers who have recently joined the RAF have mentioned that they were surprised by the numbers of aircraft involved in our raids; their previous conception of these numbers differed greatly from what they learnt after joining the RAF.'[35]

When Air Marshal Harris became C-in-C Bomber Command in February 1942 he resumed his verbal assault on 'the gutter press' and, in fact, anyone who made even the slightest criticism of bombing policy and, by extension, of his crews. In a lengthy letter to CAS Sir Charles Portal, dated 5 March 1942, he did not hold back. With prose which could be termed vituperative, to say the least, he criticised the critics. This letter provides an insight into the mind of 'Bomber' Harris and his protectiveness towards his men. It helps to understand the high esteem in which he was held by them.

> Dear CAS,
> I must bring to your urgent and earnest attention the deplorable effects on morale of the spate of largely ignorant and uninstructed chatter against our bombing policy and against the general efficiency and co-operativeness of the Air Force......... The gutter press, which deserves a full share of blame in this matter, can presumably only be got at through the sensation mongers, circulation hounds and irresponsibles who run it..........
>
> Whatever the justification for criticism those who make it in public should be brought to understand the appalling injury they are inflicting on our war effort, the fearful effects on the morale of crews, which will rise crescendo unless these mischievous tongues are bridled, and the comfort which they bring to the enemy.......... I can only assert that unless the highest influences are brought to bear in restraint on the Press, the other Services and on these MPs I cannot hold myself responsible for maintaining the morale of my crews, still less for increasing it to that pitch towards which we aspire........
>
> Yours,
> Bert.[36]

*

How did the public respond to RAF news? A Mass Observation file of 1941 reveals a variety of attitudes. Amongst such remarks as '…...they do some grand jobs' and 'There's nothing to touch them in the whole of history', some criticism emerges.[37] Some thought there was *too much* RAF news, others that it was boring:

> Interest and enthusiasm for the RAF itself is not as strong now as it was, owing largely to the fact that some of its present major activities are not so visible to the British in Britain. Our bombing of Germany is not always such exciting news to ordinary people as is apparently supposed in some quarters. On the contrary, there are a considerable number of people who are tired of the necessarily rather general news about our bombing Germany.[38]

This attitude could have had an adverse effect on the morale of the aircrews who, apart from necessary operational details, were given the same news as the public.[39] The Air Ministry thought that adequate access for aircrew to news, in the form of news sheets, notices, supplies of newspapers and radio was essential 'in view of its importance in maintaining morale.'[40] Ministry acolytes would have been dismayed to learn that, according to one Mass Observation report, aircrews were not too exercised over war news. Preferred reading on bomber stations was the *Daily Mirror*, especially the antics of *Jane*, the cartoon strip character who regularly lost items of clothing.[41]

Kellett wrote, 'Civilian attitudes to the war effort are rapidly transmitted to the combat troops through the instruments of modern communications. It is therefore increasingly difficult to assign purely institutional causes to military cohesion and disintegrations and to ignore wider societal pressures.'[42] Bomber Command aircrew, of all the services, were the most likely to fit this pattern. Despite isolation on sometimes remote stations, the opportunities for contact with the civilian population were manifold. They shared the vicissitudes of war; aircrew and public morale were inextricably linked. Bomber Command *did* receive public approbation, and it was a valuable ingredient in the maintenance of morale.

Chapter 2

Volunteers

'We were all volunteers, so whatever happened you had only yourself to blame. Some say, "Never volunteer!"'[1]

An impediment to recruitment when war came was the perception of the RAF as a privileged elite, hostile to encroachment from the 'lesser orders'. One disgruntled reader wrote to his local newspaper in early 1939:

> The Royal Air Force has always appealed to me, but evidently the Government intend to keep RAF pilots an exclusive branch of the Service. Unless you have a university education or possess a school's certificate, it is a waste of time sending an application for pilot service in the RAF. There are many young men well-educated but without these qualifications anxious to fly in the service of our country, but this 'Old School Tie' influence puts a sudden stop to their aspirations. ….. this class distinction should not exist.[2]

In the stubbornly class-ridden society of pre-war years that reader's complaint may have been justified but this was about to change. Flying was no longer the preserve of a privileged elite. If one possessed the necessary qualities, it became easier for intelligent men, without the advantages bestowed by class, to enter the Service. The volunteers who flocked to the Royal Air Force were of a high calibre. They were bright individuals, many of whom would otherwise have been at university or in the professions.[3] All volunteered for 'flying duties' and did not know to which Command they would be posted.[4]

The big increase in numbers required by war meant that the RAF could no longer rely only on those with a school certificate. It had also to take men with elementary education to train as pilots, navigators and air bombers.[5] The RAF began its appeal for volunteers to fill the large number of aircrew posts which would be needed; men aged 18 to 28 registering for national service could express a preference for the RAF.[6] The response was enthusiastic and by April 1940 the number of pilots emerging from the training system had doubled. There was still need for more, and not only pilots. One advertisement in March 1940 focused on the attractive incentive of a commission for air gunners – 'the "eyes" and "teeth" of the RAF'.[7] – and the remuneration which accompanied the commission. A further appeal, in May 1940, was made:

> In spite of the widespread response to the appeal for a pool of volunteers for Royal Air Force aircrews, there is still room for more men, states the Air Ministry. All men within the prescribed ages and conditions who have not yet attested in one or other of the services are eligible, whether they have been called up for medical examination or not. Applicants for training as pilots must be between eighteen and twenty-eight; for training as observers [navigators], wireless operators and air gunners they must be between eighteen and thirty-two. All should have received schooling up to the age of sixteen and be physically fit.[8]

Such a vast undertaking inevitably led to delay. Men would be summoned for training and then 'kick their heels' for up to three months before training actually began. It was reported that some men lost their jobs as a result.[9] The RAF acted to put an end to this delay and innovated a scheme whereby candidates of exceptional ability and leadership potential would begin a training programme immediately on enlistment.[10] At this early stage of the war an acting pilot officer would receive 11/10d per day (approximately 55p). Upon commissioning this would rise to 14/6d per day (approximately 75p). As a flying officer he would receive 18/2d (approximately 90p) and, after a year, as a flight lieutenant, 21/9d (approximately £1.08).[11]

Secretary of State for Air Sir Archibald Sinclair urged men to: 'Try again to join the RAF: Our daring bomber, fighter and coastal pilots, he said, had belied all the silly talk about the decadence of British youth......To those who have been crowded out when the Force was smaller I say, "Come along and try again"...... To others who want to join this gallant band of volunteers, whose deeds will shine with glory in the history or our country, I say, "Now is your chance to come forward."'[12] Three months later it was apparent that his encouragement had been successful: 'Rush to fly with the new RAF: There has been a quick response to the announcement that almost every man, whatever his occupation, could volunteer for flying duties in the RAF......'[13] Later in 1941, 'You men who are fit and under 33 – your place in this war is at the side of the gallant RAF flying men who are teaching the Hun what air war means. Now is the time to come forward and put your name down for flying duties at the Combined Recruiting Centre.'[14]

To reassure those harbouring doubts about enlisting the *Daily Mirror* issued an article with the headline 'Mass production doesn't kill personality in the RAF.' It described one recruit's experience, from the moment he joins the Service. At first he is self-conscious but soon, with the aid of rigorous drilling, feels more at ease. 'Through discipline he has gained confidence. He is falling into step with the Royal Air Force, and the RAF spirit of pride in the service is born in him.'[15] Thus was morale instilled at the very beginning of the airman's career. Waiting for their chance were the air cadets of schools and colleges around the nation. In 1942 200,000 of them were accepted into RAF stations to learn maintenance and to experience flights, as part of their summer camp.[16] The eventual aim, of course, was to find suitable candidates for aircrew.

The steady stream of volunteers became a flood. By 1943 there was a glut of recruits and 'Feeding into the RAF all who have been accepted as airmen is becoming one of the major headaches of the manpower authorities.'[17] One man who had been put on deferred service as a wireless operator/gunner in November 1940 had waited for twelve months before starting his duties. A possible solution to the problem of stagnation was suggested: such men could be employed on the land while serving in their holding units and continuing with their training.[18]

*

Why did young men volunteer for what they knew was a dangerous occupation? In his last letter to his mother, Flying Officer Vivian Rosewarne wrote,

'Today we are faced with the greatest organised challenge to Christianity and civilisation that the World has ever seen, and I count myself lucky and honoured to be the right age and fully trained to throw my full weight into the scale.'[19] He was killed in 1940. The letter was published by *The Times* to great acclaim. Unashamedly patriotic, it touched a nerve in the population. Alongside cruder appeals such as that of Sir William Rothenstein – 'Nothing has more raised the anger of our airmen against the Nazis than their hideous cruelties' – propagandists sought to justify the struggle.[20] The war was a crusade against evil, and although most servicemen did not think too deeply on ideological lines, a much greater number than in their fathers' generation were 'ideologically engaged.'[21] Patriotism certainly *did* play a part. There was also a deeper 'imposed code of obligated conduct accepted by youth from its elders as a natural self-discipline.'[22] In other words, duty. Coupled with this ethos, many young men realised that they were being presented with a golden opportunity to indulge in one of the great passions of the 1930s and 1940s: flying. 'Those who came to the RAF did so because they passionately, single-mindedly, unashamedly wanted to fly …… [flying] …… captured the imagination of …… young grammar school boys, of modest, conventional, lower-middle class backgrounds from which they yearned to escape.'[23] With flying came glamour. One of Bomber Command's more illustrious members, Leonard Cheshire VC, believed that war was 'joyous'.[24] It gave purpose to his life, while providing a glamorous, playboy lifestyle. This image of the pre-war flyer was fixed in the minds of the young men attracted to the service. Bill Reid, another Bomber Command recipient of the Victoria Cross, gave his reason for volunteering: 'We, as boys in school in most cases, in fact joined the Air Force because there was a war being fought and we felt this was the best service. There was a bit of glamour attached to the Air Force.'[25] He added, 'We couldn't drive, let alone fly. To fly a Lancaster was a tremendous thing.'[26] Air Gunner D.J. Gill was 18 in 1942. He volunteered for aircrew in response to 'wartime recruitment propaganda in relation to the RAF and the glamour it depicted of brave young men going to war, killing the enemy, returning as heroes.' It did not take long for him to realise that the reality was very different.[27] Future Wing Commander Jim Wright gave his reason: 'We were at war (again). It was the obvious & natural thing to do at my age (born 27 July 1922). I was a junior civil servant in a "Reserved" occupation ….. the only way to escape from "reserved" was to become aircrew or a submariner, I think. I preferred aircrew.'[28]

Family tradition played a part. Some volunteered because their fathers had been in the Royal Flying Corps in the Great War. The First World War loomed large in the minds of the generation whose fathers had fought in it. Many opted to join the Air Force to avoid the horrors of trench warfare, which they assumed might be repeated in the present conflict.[29] Future Flying Officer Pierre Richard was fascinated by aeroplanes, living as he did close to Hendon, where as a boy he enjoyed watching the Air Pageant; he was determined to join the RAF. He was intent on emulating his uncle, who had been a pilot in the First World War.[30] Revenge was also a motivator. Wing Commander K.J. Newman volunteered because his home had been destroyed by German bombs.[31]

Some rather less than patriotic reasons steered men towards the RAF. Jim Betteridge admitted, 'I joined because I fancied myself as Biggles.'[32] Eddie Wheeler: 'It was at the cinema one evening that I saw George Formby in *Something* [sic] *in the Air*.'[33] Alfred Jenner: 'My choice was based on the fact that the RAF was the only one of the services where the lower ranks wore ties; I think I volunteered for aircrew for a host of wrong reasons ….. I liked the uniform and fancied the idea of silken wings on my breast. Then too, it appeared to offer an easier way of service; bacon and eggs for breakfast, clean sheets on your bed…. '[34] As will be seen in the next chapter, a man with a spurious reason for volunteering but a genuine desire to fly *might* fool a selection board but he would have to convince sceptics that his aerial skills outweighed his dubious incentive to enlist.

Whatever the reason for volunteering, it was now the job of the Royal Air Force to train these eager flyers to kill the enemy. Volunteering implied acceptance of risk. It would slowly dawn on the enthusiastic young recruit that this was not a game.[35] One veteran recalled: 'I was a would-be hero. I suddenly thought, "Good God, I might get killed."'[36] Reality intervened and replaced any heroic, glamorous or romantic notions which had impelled men to join up. Even if, as evidenced above, some had rather bogus motives for volunteering, all volunteers were highly motivated; they believed in what they were doing. 'All shared the general public hatred of the Nazis and all desired victory.'[37]

Enthusiasm at the outset of a flyer's career could only encourage good morale. As is evident, aircrew volunteered for many reasons. They encompass family tradition, fascination with flying, a sense of duty and obligation, a desire to avoid the rigours of army or navy life, revenge after seeing their families' and friends' houses destroyed by the Luftwaffe and, yes, patriotism.

Chapter 3

A Bomber Type: Selection and Training

'Adequate training is the most important factor of all in building up confidence, from which arises fearlessness.'[1]

Selection

Experiences at selection centres could be dispiriting. When Air Cadet and future Flight Lieutenant D. Steiner presented himself in May 1941 the decidedly uncongenial officer behind the desk barked, 'What is 5/64th as a decimal?' A bemused Steiner must have satisfied the selection officer with his answer because he was soon on his way to the RAF Reception Centre at St. John's Wood in London.[2]

Bomber Command had to find the right men to do the job. The first priority, therefore, was to ensure that the selection process was rigorous. Rejection of unsatisfactory candidates would eliminate problems later. In selection, the Air Ministry was guided by principles formulated in the First World War and the role of psychiatry was only gradually recognised. Certain individuals were unlikely to cope with the stress of combat; it seemed logical to exclude such men at the earliest possible moment.[3] The 'weeding out' process began at the selection stage; the safeguarding of morale commenced at this point. Selection boards had to bear in mind that enthusiasm for flying could not hide deficiencies in the prospective flyer. Some did slip through the net, their unsuitability exposed when they became operational, or even during flying training. A medical officer with 9 Squadron noted: 'Candidates are, for the most part, very young and incapable of judging their true "metier" in the war.'[4] He went on to list the undesirable motives for volunteering: glamour, romance of flying, mercenary reasons, 'imitation based on hero worship' and the 'necessity of joining one of the services and joining the RAF because it is less hidebound by tradition and discipline.'[5] The biggest threat to morale at the selection stage was posed by the failure to recognise the warning signs given by men who had volunteered for some, or all, of the wrong reasons.

An anonymous group captain offered his own observations and suggestions for the 'right type' for bomber operations. Firstly, they should be physically strong. Flying a Wellington for hours was rather different to flying a Hurricane for ninety minutes. 'No "weeds", the fighters can have those,' he recommended.[6] Next, he believed, the candidate should be the cool, solid type, an older man than was required for fighter aircraft. Intelligence was essential. 'A bonehead in a bomber squadron is not only a menace to himself but a menace to the others in his crew……. I have had a few nitwits and they drive any Squadron Commander to distraction.'[7] Finally, he addressed the requirements for air gunners, who should possess the qualities of courage and endurance. They did not need to be intellectual giants, the group captain offering, 'I do not mind if they are really rough and "common".'[8] He would have been satisfied to know that, approximately in accordance with his wishes, tests designed to separate those more suitable for fighters or bombers had been carried out at the Initial Training Wing, Cambridge. In essence, temperamentally quick men should fly fighters and temperamentally deliberate men would be the bomber pilots.[9]

The application of psychiatric assessment of candidates was slow in evolving and at the beginning of the war selection depended very much on looking for the 'right types'. Public school boys were the 'right types'.[10] When casualties mounted and more aircrews were needed the Air Ministry was prepared to relax its rigid class view of suitability. Previously 'unsuitable types' were accepted.[11] The relaxation of standards created its own problem. Many men who slipped through the selection net and were accepted for aircrew *did* prove unsuitable, could not cope with the rigours of flying and suffered breakdowns. Up to this time it had not been possible to correlate operational success with the results of selection and grading tests. It became a matter of urgency to do so:

> Although there is a large element of chance in individual encounters with the enemy, it is quite clear that aircrew vary widely in their inherent capacity for success in action and the effectiveness of our air striking force depends upon whether we are able to select the

right people [those able to master the technically challenging heavy bombers now in service]……. it becomes more and more important to eliminate the operationally unsatisfactory pilots before their mistakes can endanger the lives of others.[12]

The Air Ministry asked whether it *would* be possible to screen candidates either before selection or at the early stages of training in order to identify 'probability of failure in operational flying because of temperamental unsuitability.' By these means wastage would be reduced.[13] In compliance with the Air Ministry's request tests using combined psychological and psychiatric methods were devised in 1943 to be used in the selection process. Medical officers trained in these disciplines would advise the boards on the suitability of candidates. They would consider family history, any record of nervous breakdown, morbid fears, timidity, lack of aggressiveness, obsessions, immaturity and any other indication that an applicant would be unsuitable material for aircrew.[14] By the following year the tests were being used. Appraisal of skills superseded subjective selection on the basis of class or demeanour.[15] Traditional aircrew selection boards looking for the 'right types' were belatedly replaced by scientific measures. These were still fallible but they were an improvement.

....

Training

The training process was long and arduous, and lasted from eighteen months to two years. When war was declared local education authorities provided classes for air cadets in mathematics and science. Courses would be organised on similar lines to those taught at Initial Training Wing schools: comprising aircrew and technical components. With the headline '130,000 ATC boys in 27 days' the *Yorkshire Post* informed its readers that: 'The syllabus is designed to develop the physical fitness, morale and leadership of cadets.'[16] By 1942 full time courses of six months were in operation, with pupils studying mathematics, science, mechanical drawing, English and history. The aim was to stimulate mental growth and intellectual self-respect. Thousands of cadets benefitted. From the PACT (Preliminary Air Crew Training) Wing students progressed to Initial Training Wing of Flying Training Command.[17] When pupils arrived at an OTU (Operational Training Unit) Bomber Command itself assumed responsibility.[18] Finally, when the 'heavies' were introduced, OTU trainees would proceed to the final stage of their training, the Stirlings, Halifaxes and Lancasters of the HCUs (Heavy Conversion Units).

Before arriving at their OTUs spirits were high, as confidence in flying had been built up and new friends had been made. Newly-arrived pilots had already done 200-250 hours flying; other crew members between 30 and 100.[19] The Air Member for Personnel, Air Marshal Sir Bertine Sutton, made clear to the C-in-C Flying Training Command what incoming trainees should know: '..... it was advisable to notify all air crew before grading commences that they were now about to start their training proper, that their duties would require a high standard of moral courage, and that if any of them felt any doubt on this score, it would be well for them to say so at once before their training had progressed further.'[20]

Air Vice Marshal Sir Charles Symonds, eminent neurologist of the RAF, undertook a tour of OTUs in the USA and Canada in July 1943. The report on his observations reinforced the belief that identifying, and removing, unsuitable aircrew during training would prevent disaster further along the line. In so doing, morale would be protected. Symonds contended that experienced instructors in constant contact with trainees should be able to weed out suspects who revealed nervousness at the controls, who found excuses to absent themselves from flying exercises and, above all, by studying the facial expressions of the trainees while they were at the controls.[21]

It was decided that 10 flying hours would be the cut-off point. Before that a pupil could withdraw from flying without disciplinary repercussions. If a trainee had continued his course beyond that point and had subsequently broken down, he would be under suspicion of wavering (q.v.).[22] 'After 10 hours flying has been completed an airman cannot plead that he did not know what flying was like and found he could not stand it as soon as he had first hand experience, and any wavering after 10 hours must be investigated from the point of view that it is a possible lack of moral fibre.'[23]

*

As he began his progression through the stages of training, recruit Steiner was sent to Brighton, where, to his delight, he was billeted at the Metropole Hotel. Not so luxurious was Heaton Park Air Crew Holding Unit, his next port of call. There was a general glut of recruits, of which he was one. 'Hanging around' constituted a large portion of a trainee airman's life, tending to dampen morale. Steiner's time at Heaton Park consisted of guard duty, picking up litter, kitchen fatigues, parade ground drill and more drill. He developed the skill of looking as if he were on an important errand; in that way one avoided the inevitable fate of persecution by NCOs looking for victims. Steiner enjoyed his next posting to Initial Training Wing at Hastings, although he still had the feeling that he was 'kicking his heels'. Eventually Moncton, Canada beckoned and after four and a half months training there he was unexpectedly commissioned, eventually finding himself at an OTU at Wymeswold in Leicestershire.[24]

Air Gunner D.J. Gill had harsh criticism for the training he received. He was taught how to use a bayonet and how to throw a grenade, two skills not needed by an air gunner. His Morse and Aldis Lamp training was useless, as neither were employed on operations. Baling out procedure did not mention the fact that one's boots could fly off in descent, leading to frostbite in winter. He was never told that surrendering to German civilians was not a wise course of action. Gill was referring to the later stages of the war, when the lynching of parachuted airmen (q.v.) was a real possibility. Finally, in his litany of complaints, 'In the aircraft I flew, I had no idea where the first aid kit was, if, indeed, there was one.'[25] All of these grievances could dampen enthusiasm and morale but it must be emphasised that highlighting the complaints of a minority should not detract from the general satisfaction felt by the majority that their training, whether in Britain or overseas, had been sound and vital to their chances of survival. Wing Commander Jim Wright was sure that, 'The Commonwealth [Empire] Air Training Scheme (q.v.) provided good basic training sufficient for wartime tasks.'[26]

*

It was on arrival at the OTU that 'crewing up' occurred, a procedure which was vital to morale. This curious, remarkably effective system was deliberately employed to form crews. All the trainees were herded into a large hall or hangar and were left to choose their future crew mates. The effect on morale was recognised in the Air Ministry: 'Aircrew personnel would be formed as crews [at OTUs]. They would know that their identity would be preserved when they went to their operational squadrons. It should be one of the most important traits of OTUs to foster and encourage in every way possible the crew spirit from the beginning.'[27] Dr. Stafford-Clark, who had spent 3.5 years caring for 4,000 aircrew on bomber stations, knew the value of the crewing up system:

> This conception of the solidarity and integrity of a crew begun and fostered at this stage of the men's flying career was a tremendously significant influence in their lives and their attitude to their job. The fundamental and insistent need which all men have, to identify their greatest efforts with something beyond and bigger than themselves, found here a temporary expression. A good captain's concern for his crew, each individual member's sense of obligation and responsibility towards the whole was more than simple comradeship ...... it had become an act of faith.[28]

The aircrews themselves were well aware of the importance of this process; their lives might depend on the choices they made. Quiet men sought out men of similar temperament; married pilots were popular – they were considered more careful. Choices were not always rational and superstition played a part. If a pilot had been involved in a flying accident, some men would be drawn to him on the assumption that he would, as a result of the accident, now be more cautious in the air; others would steer well clear, not wishing to attach themselves to a potentially dangerous pilot. F/O. Fairhead recalled, 'We milled around talking to each other until I found the ones I liked best, and I assumed they felt the same way. We shook hands and I was now "crewed up".'[29]

Wing Commander Newman described his 'crewing up' experience: 'When all the pilots were assembled an equivalent number of navigators were sent into the room and we were told select one. I chose a flying officer – Eddie Hall, only officer in the crew – on the assumption that as he had gained a commission he might be better than average. He too was a married man – an essential requirement I felt, as our joint will to survive would be stronger.' Newman chose an older man whom, he reasoned, would be a steadying influence.[30] Then bomb aimers were sent in, followed by wireless operators/air gunners, to be absorbed into crews in their turn. Trainee Steiner crewed up: 'We were assembled in an empty hangar and given a "pep" talk by the CO who advised us that this was the time to withdraw from operational flying if we had any doubts, but that the future would be rather unpleasant if we chose to do so.' The assembled airmen were given an hour to complete their crews. 'Lady luck was riding on some shoulders and not on others and you did not know whom she was favouring.' Two pilots asked Steiner to join their crews. He declined. Both were killed.[31]

After the formation of the crew there would be up to two months training, comprising lectures, cross-country flights and emergency drills. This with only five crew members; the flight engineer, who typically had far less flying experience, and mid-upper gunner would join at the HCU.[32]

*

In April 1940 the Empire Air Training Scheme came into effect, whereby British volunteers were sent to Canada, Australia, New Zealand, South Africa, Rhodesia and the USA.[33] Anthony Eden, Secretary of State for Dominion Affairs at that time, commenting on the Scheme, was quoted in the press: 'There has never been any development of this kind or any scheme which involves so important a measure of cooperation for the future of air warfare.'[34] F/O. M.C. Wright recalled, 'From an enjoyment point of view, what greater adventure could a teenager wish for than going to Canada? Away from the dreariness of 1942 wartime Britain into a vast beautiful land of plenty.'[35]

F/O. R.J. Fayers was another who crossed the Atlantic for training. After attending the Electrical Wireless School, RAF Yatesbury, he found himself in a rather different environment, the Deep South of the USA, in Montgomery, Alabama. There he failed flying training, proceeded to Jacksonville, Florida, and became a navigator. His diary reveals a certain contentment with his lot: 'For the first time I'm willing to admit that American girls have something. That impression came mainly after yesterday afternoon on the beach which is pure Hollywood movieism. The pond and girls are all background and extras

…….. and the sky has technicolor.……. I live at the San Sebastian Hotel ……. clean sheets, an extra comfortable bed, a towel per day, a bathroom, super food, an interesting course, England in a few months, I have no grumble.'[36] A visit to the cinema gave him a chance to evaluate life in his homeland: 'I saw the best film to come out of this war [*Mrs. Miniver*] – it was beautiful and true – The American audience clapped as Spits took off "to save England". America has taught me how to love this old life I had and strangely to be almost proud of the RAF.'[37] F/O. Fayers sailed home on 9 September 1942, ready to play his part.

Wing Commander Newman was another EATS trainee, learning his trade in Waterkloof, South Africa. Returning to England he attended Advanced Training School Unit 1 at Shawbury, near Shrewsbury, before allocation to 30 OTU at Hixon, near Stafford. It was a comfortable billet, a pre-war station. An eye-opener for Newman was the propensity for swearing amongst air gunners and bomb aimers, these often the products of working class backgrounds; pilots, navigators and flight engineers tended to be from public or grammar schools. Newman acknowledged the differences between the two groups: 'Without wishing to sound snobbish, their attitude to life was quite different from mine and some seemed very coarse by comparison with my former room-mates.'[38] Incidentally, it occurred to Newman that perhaps the reason that tour-expired aircrew happened to be his instructors was that 'their presence was intended to show us that it *was* possible to survive a tour of bomber operations.'[39]

*

The Air Ministry was proactive in preventing pupils on the EATS 'going soft'. A report on trainees in the USA by Air Marshal A.G.R. Garrod, Air Member for Training, noted: 'The discipline question is going to be difficult with the large number of pupils involved, and the infectious lax discipline of the US cadets ….. it must be borne in mind that Miami is hot and humid, the "playboy" attitude to life is universal there, and we expect our pupils to work.'[40]

Those lucky enough to go abroad on the EATS lived a comparatively luxurious life but a trainee's life abroad was not always a bed of roses. Future

Dambuster Johnny Johnson was one of those who trained in Florida, on a station at Arcadia. He remembered the lack of discipline which permeated the ethos of the American cadets: 'I didn't really get on with the Army Air Corps discipline, or *lack* of discipline, the way they just sauntered around, never marching properly.'[41] It could not be said, however, that the American *instructors* exhibited lax discipline. Johnny also remembered, 'We had a system where they made you get out of bed in the morning and you had to fold the top blanket at an angle of 45 degrees from the bottom and the inspecting officer would go round with a protractor, measuring them. If it wasn't at 45 degrees, you got stripped off.'[42]

When trainees returned to Britain there was a danger that spirits would flag but this was usually offset by the enthusiasm of the pupils for flying and by their desire to 'do their bit'.[43] At the same time hundreds of airmen from the Dominions left their homes to train in the Scheme and then proceeded to Britain to become operational. This often involved lengthy delays, with resultant sinking morale. One contingent of Dominion aircrew was unimpressed by the RAF. No-one met them on disembarkation in Britain when they believed there should have been 'a good welcome by the RAF authorities.'[44] Another group, of Australians, spent eight weeks travelling to Britain, during which time they lost their edge and, according to Sir Philip Joubert, 'having forgotten to fly even a light aeroplane.'[45]

In May 1943 Joubert, whose job as joint Inspector General of the RAF took him to the various training establishments around the country (but not EATS countries), wrote a minute to the CAS titled 'Discipline and the Fighting Spirit in the RAF.'[46] Joubert found that training was, by and large, of a good standard. He did, however, produce a list of areas where improvements could be made, most notably deferment of posting. It could take up to two years to complete training and delays at any point in the process had serious repercussions on morale. 'This irregular movement of personnel is one of the major causes of inefficiency, loss of morale and indiscipline.'[47] Movement from British and EATS OTUs to HCUs and operational squadrons involved large numbers of newly trained pilots, a logistical challenge. Result: delay. 'It was inevitable that airmen would chafe and grumble. Any unforeseen delays which prevented moving to the next stage of the process had a serious impact on morale.'[48] The Bournemouth Aircrew Reception Centre was subjected to particularly harsh criticism: 'By far the larger number [of aircrews] spend their time hanging around the hotels and flats in which they are quartered, or lounging aimlessly about the streets. Their discipline is bad and their morale is at a low ebb.'[49]

Despite the occasional hiatus, the EATS scheme was recognised as extremely valuable. Imaginative and useful instruction prepared aircrew for the time when they would take to the air over Germany. One drawback to training in the USA, Canada or South Africa was the very different weather conditions which would be encountered in Europe. Those trained in Britain had an advantage over the EATS men, who, as well as learning to fly in hostile skies, had to adapt to the notoriously changeable weather. In the final analysis, while training was vitally important, it was experience on operations, and a modicum of luck, which *might* ensure survival.

*

Not every British trainee experienced the delights of the USA, Canada or South Africa. F/O. R.J. Fairhead's first experience of RAF life was not a happy one. From the Uxbridge Receiving Centre, 'a dreadful place' with inedible food and tough discipline designed to 'knock the civilian out and the serviceman in', he moved to Initial Training at RAF Usworth, near Sunderland. For those in despair at their predicament it was possible to buy oneself out of the service for a mere £20, a sum not readily available to most recruits. Harried by Service Police and dour instructors, and lacking £20, Fairhead suffered. 'The constant repetitive drilling, marching, kit inspection, barrack room inspection and the rigid obedience to any order – no matter how stupid! – was, I was later to find out, very necessary to ensure that orders were instantly carried out, as, at some time, any fractional delay for explanation could be fatal.'[50] He had a low opinion of those distant figures in control of his life. When stationed at Tangmere, before going to an OTU, he witnessed a Whitley bomber refuelling to be ready for a nickel (leaflet) raid. 'It did nothing good for our morale to realise that those in charge of the country and services had so little intelligence.'[51] Fairhead trained at 57 OTU Hawarden, then on to a flight engineer training course at St. Athan, Wales and then to an operational squadron, No. 207.[52]

A Bomber Type: Selection and Training 25

The final stage before joining an operational squadron was the HCU, where newly-trained pilots and those who had flown twin-engined bombers became familiar with the 'heavies', first the Stirlings and Halifaxes and then the Lancasters. A warning from Air Vice Marshal A.J. Capel, AOT, reminded OTUs that pilots should only proceed to HCUs if they were considered ready to fly 'heavies'. Unsure pilots and navigators were of no use. The best OTUs would be the ones with a high percentage of crews who converted successfully and not the OTUs which passed 100% of their crews, only to have some failing at the HCU.[53]

K.J. Newman was a trainee at 1656 HCU, Lindholme, near Doncaster. His accommodation was at Boston Park, in Nissen Huts which were damp, cold and permanently bereft of fuel for the stove. There was much parading and marching. 'Sometimes we were marched up the road and back again – sometimes we were marched down the road first for a change.' The further one got from an operational unit the more traditional discipline of the 'bullshit' variety was in evidence and imposed. As a consequence, 'Morale at Boston Park was at a very low ebb indeed. Our conditions were bad enough but daily came news of Bomber Command's heavy losses.'[54] Delays, frequent postings, miserable living conditions and unwelcome news: all could very easily strike at morale.

*

Indispensable to the effectiveness of the OTUs were the instructors. A further potentially harmful factor determining morale at the training stage was the quality and commitment of these men. The policy of using tour-expired aircrew as instructors at OTUs was not universally liked by them and there was a reluctance to participate. Their grievances were recognised by the AOC Flying Training Command, Air Marshal Sir Philip Babington. He listed them in a letter to Under Secretary of State H.H. Balfour. As non-operational pilots, any instructor living a mile or more away from the OTU station was not entitled to medical treatment; similarly, free vitamin pills were not available to non-operational pilots. They were denied special leave petrol allowance and extra rations were not issued to non-operational men.[55] Having completed thirty operations, it was in a disgruntled state of mind that those instructors nursing these feelings of resentment proceeded to their OTUs. On top of these grievances, facing a combination of nervous young trainees and 'clapped out' aircraft in which to train gave rise to trepidation. The medical officer at one station, Wyton, confirmed the disquiet felt by aircrews about to embark on training: 'The method of resting by sending a man to an OTU is most unpopular with aircrew. They feel that they cannot rely on their aircraft at OTU or on their pupils. They still have operations hanging over their heads for total effort sorties [when they would be recalled] with the additional factor of their aircraft being less carefully maintained.'[56] One tour-expired pilot/instructor felt that: 'The OTU is a relief from nervous tension but it is no rest physically.'[57] Another, a squadron commander judged unsuitable for flying instruction, agreed, 'I went to an OTU and I was dead tired in no time, and frightened stiff too.'[58] Instructor efficiency also came under scrutiny beyond OTUs. Flying Training Command was aware that some instructors employed on tours at pre-OTU training centres which lasted 24 months became stale and enervated. The result was a dampening of morale.[59]

The lacklustre performance of tour-expired instructors was noted by the Air Council, which commented on: '..... the poor quality of the pilots coming from operational squadrons to act as instructors. All the Commanders-in-Chief agreed that pilots coming direct from operations were not in a fit state to instruct without rehabilitation.'[60] Tired instructors could not give of their best and pupils would suffer, perhaps catastrophically, when they arrived on an operational squadron.[61] Many instructors, in fact, yearned for a speedy return to operations and a second tour. 'They missed the excitement of an operational station and the pride of being in the front line.'[62]

In 1943 a proposal was put forward for men who had completed *two* tours to go back to an OTU for another instructing stint. ACAS Sir Norman Bottomley believed it would have a beneficial effect for trainees, who would 'have evidence that the hazards [sic] of two operational tours are not as desperate as they might imagine.' Especially good for morale would be the appearance of second-tour men with decorations.[63] From the instructors' point of view, they would make better trainers, not having the dread of a further tour hanging over their heads.[64]

*

A Bomber Type: Selection and Training

In April 1941 a training manual came into being. *Training Memorandum* became *Tee Emm*. Aimed initially at officers, it had been decided to present serious subject matter laced with an element of mild humour. It was given approval by the CAS, 'I hope that these Training Memoranda will be widely read and studied, since I am certain that they will help us all to improve our efficiency, not only in our training but also in operations against the enemy.'[65] Enter the cartoon character Pilot Officer Percy Prune, a recognisable figure to the many public schoolboys who peopled the RAF at this stage of the war. An affable dimwit, he would be used to demonstrate the mistakes in flying to be avoided, with slogans such as 'Careless flying costs lives', a slight adaptation of 'Careless *talk* costs lives', or 'Is your accident really necessary?', adapted from 'Is your *journey* really necessary?' He would act as a warning to bad, sloppy or dangerous flyers. It was felt that the messages on flying safety would be absorbed more readily in humorous form and that, indeed, appeared to be the case.

The Awful Tale of P/O. Prune

This is the tale of P/O. Prune
Now in hospital in Frome
Who, though industrious and keen
The type who keeps his buttons clean
Earned for himself a bitter fate
Because he could not concentrate[66]

Tee Emm soon had a circulation of 30,000 monthly copies and P/O. Prune became a household name.

*

The dangers of training are reflected in the appallingly high fatal accident rate. During the War, 5,327 men were killed during training, nearly 10% of all Bomber Command deaths.[67] It is remarkable that morale was not seriously compromised, as the young trainees gradually learnt that flying brought danger as well as glamour. The realisation that one could die before even arriving on a squadron gave many airmen pause for thought. Sir Lewis Hodges, a pilot, remembered: 'Of the 21 crews on our OTU course, six were written off before we even got to a squadron.'[68] Douglas Knight Williams, a Pathfinder navigator later killed on operations, described his emotions when confronted by death at an OTU: 'Fortunately for us …… we can never realise they're dead – it just seems as though they've been posted to another station ….. I think this is a very good attitude to take as it does not strain your nerves and the fatality does not treat you with such a rude shock.'[69]

On his return from EATS training in Canada, the then Sergeant Pierre Richard was, 'prepared for whatever we had to do. To an extent, you were brainwashed. You lived and thought of nothing but flying.'[70] The embryonic crew was now prepared to face its test on an operational squadron.

Chapter 4

The Crew

> The aircrew without the Wop/AG cannot succeed
> The aircrew without the navigator/bomb aimer cannot succeed
> The aircrew without the pilot cannot succeed
> And these together make THE SUCCESSFUL TEAM
> Without which nothing can succeed.
> *Tee Emm, Volume 1, No. 6, September 1941*

Pilot Officer J.R. Byrne wrote eloquently of his love of flying and his admiration for his fellow crew members:

> The thoughts and feelings of a Wop/AG. Friday 26 May 1944.
> To whom this may concern.
> Flying is a funny thing. It gives one a somewhat independent outlook on other non-flying people's [sic]. I love my flying. Always did and always will. I respect all other aircrew. Owing to their taking a risk every time they leave the ground. During my aviator career I have met very many different types and nationalities of air crew personnel. Many of the Air Gunners here at OTU are from Canada. Pilots from New Zealand and Australia. All united together. Because they have one outlook on life – to fight and fly for everything that means so much to them.
>
> It is a funny thing this respect for each other. I respect the pilots firstly. Navigators and Air Gunners. One pilot in particular, the skipper I should have had – Sgt. Paige (Canadian) at only 19 years of age. Paige is destined to become Captain of a bomber aircraft. In his hands alone rests the fate of 6 other members of his crew.
>
> That is the respect all aircrew have for each other.[1]

P/O. Byrne was expressing, with passion, what all aircrew felt. Crew cohesion was essential, with the aircraft captain the key component. An Air Ministry report noted that:

> A very high standard of morale is necessary among air crews of bomber squadrons. Under present conditions each aircraft is operating independently at night and the entire responsibility of [sic] the success of the operation faces on the Captain (pilot) of the aircraft, who may be relatively junior and inexperienced, and members of the aircrew are robbed of the encouragement afforded by the presence of other aircraft of the same squadron. While much can be done by Squadron and Flight Commanders in the matter of leadership on the ground, the full brunt of leadership in the air must be borne by the Captain of the aircraft.[2]

Each crew member depended upon the others and it became a matter of life and death to ensure that the crew became welded together as a *team*. The crew was the foundation upon which morale was built. Station commanders could be bombarded with limitless numbers of Air Ministry directives regarding morale but these counted for nothing against a happy crew. Without the interacting forces which glued a crew together, all other aspects of morale would be rendered useless. Whether a machine gun crew, an artillery team, a tank crew or a 5 to 7-man bomber crew, the actions of each member of the team were directed towards not letting the side down and never displaying weakness. Aircrews emulated exceptional leaders but, in the final analysis, crew members fought for each other and this was the primary reason that they could continue to board their aircraft night after night. In Bomber Command, according to Dr. Stafford-Clark:

> ...... everyone looked forward to the completion of his tour, but so strong was the crew spirit that it was not an uncommon occurrence for a man to volunteer to do as many as ten extra trips so that he and his crew could finish together, if for any reason he had joined them with more to his credit than they had done.[3]

When Symonds and Williams carried out their exhaustive study of psychological disorders in Bomber Command personnel (q.v.) they soon learnt what station commanders regarded as the most important component of morale: the crew. One CO told them, 'Crew confidence is often intense and you cannot run a crew without it. The crew should be kept together and strangers should not be put into it.'[4] There must be no Achilles' Heel. Another CO offered, 'If a man is weak but is an accepted member of the crew the rest will nurse him along, but if he ever seems likely to jeopardise the safety of the aircraft they as a crew will report him to the squadron commander.'[5] The key to a happy crew was a captain whom all could trust and an unsuitable one would cause a rapid decline in morale in that crew. Wing Commander K.J. Newman remembered his responsibility many years later: 'The thought of being in sole charge of a Lancaster bomber with seven tons of bombs on board and six other young men whose lives depended on my skill, or lack of it, was a heavy responsibility for me at age 21.'[6]

Air Marshal Harris was well aware of the importance to morale of keeping crews together. Replying to the Air Ministry on a proposal to split crews in early 1943, he argued, 'Crews are trained as a whole and the disorganisation caused by splitting crews during their thirty sorties in order to provide experienced captains for new crews would be disastrous.'[7] One of Harris's first forays, as C-in-C, into the question of crew composition was a letter to the Under Secretary of State for Air H.H. Balfour on 27 February 1942, just five days after his appointment. (He took command on 18 March). Harris was concerned that the number of available pilots was too few and believed the situation could be alleviated by abandoning the practice of carrying two pilots in each aircraft. The new 'heavies' should have a pilot's mate, he thought, trained as a flight engineer but able to take the controls should the pilot be incapacitated. The exception to this would be long haul trips, which would use the automatic pilot, dispensing with the need for a pilot's mate. Another member of the crew must receive sufficient training to be able to bring the aircraft back should an emergency arise.[8] F/O. R.J. Fairhead was aware of the unpleasant implications of switching places in the aircraft:

>.....although it was never stated officially, it was obvious that flight engineers had to be able to act as Second Pilot, without the full flying

training that pilots received. The ability of one crew member to take over the job of another was not discussed, as the circumstances under which it might become necessary was not attractive....... Obviously Bomber Command would expect this to be done [flight engineers taking the controls when a pilot was killed or wounded] by engineers, although it was officially declared as prohibited.[9]

In spite of his desire to keep crews together, Harris had to face the fact that it was not always possible. He wished to eradicate the situation whereby an NCO pilot could exercise seniority over an officer when in the air. 'We cannot go on any longer as we are,' he wrote to the AMP, Air Marshal Sutton in January 1943, and continued, 'the present system of NCO pilots in heavy bombers is hopelessly unsatisfactory.'[10] And on 29 April that year he expressed his dissatisfaction to the Under Secretary of State for Air:

> A sergeant pilot of an OTU crew is ..... frequently crewed up with Officers in the crew, over whom he has to exercise the duties of a captain .... a sergeant pilot who is captain of such a crew has no real authority over Officers in it, who are his superiors .... it is difficult for an NCO to enforce his instructions if the Officer shows reluctance to take orders from him..... I must again assert that all captains of bombers should be Officers.[11]

His argument rested on the premise that, in moments of crisis in the air, an all-NCO crew would behave in the manner of a 'mother's meeting', unable to come to a decision, as an NCO could not exercise rank over another NCO. Air Vice Marshal Capel, AOT, agreed with Harris, albeit using alternative terminology. Capel substituted 'soviet' for 'mother's meeting', the collective into which an all-NCO crew degenerated when a decision was needed.[12]

Navigator Jim Wright did not care if his captain was an NCO or an officer. All that mattered was that the team worked together. 'Every position in a bomber aircraft was a demanding one and team-work was vital to survival. Rank did not enter into it. A Sgt. Rear Gunner was the equal of a Sqn. Ldr. Gunner in practice. Everyone generally accepted that the pilot was the skipper regardless of rank.'[13] It was, in fact, quite common for an NCO to pilot a mixed-rank aircraft. He automatically became 'skipper'. Any officers in the crew would defer to him as the man in command. Portal summoned the Cs-in-C of all Commands to a meeting on 11 August 1943 to discuss the matter. They agreed that the then current practice of allowing NCOs to captain crews which included officers was regarded as unacceptable. It was bad for discipline, destroyed the self-respect of the officers and lowered their morale. It also made the exercise of captaincy by the NCO difficult, him feeling unease at giving orders to an officer. Therefore, it was thought necessary to ensure that officers joined crews with officer captains and NCOs with NCO captains.[14]

Air Vice Marshal Ralph Cochrane, just appointed C-in-C 3 Group, had long shared Harris's and Capel's misgivings about mixed rank crews. He had brought the matter to Harris's attention nearly a year before, in September 1942. He described a recent operation by squadrons in his Group, on which four aircraft did not even take off and nineteen planes turned back. Of these, only two had valid excuses. Cochrane placed the blame for this lack of 'press-on' attitude squarely on the shoulders of NCO crews. 'The real cause was the failure of the Captain to take command of his crew.'[15] One NCO explained, 'We are all sergeants together and I felt therefore that we should all have a say in deciding what we ought to do.'[16] An example of Harris's 'mother's meeting' at work. NCOs commanding officers in the air, 'strikes at the root of any organised system of leadership,' believed Cochrane and the solution would be for a commissioned officer to lead each crew, from the HCU stage.[17]

Harris agreed. An officer should be in command of the aircraft; all captains should be flight-lieutenants, in his view. He again contacted Sutton, AMP, in February, stating, 'Any NCO captain of a heavy bomber who is not deemed fit to hold a commission is in my view not fit to be the captain of a heavy bomber.'[18] He also believed that in all-NCO crews the senior NCO should be the captain and all NCO captains should be commissioned, or, if unfit for commission, they should be warrant officers.[19] Any such alterations in crew composition would create problems. It was highly undesirable to split crews at any stage, even more so when they had melded as a team half-way through a tour. This dilemma was not insuperable. New pilots were 'blooded' on arrival at operational squadrons; some became casualties on their 'dickie' (second pilot) ops, leaving their original crews 'headless', as Harris put it. In such cases it would be possible to split the crew to which the unfortunate 'dickie' pilots had been assigned and to scatter the members to other crews which had incurred casualties, creating new crews.[20] This naturally upset the desirability of keeping crews intact from the start but it was one solution to manpower logistical problems.

*

Another threat to morale was the realisation by acting captains of aircraft, appointed at times of heavy losses, that when they finished their tour they would revert to their original rank. This procedure had to be made clear at the earliest possible opportunity to pre-empt morale erosion. As so often, Arthur Harris provided an uncomplimentary assessment of higher authority inactivity, the Air Ministry having done nothing to clarify the acting captain issue: 'My own conviction after so many fruitless endeavours to get things put right is that until the Air Ministry resolves to approach the question in a new spirit with the intention of getting something done instead of obstructing all attempts at improvement it is completely futile to discuss the matter further.'[21]

On the subject of scattered crews, Donald Bennett, C-in-C 8 Group, Pathfinder Force (q.v.), did not tolerate 'odd bods' stooging around stations with nothing to do, which, apparently, was the case at some Pathfinder stations. Bennett believed, 'It is particularly important that the morale of our spare crew members should be maintained at as high a level as possible. "Hanging round" unemployed is a state of affairs which cannot be tolerated.'[22] These 'spares', bomb aimers, for example, could join crews and do alternate trips with that crew's regular bomb aimer. The morale of the 'odd bods', engaged in meaningful tasks, would be sustained.

*

When crews did stay together they produced better results than crews which consisted of a collection from other crews which had been split. The interaction between pilot and bomb aimer resulted in better bombing results when the pair had been together for a while than in inexperienced crews which had only been operating for a short period.[23] Despite the universal acknowledgement that crews must remain intact there were, of course, occasions when circumstances required the replacement of a crew member by another man, in cases of, for example, sickness, injuries or death. This was accepted. What was not accepted were deliberate attempts to break up crews, which was exactly what Pathfinder C-in-C Don Bennett desired.

There was a lengthy correspondence between Bennett, his Group Commanders and Air Marshal Harris on the subject of interchanging crews. Bennett had decided that a new system of marking by Pathfinder crews would be introduced and this would require changes in PFF crew tasks, which, in turn, would require breaking up crews. He knew that the policy of changing crews once or twice in a tour 'is generally unpopular with the majority of thoughtless aircrew' because the importance of the crew had been drilled into them from the start of training.[24] He intended to disrupt this system, or, at least, render it more flexible. A minute sent to 8 Group commanders from the Senior Air Staff Officer at PFF HQ made it clear that dissent would not be tolerated: 'In order to make this scheme a success Squadron Commanders must be absolutely ruthless in breaking up crews and personal preferences must be ignored.'[25]

Given the strong opposition to breaking up crews, from the Executive and aircrew alike, it is surprising to discover that the matter was even considered. Bennett reasoned that while team spirit was:

> sentimentally attractive to the aircrew members concerned it appears that the policy has gone too far. Aircrew members go almost hysterical if it is suggested that any interchange should take place. Their crew spirit is so highly developed that most crews would hesitate to exchange their own perhaps indifferent captain for the finest pilot and Captain in the whole of Bomber Command. Their team spirit has become wholly irrational.[26]

He added, 'Their real crew work as opposed to their vague non-productive team spirit would be far better.' Bennett pre-empted Harris's reaction to his views by writing to all his group commanders the day before he contacted the C-in-C, informing them that it was now official policy to interchange crews, when thought necessary, in the PFF.[27]

Air Vice Marshal Capel contacted Donald Bennett on 12 May 1943. He profoundly disagreed with Bennett's new policy. Keeping them together 'has been done mainly to enable crews to get to know each other and thereby engender confidence and good morale because it is considered that the operation of a heavy bomber by a team of 7 is best carried out when all members of the crew know each others [sic] capacity accurately.' If the new policy were to be implemented, it 'is likely to have serious disadvantages and to be most unpopular and it is doubtful whether the loss of morale which might follow would be outweighed by any compensating increase in operational efficiency.'[28]

The wing commander of 7 Squadron let Bennett know that interchange of crew members had occurred when necessary but that 'Crews do not appreciate being broken up unless they know it is for a sound reason. The team spirit is so deeply embedded in aircrew right from their first period of training that it is hard to make them understand that a chain is as strong as its weakest link.'[29] The 56 Squadron group captain replied to Bennett that he too had made changes when necessary for reasons of sickness or inefficiency, when a crew member had started his tour at a different time to the rest of the crew, or when a captain ends his tour, leaving the crew 'headless'.[30] All of Bennett's group commanders were opposed to the breaking up of experienced Pathfinder crews. The effect on morale of splitting a crew was obvious. 'With some aircrew it is a great hardship to be broken up. They have learnt to cooperate well and to trust one another. Having built up a crew esprit-de-corps they feel that it is a poor reward to be purposely torn apart and to do so only causes discontent.'[31]

The most robust defence of the intact crew came from the group captain of 97 Squadron:

> A very real advantage in keeping crews together is that individuals derive added courage to face up to the dangers of operations from their friendship with others in the crew. Also, should they have done a good number of operations with a particular captain and got away with it, especially if they have escaped on some occasions from tight corners, their morale rises accordingly. If they should change crews, they have to regain their confidence all over again. One of the

outcomes of this is that some individuals will never let their captain or their crew down. When he is a bit off colour he sticks it for their sake ….. Evidence of this good spirit is apparent every day when a member of a crew who has done more than his mates volunteers to stay on to see them through their tour.[32]

He was emphatic that deliberate changes should *not* occur. Capel weighed in, with a letter to Bennett: '…..the advantages of the crew spirit and crew cooperation outweigh any possible disadvantages which may arise due to the fact that crews dislike being subsequently broken up otherwise than for reasons which are inevitable – such as sickness, casualties etc. It is therefore intended to continue emphasising the crew aspect of training at all stages.'[33] Bennett probably accepted that interchanging of crews on a large scale would not occur but changes made for operational efficiency would continue, as was the case in the Main Force.

*

Another lengthy correspondence between Bomber Command Headquarters, the Air Ministry and group commanders concerned the wearing of armlets by captains of aircraft. This apparently innocuous innovation of 1944 caused considerable hostility, not just among aircrew but between representatives of the Executive. In March 1944 Air Marshal Robert Saundby, Harris's deputy, asked him to approve the new armlet to be worn by captains, as the Air Ministry was apparently incapable of making a decision on the subject and Harris's authority was needed to spur the Ministry into action.[34] This ploy worked and all Bomber Command groups received an instruction on 5 July 1944 that armlets of blue grey serge, with the letter 'C' in the centre were to be worn by captains of aircraft at all times when on duty, either on the ground or in the air.[35]

The first voice of dissent came from A.J. Capel, AOT, who had believed that the armlet was only intended for captains in training and not in all operational units. 'Is this really necessary or even desirable?', he questioned.[36] Capel appeared to relent and on 16 July 1944 ordered compulsory wearing of the armlet in all units.[37] More dissent followed, with senior officers reporting the intense dislike of the armlet among captains of crews. Air Vice Marshal Edward Addison, in command of 100 Group, informed Bomber Command HQ that, 'It has been found that a greater spirit of cooperation exists in a crew when the captain does not wear an armlet.'[38] Apart from its impracticality – getting caught on projections in the aircraft, for example – its wearing invited sarcastic comments because it resembled the armbands worn by service police and orderly officers. Crew spirit and morale was being eroded by this seemingly trivial matter.

Eventually Bomber Command HQ informed the Under Secretary of State for Air that 'the armlet referred to is not popular in Bomber Command and there is considerable reluctance to wearing it. The general consensus of opinion is that it serves no useful purpose and should be abolished. This Headquarters has never been in favour of the armlet outside the training sphere.'[39] Only after the war had ended did the compulsory wearing of the armlet cease, the Air Ministry writing to Bomber Command Headquarters, '...to request that you will confirm that armlets for captains of aircraft of Bomber Command can now be withdrawn.'[40]

*

In a move designed to encourage crews to greater effort HQ 3 Group proposed that reports of personal experiences could be widely distributed amongst the crews. 'It is thought that reports on these lines in "crew language" would be of value in promoting a spirit of competition and in enhancing morale.'[41] One report extolled the virtue of a cool-headed captain whose crew baled out of a Wellington in February 1941. He inspired confidence in his crew.[42] Another recounted the experience of P/O. Freberg, a navigator with 7 Squadron, who baled out of his Stirling at 7,000 feet on his eighteenth operation, on 10 September 1942. He was keen to return to the fray.[43] P/O. Watson, a navigator with 419 Squadron baled out from a Wellington on 16 June 1942. He survived but his pilot died when the aircraft crashed.[44] Whether reports of crashing aircraft would help to raise morale is a moot point.

All the efforts of the Air Ministry and of the upper echelons of Bomber Command to promote a high sense of duty were as nothing compared with the brotherhood of a happy crew. This, above all, was the key to survival. Luck did play a part but without harmony a crew was doomed. A contemporary observer wrote, 'Each one [crew member] has his own specialised job and does not go outside it. For the crew to be a happy one, each man must have complete confidence in each of his companions. If there is a weak link in the chain, all suffer.'[45]

A happy crew P/O. Byrne's was not. He was assaulted by his own mid-upper gunner in a cinema. After a sympathetic hearing from the station commander of the HCU at which he was training, Byrne resigned from his crew on 8 September 1944.[46] It would not have survived long on an operational tour. If one was unhappy with a crew, switching to another did not guarantee survival. A Wop/Ag. in F/Lt. Newman's crew had had enough after three gruelling trips to Happy Valley (The Ruhr), the first three of their tour, and refused to fly with them again. He thought they were inexperienced and decided to join a crew which was halfway through its tour, a safer bet, he believed, for survival. That crew did not survive.[47]

There was no guarantee that the very best crews would survive either. On 31 August 1943 P/O. Vandekerckhove (q.v.) and his crew of 427 (RCAF) Squadron (q.v.) failed to return from a raid on Berlin. He, four members of his crew and an unlucky second pilot gaining experience were killed. It was the last trip of their first tour.[48] F/O. Fairhead, who did survive, believed that, 'Experienced crews knew who had a chance of surviving with luck and we were usually right.'[49] P/O. Vandekerckhove and crew was a sad exception.

All the decisions on crew composition outlined in this chapter had an impact on morale. Despite the best efforts of the Air Ministry and of Bomber Command senior staff to disrupt their cohesion, the aircrews quietly got on with their job. 'There was no question of mindless obedience to orders; the very nature of aircrew duties of all types demanded men with intelligence, above average education, and individual initiative. Such men are bound to their duties and fellow crew members by a self-imposed discipline, a willingness and resolution, with no regard to bureaucratic rules and regulations.'[50] Johnny Johnson put his trust in his skipper: 'I can honestly say that I never once felt I wasn't going to come back. I'm sure that's because I had confidence in Joe [his pilot, Joe McCarthy]. He was a big man, six foot two; big in size, big in personality. Also big in pilot ability, which kept the crew together. We very much depended on him getting us there and back.'[51]

Chapter 5

The Squadron

Martin Middlebrook claimed that the squadron and even the flight meant almost nothing in comparison with the crew.[1] The crew was everything. One navigator recalled:

> We were intensely preoccupied with our own crew and very strongly motivated not to let it down. Apart from our commanders and three or four other crews that were close contemporaries, we knew few other aircrews on the station as more than passing acquaintances. The effect on morale is less severe if casualties are not know to one personally.[2]

It could be argued from Middlebrook's statement that the squadron was of no consequence and was not a factor in the equation of morale. Was it?

The primary group is of most significance to the man in combat but 'the widening ripples of secondary groups are also important.'[3] The squadron provided a spiritual home for career airmen and the young wartime volunteers alike.[4] It could promote a sense of community, even though primary group allegiance is in direct opposition to squadron allegiance. One view has it that small group allegiance *is* a factor in morale; regiment or squadron spirit is not.[5] A contrary view maintains that fostering pride in a regiment or squadron is essential to nurturing morale.[6] One medical officer in Bomber Command subscribed to the latter opinion: ' … it has been proven that the element of tradition drawn from a squadron's past operational record has a powerful effect.'[7]

Aircrew had no choice in which squadron to which they were posted. Once there, they began the process of assimilation into the culture and mores of their new squadron. Don Charlwood reminisced, 'We who had once laughed at the handle-bar moustache and the exaggerated speech had found the life of which these things were the symbol. And that life had become our life.'[8] Remembering his former squadron in 1943, Leonard Cheshire wrote of 'the carefree, cheerful life, the trust and companionship in danger, the splendour of success, the frustration of failure.'[9] Further contemporary evidence of this sense of belonging is provided by F/O. Horner. He had just finished a tour of operations and was relieved but despondent. 'There's a unity in the life of a squadron which you don't get anywhere else and I'll miss it.'[10] In time, newcomers' indifference evolved into pride. Jim Wright thought, 'It was simply natural to have pride in one's squadron, station, and in the whole of the armed forces of which we were a part.'[11]

Guy Gibson wrote of the rivalry between Bomber and Fighter Command. While *all* airmen were highly regarded during the war, there was irritation at the perceived superior status of 'the flying-booted, scarf-flapping glamour boys [of Fighter Command].'[12] Friendly inter-squadron rivalry was common among bomber squadrons. When they met on social occasions there was a chance to compare notes, to sing the praises of a particular aircraft or playfully boast about the bombing success rate of one's squadron. 'Rivalry in healthy form grows between this and 57 Squadron, also stationed at East Kirkby,' wrote the adjutant of 630 Squadron in January 1944.[13] Rivalry between squadrons existed and Bomber Command exploited it. As one senior officer noted: 'Without exception, every squadron threw out dark hints about the inaccurate claims of the other squadrons.'[14] Thus was competition encouraged and the state of morale measured.

When technology made it possible, photographic evidence of bombing became the means by which results could be assessed. Photographs were therefore extremely important in determining squadron success. Knowledge of good results meant improved morale. Guy Gibson explained:

> All squadrons must get photographic-minded ...... There would be a photographic ladder in the Group and in Bomber Command .... it would be easy to see which was the top squadron and which was the top crew. Moreover, it would introduce a high degree of competitive spirit between the squadrons ...... thus doing a good job in trying to make each beat the other.[15]

Cecil Beaton, the fashion photographer, who was employed at the Ministry of Information during the war, realised in 1942 that 'the spirit of a squadron is enormously dependent upon the personality, vitality or even wit of certain of its members. A squadron is keyed up to produce the best results when it feels itself to be in fine form. The whole fabric can become slackened by the removal of a few of its compelling personalities.'[16]

*

There was strong disagreement over the assertion in some quarters that squadron commanders should not fly. It was essential that they did – their men expected them to and morale was usually high on a squadron with an operationally active leader. There was a downside to this ethos. It was bad enough when the average crew was lost but when squadron commanders went missing the effect on morale could be severe. On the newly formed 630 Squadron at East Kirkby Wing Commander J.D. Rollinson returned from leave on 21 January 1944 and one week later went missing on a raid to Berlin.[17] Group Captain K.J. Rampling DSO, DFC of 7 Squadron was lost on a raid to Frankfurt on 22/23 March 1944.[18] No. 427 (RCAF) Squadron took part in the raid on Nuremberg (q.v.) which saw Bomber Command's worst night of the war in human terms, 30/31 March 1944. 'The squadron suffered a heavy loss this night. Both our "A" and "B" Flight Commanders failed to return. "A" F/L. G.J. Laird DFC in "W" Willie, "B" A/S/Ldr. J.M. Bissett DFM in "D" Donald and P/O. McPhee in "E" Easy, a new crew.'[19] Perhaps P/O. McPhee's crew was unknown to other crews of the squadron but losing two experienced crews in one night was a bitter pill. Temporary demoralisation customarily followed such losses but the squadron would soldier on. What other course of action was there? The loss of commanders, and, indeed of all fellow aircrews, could be borne if results at the time of the loss were satisfactory. Such valuable men, it was felt, had not been sacrificed for nothing. Andrew Brookes wrote, 'We were a happy squadron. The vacant chairs around the breakfast table spread gloom for a while, but then new crews came to take their place and we got on with it.'[20]

For the crews of a squadron, losses caused temporary depression in some and fatalistic acceptance in others, with no effect on morale; a long run of heavy losses inevitably dented morale. Most crews in F/O. Fairhead's

Squadron were sergeants or flight sergeants, many of whom were destined to be absent at breakfast tables. 'It was not a lively breakfast, partly due to knowing they were most likely dead and would it be our empty table next time? These thoughts were never voiced.'[21] When experienced crews 'got the chop' new crews naturally pondered on their own chances of survival. Two crews of 427 Squadron were lost on 6 September, raiding Munich. One was untried, the other vastly experienced. The crews were captained by P/O Biggs DFM and F/O Pery-Knox-Gore. 'The loss of these two Captains will be a serious blow to the Squadron. Biggs being an original member of the Squadron and Pery-Knox-Gore showing enough stuff in the short time he was with us to convince all that he was ace material.'[22] When the 'chop rate' was high established crews did not even know any new crews which had gone missing. The effect on morale in those cases was almost negligible.[23]

The chronicler of 630 Squadron's operations record book had this to say: 'Much progress has been made in the "knitting together" of the squadron at East Kirkby. The Squadron was beginning to "feel its feet". The loss of its Commanding Officer [Wing Commander Rollinson] ...... so early in its career was a grievous blow.'[24] The optimistic tone was sustained in the adjutant's summary of events in April 1944. Losses were relatively light, considering the number of operations carried out. The adjutant wrote, 'This unit has now developed a very sound and decided squadron spirit...... Considerable pride is noticable [sic] amongst both air and ground crew in their membership of the unit. Discipline and good behaviour are gratifyingly high ..... A Squadron photograph has been taken and has done much to knit together the various sections and help along the growing spirit of willing cheerful effort.'[25] Here we have contemporary evidence of high squadron morale in the later part of the war.

In a constantly changing squadron cohesion was difficult to maintain, yet morale held. The apparently callous shrugging off of deaths on the squadron was part of the defence mechanism necessary for warding off stress. Even during periods of very high losses a squadron could remain resilient. Prolonged activity prevented crews from dwelling on the subject. Losses were absorbed and forgotten. The squadron provided a spiritual home for aircrews. There was pride in serving with a particular squadron. It contributed to an individual's sense of belonging and feeling of worth, and was therefore beneficial, rather than essential, in sustaining morale.

Chapter 6

The Bomber Station

Lincolnshire Bomber Station
by Flight Lieutenant Henry Treece

Across the road the homesick Romans made
The ground mist thickens to a milky shroud;
Through flat, damp fields call sheep, mourning their dead
In cracked and timeless voices, unutterably sad
Suffering for all the world, In Lincolnshire.[1]

*

Operational Squadron
by Ronald Wilcox

We'll listen to no peroration
but to the haunts of love and wine
to run the gamut of sensation
to laugh and weep while yet there's time.[2]

*

Introduction

To state the obvious, a serviceman who is provided with adequate food and shelter, and opportunities for entertainment will be more content than one who is denied these necessities and pleasures. Armies and navies are separated entirely from society when they do battle. The men of Bomber Command fought a different kind of war, in which they returned to relative normality after each operation. Each bomber station was, in effect, *two* communities: one for officers, one for NCOs, both closed to the outside world. Although the stations in which aircrews lived were often isolated, they still afforded opportunities to remain in contact with the wider community.[3] The question of morale in relation to life on a bomber station is twofold: how did station facilities impinge on morale and how did constant contact with the outside world *affect* morale?

Conditions

The stereotype of a bomber station is one of a damp, windswept airfield, dotted with draughty Nissen Huts, rather than the comfortable accommodation provided by pre-war permanent stations. This is not far removed from reality for some unfortunates. The hastily-constructed stations which mushroomed after the outbreak of war were often spartan. George Hull wrote to a friend: 'The camp [Wigsley] is dispersed beyond reason .... messing is terrible .... washing facilities are confined to a few dozen filthy bowls and two sets of showers and inch deep in mud and water.'[4] Hull's description is borne out by an official report: 'The conditions are very uncomfortable. There is continual dampness. The conditions have certainly a direct bearing on the number of cases of rheumatism.'[5] In winter an eerie silence would pervade the station. Pilot Officer M.A. Scott wrote in his diary: 'A mist-drenched thaw, damp fingers everywhere, reaching into every corner of an ice-cold building. An odourless, fishy atmosphere everywhere.'[6]

Men often had to sleep fully-clothed, steal wood for fuel to feed into the tortoise stove, bicycle a mile to the mess and dodge the omnipresent mud.[7] Future Wing Commander K.J. Newman spoke of his accommodation in a Nissen Hut at Seighford. It was cold and damp, hot water was occasionally available in a nearby bath house and any food left lying around was gratefully received by mice and rats. His morale was restored at Hemswell, where comfortable rooms awaited.[8] Future Flight Lieutenant D. Steiner remembered the dispersed station at Elsham Wolds, where a bicycle was essential. He was then posted to Fiskerton, opened in 1943. The ubiquitous Nissen Hut provided accommodation, in which he was frequently awoken by various crews leaving for, or arriving back from, operations. His hut was surrounded by a sea of mud and freezing cold; if the coke provided for the tortoise stove was not assiduously guarded, it would be 'liberated' by light-fingered occupants of other Nissen Huts. Steiner's morale, like Newman's, revived dramatically when he, too, found himself in a comfortable room at Hemswell.[9]

An airman lucky enough to find himself on a pre-war permanent station could expect a degree of comfort perhaps previously unknown to him. Flight Lieutenant Rupert Cooling wrote: 'At peacetime stations like Harwell or Honington in 1940 one lived in greater comfort than one had hitherto enjoyed at home. Warm, well-furnished Mess with waitress service, billiard rooms and a bar. Home is what you make it.'[10] The airman's individual morale would no doubt be boosted by such luxury, at least until other factors came into play. Although depression, or at least discontent, could be induced by unsatisfactory conditions, general morale was not affected. There was always the optimistic belief that things could improve and George Hull eventually found himself in a more agreeable environment than Wigsley. 'Coningsby the beautiful, Coningsby the comfortable! .... lording it in a double bedroom which contains a real deal table and a radiator! Hurrah for the RAF! Well, anyway, it's about time.'[11] Agreeable accommodation worked wonders for morale.

Welfare

In 1942 Cecil Beaton wrote, 'It is said that the further removed from a large town with its girls, colour and distractions, the better is the spirit and morale of the station.'[12] Beaton's assertion is at odds with Air Council thoughts on the matter. There are numerous mentions in its files of the deleterious effect on morale of boredom. For example, 'The isolation of certain dispersed stations and lack of transport which prevents crews leaving the vicinity undoubtedly will be a factor resulting in boredom, and this is likely to lower efficiency.'[13] The council knew that constant monitoring of conditions was necessary. An Air Council meeting took note of the 'urgent need for energetic measures to combat boredom and maintain morale during the winter, especially at remote stations.'[14] Diary entries by aircrew demonstrate that the enervating effects of inactivity could be a threat to morale. 'I have been feeling ill-tempered most of the evening. It is probably loneliness more than anything else, though inactivity has a lot to do with it,' wrote M.A. Scott in 1941.[15] Before he found himself in a more agreeable environment George Hull had complained, 'Wigsley, the antithesis of all things good, and the apotheosis of boredom and decay …….. just sat around the crew room in the state of completely browned off.'[16]

Complaints of a medical nature arising from bad station conditions feature regularly in Bomber Command medical reports.[17] One stated: 'It is a continual source of surprise that the relatively overcrowded condition of all ranks accommodation has not given rise to more epidemics.'[18] Medical officers constantly monitored the welfare of crews; any measure which decreased the risk of flying stress (q.v.) was employed. Consequently, the aircrews were considerably pampered, receiving ultra-violet lamp treatment, dosages of vitamin tablets, orange juice, paradine eye-drops for improved night vision and caffeine supplements. Benzedrine was administered to promote wakefulness. Crews received constant reminders on how to avoid frostbite and anoxia,[19] and were encouraged to take as much exercise as possible. 'MOs are universally aware of the importance of physical fitness and the direct influence this requirement can have on morale and fighting efficiency,' noted one report.[20] The solicitous treatment given to aircrews undoubtedly had the desired effect. Although some of the treatments were of dubious value, and, in the case of benzedrine, potentially harmful, they gave the crews the impression that someone *cared* about them.

There was, however, one problem which exercised the Air Ministry for the duration of the war. The incidence of venereal disease, a serious, potentially fatal condition before the advent of penicillin, increased dramatically. The reasons are obvious: wartime produced a slackening of moral restraints; a highly mobile population produced greater social interaction and 'the thought that death might be around the corner was a powerful incentive towards promiscuity.'[21] Bomber Command aircrews had ample opportunity for sexual adventure. They were the subject of considerable adulation from the civilian population, with whom it was easy to socialise. The RAF was concerned about venereal disease chiefly because it affected the efficiency of the Force. One training manual spelt out this attitude: 'We are not concerned with men's morals but with their health and fitness for duty in this tremendous effort we are making ……. The serious thing is not whether he has shown a lack of morals but whether he has failed in his duty to the cause.'[22]

It was necessary to take steps to improve self-control by airmen, 'particularly aircrew', wrote Bertine Sutton, the AMP.[23] Venereal disease rates in Bomber Command had risen from 8 cases in 1,000 during the period September 1939-December 1941 to 11.5 cases per 1,000 during the period January 1942-April 1943.[24] The Inspector General, Sir Philip Joubert, reported:

> Bomber Command has shown a tendency to have a definitely higher venereal disease rate than all other Commands, except Coastal Command, up to the end of 1941. Since the beginning of 1942 the incidence has steadily and markedly increased in Bomber Command, and still remains unsatisfactorily high, particularly in air crew. It is for consideration whether this increased incidence is connected with the stress and strain of the increased intensity of bomber operations. Previous to 1942 many sorties were easy; now-a-days practically all trips are difficult, tending to impress on air crews that they are living dangerously.[25]

Joubert continued:

> The increase of the disease among flying personnel from the flying training to the operational flying stage is disquieting. It is considered that several factors are concerned, such as the glamour of being a flying man, which appeals so much to the ladies; the extra pay of aircrew which tends to take them to places of amusement, with attendant dangers, and last but not least the fact that they are living dangerously and so a certain number are apt to adopt the attitude of 'eat, drink and be merry ......'[26]

This 'eat, drink and be merry' attitude was cited, in a minute accompanying Joubert's report, as the reason for increased venereal disease rates, along with 'the glamour of RAF uniform'. Attracting members of the opposite sex was easy; it was equally easy to ignore the potential consequences of sexual liaisons.[27] The report concluded that good leadership, good aircraft, activity and success on operations would lessen the incidence of venereal disease.[28]

The author of the minute writes in charmingly unofficial style that venereal disease is rampant in the summer months when, '...... there is long daylight conducive to wandering abroad, love and other eccentricities .... this defect of man is age old, as poets refer to June as the month of love, and talk of midsummer madness.'[29] Perhaps the minute's author was just a frustrated Romantic poet.

The issue of prophylactics might have decreased the incidence of venereal disease. Before the war it had been decided not to issue them to personnel. 'The view was then taken that the issue of these articles, at any rate to personnel in Britain, would have affronted certain sections of public opinion.'[30] Then, during the war, it was decided that '.... the free issue of condoms may encourage Service personnel to take risks they would otherwise avoid.'[31] Statistics from 1943 show that their availability in RCAF and American units led to an incidence of 20 and 30 infected men in 1,000 respectively, compared with 11.5 in 1,000 in the RAF. '...the countries which have the highest incidence of venereal disease are those whose personnel expose themselves most to the risk of infection by the company they seek and by their habits in regard to intoxicants.'[32] It was concluded by the Air Ministry that there was no evidence that condoms controlled infection; on the contrary – the statistics indicated that it *contributed* to the rate of infection. If free condoms were available, it would be perceived as a condoning of promiscuity. Moral outrage would ensue. There would be no change of policy and no free issue.

Lectures rather than condoms might be the answer. An Air Ministry minute directed that a bawdy approach to the subject was not appropriate with an audience of decent, clean living young men. More effective would be: '....... a quiet statement of fact [rather than] a rhetorical description of horrors.'[33] The goal of such lectures would be the sublimation of the sexual instinct by concentrating on the task at hand. Hobbies, games and sport would provide the ideal tonic.

*

Whether or not aircrews were aware of so much energy being expended on their well-being in the interests of morale, they had their own ideas about keeping up their spirits. A Mass Observation report found that: 'Eating, drinking, dancing, women and the pictures are the five main activities, (possibly in conjunction with each other).'[34] Sir William Rothenstein, an ardent propagandist for the RAF, made the same observation, in gentler language: '…. their pleasures and dissipations are simple – visits to neighbouring towns, the pubs and cinemas. So too, they read detective stories and light novels, which make little claim on their mental powers. In the Mess they played bridge, billiards and ping pong, draughts too, and a few played chess.'[35] Rather more robust language was employed by Wing Commander Evan Gwynn Jones, who recalled fondly, 'Piss-ups were very frequent. In addition to flight piss-ups, there were squadron piss-ups, stand-down piss-ups and, as good as any, gong list piss-ups. Inter-squadron drinking matches were a highlight.'[36] F/O. Pierre Richard believed that, 'Rather heavy social drinking had been encouraged in Bomber Command. Take their minds off the carnage, was the idea, I think.'[37] If spirits were kept up by drinking, its long-term value to morale was doubted by one Mass Observation reporter: '[the] occasional organised piss-up, which perhaps steps up morale for a short time, leaves both a physical and a mental hangover.'[38] Nevertheless, drinking sessions provided comfort and companionship for the crews. Guy Gibson's frequent references to his drinking escapades are a strong feature of his autobiography *Enemy Coast Ahead*.

*

In 1940, the *Daily Mirror* gave its readers a glimpse into life on a bomber station. In an article with the headline 'RAF's own leaflet war' it reported the friendly rivalry between two stations:

> The pilots and crews of two Yorkshire RAF stations ……. have been 'raiding' each other with leaflets, some in verse. One station apparently received more publicity for their part in the raid [on Sylt shipping] than their comrades at the second station. The latter set out for the first station and plastered the officers' mess with leaflets ironically congratulating them on 'their heroism' on the Sylt bombardment.

'Reprisals' were not long delayed, for yesterday printed leaflets ...... were picked up on the first station. An extract read: 'You must be frightfully jealous but then you came in rather late. It must be galling to have your thunder stolen. We sympathise. There are tales of indiscriminate bombing of mackerel in the North Sea, but we accept all these stories with a large pinch of Sylt.[39]

Such high jinks were no doubt a tonic for morale, both of the readers of the *Daily Mirror* article and of aircrews, at that early stage in Bomber Command's war.

The Mess

'I shall now take you non-flying people's [sic] into an aircrew's Mess,' wrote P/O. Byrne. 'You will find most of the boys asleep in the armchairs around the perimeter of the room. A few will be reading a paper or a magazine. The most energetic will be playing billiards and snooker. Two playing table tennis at the top quarter of the room. This does not seem the place fit for heroes to live in.'[40]

Mess life was important to the crews. A medical officer observed: 'To their messing the aircrews customarily pay more attention and any lowering of the standard can easily lead to discontent and encourage grumbling habits.'[41] At the same time it was realised by most aircrew that they were better off in terms of material comfort than many civilians.[42] Mess life could assume Jekyll and Hyde qualities. On the one hand it could be likened to 'a camp for overgrown schoolboys' where high spirits, pranks and games created a fine *esprit-de-corps*.[43] Don Charlwood recalled that anything could happen in the mess: 'Bike races occurred; men left footprints on the ceiling; the piano was plied with beer by grateful singers; the furniture was turned upside down so that aircrew men could fling themselves over it.'[44] On the other hand it could be a haven for escape. The mess '...... was like a 6th form room .... the comfortable, warm room, the pleasant tap of the ping-pong balls and the homely schoolboyish atmosphere seemed fantastically unwarlike.'[45] The calming effect of the mess was captured in lyrical prose by George Hull, presumably after he had escaped from Wigsley and found himself at Coningsby: 'I am sitting in a darkening Mess writing in the dark almost, watching the flickering fire and listening to the strains of the "Warsaw Concerto" being bashed out on the piano. I am almost happy at the moment.'[46]

One observer did not share Hull's state of near elation. If the inmates were not gambling, listening to non-stop dance music on the wireless or following the adventures of *Jane* in the *Daily Mirror*, 'the most popular leisure activity was to sit in a chair .... and either talk or sleep, or as likely as not, do neither but just sit (or lie).'[47] The remedy for this inactivity, the observer concluded, was to move men nearer to their homes and families, which would do more that anything else to raise morale in the RAF.[48] This was a forlorn hope, as it was in direct opposition to Arthur Harris's views on 'living in', the requirement that married aircrew should be separated from their families and live on the station. The despair of this same observer at the lack of culture in the mess would have been alleviated if he had read M.A. Scott's diary: 'I found the wistful 5/4 movement of the Pathetique as moving as ever' and two days later he recorded the fact that 'I won 7/- at poker tonight in 50 minutes, and then left to listen to Brahms.'[49] Like Hull, another satisfied mess customer.

The Air Ministry, recognising the problems associated with throwing together such a disparate collection of individuals from all strata of society, made efforts to highlight the need for tolerance of others. Guy Gibson, a man uncomfortable in intellectual company, had an uneasy relationship with his one-time flight commander, John Wooldridge, an aesthete who would prefer to read or listen to music, while Gibson would be in a drinking session in the mess.[50] Of Wooldridge, Gibson himself wrote, 'He had amazing habits, and at the time he joined he was engaged in the doubtful art of composing a concerto.'[51] Gibson continued: 'He couldn't drink a lot .... poetry was his line as well, but he was an excellent type.'[52] Gibson's Philistinism may or may not have been shared by others in the Command but his attitude toward Wooldridge exemplifies the necessity for acceptance of one's fellow's foibles if any semblance of comradely cohesion were to be achieved. Wooldridge, with handlebar moustache and quietly-spoken understatement, the epitome of a British RAF pilot, went on to write the script for the 1953 film *Appointment in London,* based on his own experience in Bomber Command, and was killed in a road accident in 1958.

Men of a sensitive nature or serious thinkers who did not conform to the 'heavy drinking' ethos which was prevalent, could find themselves isolated on stations. RCAF crews were reminded that, 'The cameraderie in the Mess should be such that no man should be thought a sissy because he prefers a book, even a highbrow one, or solitaire to a game of poker. All are in the Service to do their best.'[53] Segregation of officer and NCO messes was an unfortunate arrangement, affecting the morale of mixed rank crews, as one crewman with the RCAF pointed out. There was 'Injury to team spirit when the crew, as an entity, is not able to live and fraternise, the one with the other, during leisure and off-duty hours.'[54]

*

Administration

'...... the first essential of good discipline is a clearly defined and thoroughly understood chain of command and responsibility; and the key position in this chain is held by the Station Commander.' So wrote the CAS to Sir Philip Babington, AOC Flying Training Command, on 3 December 1942.[55] A view endorsed by VCAS AVM C.E.H. Medhurst in November 1942: '.... the influence of a good Station Commander is soon felt throughout the whole station ...... those which show up to the best advantage are invariably commanded by energetic Station Commanders who have a complete knowledge of everything which is going on within the station.'[56] Ruthless methods to remove inadequate station commanders should be employed, Medhurst instructed.

As I.G., Sir Philip Joubert had his own opinions on the running of a good station. Commanders were entitled to more support than they were receiving from HQ and from group HQs. His observations from station visits resulted in some caustic comments. There should be no loitering or ambling around aimlessly. Squads of aircrew or ground crew should be marched around the station. He was shocked by sloppy saluting and by the indiscipline of Dominion aircrews, both of which misdemeanours could, in his opinion, affect morale. Aircrews moved from one squadron to another with frequency. This policy, believed Joubert, '.... made it impossible for officers and men to get to know each other and for units to attain that cohesion and esprit de corps which were necessary for good discipline.'[57]

With victory in sight the Air Ministry did not flag in its promotion of good management of bomber stations. 'Relations between officers and men are fundamental to the maintenance of a satisfactory state of morale and discipline.'[58] Maximum operational effort had created a distance between officers and men. Now that operational effort could be relaxed it could provide the opportunity for that situation to be remedied.

Entertainment

The cinema, either on the station or in the local towns, provided another means of escapism for aircrews, and indeed, the entire population. Weekly attendances 'at the pictures' rose from 19 million in 1939 to 30 million in 1945 and films were a major influence on the mores of wartime Britain.[59] One member of Bomber Command, Sergeant Wiggins, revealed his passion for films in his diary. Whenever possible, he made the trip to his local picture house or to the camp cinema. On 5 June 1944 he made the entry '"They got me covered", Bob Hope and Dorothy Lamour. Good entertainment. Station cinema!'[60] He was killed the next day, D-Day, on a raid to Caen. This poignant last entry in his diary illustrates the bizarre world in which aircrews lived. Whatever activity in which they were engaged, death was never far away. Perhaps it *was* better to adopt the 'eat, drink and be merry' philosophy rather than brood on possible imminent mortality.

Dances were a popular diversion. Chain dances, like the Lambeth Walk and the Hokey-Cokey, were favourites. They reflected the intense community spirit of the time and, of course, one met girls at dances.[61] The newly-formed 630 Squadron celebrated Christmas 1943 with a dinner and dance. On the 23rd the squadron took part in an attack on Berlin. There were no losses. Then on Christmas Day 'Officers helped to airmen's Christmas dinner and entertained Sergeants in Mess at 19.00 hours. Dance and cabaret held in No.2 Dinning [sic] Hall was a great success.' The adjutant added, hopefully, 'There is rather a lack of entertainment on the station but the position is expected to improve.' Summing up the squadron's first month at East Kirkby the adjutant commented indignantly, '48 officers have still no batman at all!'[62] But it was a contented squadron.

In May 1944 Folliott Sandford of the Air Ministry wrote to the VCAS regarding 'all ranks' dances at stations. There was a lack of partners at segregated dances and it might be good for morale if officers and NCOs, and WAAFs of all ranks, were given the chance to mingle. The Air Ministry approved the idea but not on stations where bad discipline was evident. On stations where 'all ranks' dances were permitted, they would be cancelled at the first sign of trouble.[63] This concern is perhaps understandable when one reads an account by George Hull of one such shindig:

> The station warrant officer [responsible for discipline] did an Apache war dance with a red-haired bit of stuff from the Orderly Room, two squadron leaders played rugger with a squashed bun and ended up under the billiards table, two flight sergeants fought a bloody battle on the stairs …….. apparently I made four dates for tonight. [The dance was] ….. one of those 'drink up, mates, you may go for a Burton tomorrow' efforts.[64]

Hull was killed six days later.

Other camp entertainment was provided by ENSA (Entertainments National Services Association or fondly remembered by some as Every Night Something Awful). The civilian Robert Nichols, a distinguished poet of his day, who was attached to RAF Oakington, wrote on many aspects of life in Bomber Command and his voluminous correspondence made its way to the very top of the Command. On station entertainment he thought, 'Something should be done about ENSA.' Only one in three shows was worth seeing. 'It must be understood that a really good show such as "Ladies of the Night" goes really big and constitutes a real tonic to the station.' Nichols suggested more concerts by CEMA (Council for the Encouragement of Music and the Arts).[65] One wonders how they would have been received by Norman Bottomley's criminal NCOs (q.v., see Chapter 9), for whom such cultural refinement was not standard fare. Despite a reputation for poor quality shows, at least some Bomber Command men appreciated the efforts of ENSA, as an Air Ministry report on morale in August 1945 showed.[66] Most were only too glad to have another diversion from reality and boredom, whatever the quality of the ENSA concerts.

The Local Community

Contact with the local community could have its own effect on morale. Reflecting the popularity of aircrews with the general public, local populations usually welcomed airmen. There were exceptions. The invasion of rural areas by large numbers of RAF personnel did bring problems. Farmers lost land under runways, aircraft noise caused discomfort, there was risk of attack by German intruder aircraft and in one area at least, a complaint from the local hunt at the loss of fox-hunting land.[67] Boisterous behaviour was usually tolerated but, presumably because it was the centre for so many off-duty crews, some of Lincoln City's inhabitants were hostile. Aircrews were refused service in some of the city's restaurants. George Hull may have contributed to this hostility: 'We can be a bit boisterous in Lincoln on occasions – it's a case of letting off steam or bursting – but I think a little toleration on the population's part is required.'[68] The high spirits of airmen, however, were generally accepted. Village pubs and local families were welcoming and it can be stated with certainty that general morale in Bomber Command only benefitted from good relations with local communities.

Leave

When airmen went on leave the opportunity for disenchantment with Bomber Command was at a high level. This statement may seem odd, because surely the temporary release from the constant fear of injury or worse would induce something approaching euphoria. Yes, but the knowledge that an airman had to return to that world of ever present danger could be a strong incentive to melt into the population at the end of his leave. That this was an extremely rare occurrence is testament to aircrew fortitude, discipline and sense of duty. George Hull resisted such action and confided:

> Somehow, just after returning from leave, I am always struck with the uselessness of all this waste of time in the service. At other times, caught up in the enthusiasm of the moment it does not seem a bad life at all, then you go home on leave and do all the things that you did before the war, dropping back into civilian life for a few glorious

days with ease. Then in a flash it's goodbye to all the things you realise that matter and you're left feeling a little stunned by it all.[69]

Heartening as it was to receive the public's adulation, aircrews must have had pause for thought when they inhabited a world free of danger for a few days; the urge not to return to possible death must have been a strong one. Approximately 6,000 RAF personnel deserted during the Second World War. A breakdown of all the Commands is not available but Bomber Command airmen are undoubtedly represented in that number. RAF desertion is outwith the scope of this study but it must be recorded that it *did* occur and those relatively few men who chose to renege on duty had suffered breakdown of morale. It could be surmised that desertions were most frequent at times of leave. The vast majority of men did not choose this course of action and returned to their duties.

Unreality

Even while on station the crews lived a double life of unreality which encompassed tranquillity and terror within a few short hours. Pierre Richard observed, 'It was a strange way to live, on the very edge of death.' When he joined his first operational squadron it was, 'as if I were looking at a dream world……. I never lost that strange feeling of unreality.'[70] Lord Moran recognised this phenomenon: 'One night the pilot lives amongst civilians in soft security. The next he spends in a bomber over Germany. The sharp contrast adds to his troubles by keeping alive the idea of another way of life – the chronic danger of an alternative to war.'[71] Leonard Cheshire wrote in 1943: 'All the time during the film I kept thinking, "What a funny war this is! One minute you're in the middle of guns and blood and the next you're watching Bing Crosby playing the fool." But as they say, I will have to get used to it.'[72]

Don Charlwood, made a fair attempt at explaining the phenomenon: 'Life on the squadron was seldom far from fantasy. We might, at eight, be in a chair beside a fire, but at ten, in an empty world above a floor of cloud. Or at eight, walking in Barnetby with a girl whose nearness denied all possibility of sudden death at twelve.'[73] He, Cheshire and all aircrews, *did* get used to it although they found it impossible to articulate to anyone who had not experienced it. Guy Gibson derived great satisfaction from the fact that Richard Dimbleby, the BBC journalist who had flown on a raid to Germany with Gibson, was able to express clearly what Gibson himself did not have the eloquence to convey.[74] The artist Sir William Rothenstein provided a succinct description of the unique nature of Bomber Command's war:

> After a night's operations the young men to whom I was talking might dash into a neighbouring town to see a film or visit a friend. But this contact with normal humanity is superficial, haphazard, ephemeral, compared with their relationship to one another, cemented by dangers and difficulties shared, and pervaded always by the consciousness that death was close to them, as it could not be to their fellow civilians.[75]

There were 'grouses', men became 'browned off', conditions and entertainment varied from station to station, contact with the civilian population provided opportunity for reflection on the life they were leading. Individuals could suffer temporary depression. All the evidence indicates that the elements of station life which constituted the daily existence of Bomber Command aircrews *contributed* to maintaining morale.

Chapter 7

Collecting a Gong: Incentives

'Incentives' encompasses remuneration, commissions, promotion, and decorations. The intensity of operations and the high crew loss rate provided accelerated opportunities for both gallantry decorations and promotion. Would these incentives have had any part to play in maintaining morale?

Remuneration

'No-one can have joined Bomber Command for the pay,' wrote Norman Longmate.[1] A contemporary report bears out this opinion: 'You will never meet an airman ...... who does not regard 2/6d [12.5p] a day as a swindle and a humiliation.'[2] Wing Commander Jim Wright disagreed. 'I don't think anyone seriously grumbled about PAY – may have been some humorous references to American/Canadian rates of pay (which were higher than ours for similar ranks) but I don't think it was a problem.'[3]

There *was*, though, discontent. 'The RAF grumbles – with good cause,' read a *Daily Mirror* article headline. It continued, 'Sir Archibald Sinclair, the Secretary of State for Air, is gravely concerned over RAF morale and is following with keen personal interest every effort made to make the youngest Service a more contented Service........ Sir Archibald Sinclair does not favour any discrimination which may affect discipline. It is the lower strata of his Ministry who are responsible for this discontent-breeder.'[4] The *Mirror*'s 'Question Time in the Mess' argued that 'welfaring' was the most neglected side of RAF administration. Disgruntled Air Force personnel who wrote to the newspaper overwhelmingly focussed on pay, promotion and leave. An example cited in the article was the fact that sergeant pilots and navigators were paid 13s (65p) daily, while flight sergeants received 15s 6d (77.5p). Both took equal risks; why not equal pay? From such trivial concerns discontent could spread.

As usual, the Air Ministry had an eye on the potential damage to morale caused by aggrieved airmen. In a report in 1944 it was noted that there was an '....... adverse effect on the morale of RAF personnel of the mounting wages of civilian car workers.'[5] Arthur Harris wrote to the AMP Air Marshal Sir Bertine Sutton on 19 February 1943 in support of his crews and on the subject of the pittance with which, in his view, they were paid:

> These youngsters, who bear almost the whole brunt of the War, are doing magnificent work and we appear to grudge them everything ....They do not fight for money ...... but they and their families have to compete in a very restricted market for the necessities and amenities of life with the bloated plutocrats who call themselves the 'workers'. Ye Gods! Who does the work in the War, anyway?[6]

Sutton replied on 13 March. Quoting Ministry of Labour statistics, he compared favourably the rate of pay for a mechanic in an aircraft factory, or, as Harris would prefer to call such a worker, 'a 21 year old idle scruffy mechanic', with a flight lieutenant's. The mechanic earned 21/- per week (£1.05); the flight lieutenant 21/9d per week (£1.08). In inimitable style, Harris replied,

'I am quite frankly astounded to see that you attempt to justify (?) the existing state of affairs. The morale of the service will not held [sic] up indefinitely while the men are subjected to intense financial worries and their wives and families are put nowhere in competition with the overpaid, so-called "workers" ...... I do implore you to treat this question as a matter vitally and closely connected with the morale of the Services now, and the welfare of the whole nation in the immediate post-war period.'[7]

Harris was referring to the advantageous conditions in which civilian workers would find themselves after the war, compared with the 'penniless demobilisees of the Services'.[8]

Despite these concerns, and Harris's protestations, it appears that pay did not enter into the equation where morale was concerned. Grouses and grumbles there were, but considering the danger faced almost daily by aircrew, the meagre remuneration on offer was never a cause for widespread discontent. Writing in 1940, Sergeant W.D. Morrison seemed happy with his lot: 'I do all right on my two bob a day …. everything we need is supplied and we often get oranges after our meals so anything we *do* buy is a luxury.'[9]

Commissions

The RAF in the Second World War was never able to rid itself entirely of its class-based notions of leadership. The public school ethos was maintained throughout.[10] One report concluded: 'The overwhelming majority of the rank and file resent intensely the segregation between officers and men'; the same report included the thoughts of a warrant officer: 'We're just dirt – that's how they (officers) look on us. They won't get me in one of their wars again. No sir.'[11] Despite class antagonism, evidence suggests that it rarely mattered to aircrews. There was never general discontent, rather an acceptance of a system in which one day one might obtain a commission. The pride in wearing an officer's insignia was something to look forward to, an incentive.[12]

Nevertheless, the Air Ministry still frowned upon the idea that a commissioned officer should serve under an NCO captain.[13] Harris considered that if it were obvious that an NCO deserved a commission for his exemplary conduct in the air, he should receive that commission immediately. Such an award would raise the morale, not only of the man himself, but also of his comrades. He asked the Under Secretary of State for Air H.H. Balfour to consider the following:

> Cases arise where airmen members of aircrews operating against the enemy display high qualities of gallant leadership sufficient to justify the grant of an immediate commission, quite apart from an award merely for gallantry …. it is inevitable in a major war that the qualities of born leaders will become apparent and immediate recognition of these qualities will be appreciated by other aircrew members, and act as a stimulus to greater effort.[14]

Air gunners, in particular, were regarded as poor material: 'Very few air gunners are suitable for commissioning. The standard leaves much to be desired.'[15] The Air Ministry was reluctant to pursue an intensive commissioning policy but was left with no alternative in the face of manpower requirements. Harris shared the Ministry's misgivings regarding poor standards. He was dismissive of officer selection boards, which he termed 'useless'.[16] Still in favour of a limited number of commissions for outstanding NCOs, he realised reluctantly that the commissioning of large numbers of NCOs must proceed, even with inferior material, as a matter of operational necessity.

Harris then wanted to see commissioning at OTUs to relieve his group commanders, who were responsible for commissioning, of a considerable workload. He had received a plea from Ralph Cochrane, now AOC 5 Group, who held exactly the same view. 'It is most unsatisfactory that Captains of aircraft should have their commissioning deferred until they are posted to operational Squadrons. I must therefore take action as soon as they reach the Group to make good the failure to initiate commissioning at an earlier Training stage.'[17] Commissioning must take place at the OTU stage.

To which AMP Air Marshal Sir Bertine Sutton responded, 'To commission at OTUs is at present contrary to the policy that aircrews (except those commissioned on graduation from training) should not be recommended until they have proved themselves either in operations or as instructors.'[18] Harris replied, 'I am sorry to see that you are not willing to relieve Group Commanders of their intolerable and indeed fruitless task of personally interviewing vast numbers of recommendees for commissions.'[19] Reluctantly, he gave way on that occasion. In July 1943 he tried a different approach, in order to help his beleaguered group commanders. This time it was an appeal to let them delegate their commissioning responsibilities to squadron and station commanders, who were in a far better position to judge the qualities of commission candidates, men who would be known to them personally.[20]

By 1945 44% of crews arriving from OTUs at 3 Group were captained by NCO pilots.[21] It would be a similar percentage at other groups. It was now the responsibility of junior commanders to select those NCOs suitable for commissions.

Promotion

Commissioned officers often found their rise up the ranks to senior positions occurring at an alarmingly fast rate. In peacetime, it would take rather longer to become a squadron leader or wing commander. The terrible losses sustained by Bomber Command in the war meant that inexperienced men, perhaps with only a few 'ops' under their belts, suddenly found themselves leading squadrons. Wing Commander A.J. Wright remembered that:

> Promotion was largely a routine sort of thing. Sgts automatically went on through F/Sgt WOs and were commissioned if they survived long enough and had earned such recognition. Many (about 20 – 25%) were commissioned at end of basic training as Pilot Officers – 6 months to Fg/Of. & about another 18 months to Flt./Lt. But pilots were often promoted to Acting Flt./Lt. on squadrons to fill necessary posts. The 'chop rate' on squadrons in my time was severe and it was often the case that if COs and flight commanders did not return, someone had to step in and take their place. Hence 21 year old pilots with operational experience could well hold senior squadron leader or wing commander ranks on an acting, temporary basis.[22]

Promotion in Bomber Command was automatic; it was merely a question of staying alive long enough to qualify for it.

Decorations

Immediate awards of the Distinguished Flying Medal or Distinguished Flying Cross were a boost to morale, both of the recipient and of his comrades; awards which took time to reach their recipients less so. In the intervening period the man may have been posted to another squadron – or killed or gone missing. An officer quoted in a post-war report believed that morale could have been raised by *immediate* awards, while the man concerned was still with his squadron. 'All the crews got uplift from it.'[23] Awards which took longer to be processed, on the other hand, had no benefit for morale. They often '....do not come through until the man has left the squadron so that they have no personal value for the crews.'[24]

There were those who thought that decorations should be awarded to an entire crew if it managed to reach the end of its tour without 'putting up a black'. This would give crews a target, an incentive.[25]

It was a view shared by Oliver Stewart. In his column *Air Eddies* he wrote in October 1941 that,

> ……..it is wrong that those who have done this [completed a given number of operations] should have no distinction from those who wear wings – and often other decorations too – but who have never been shot at in their lives…….. We must show that the country appreciates the vital work of endurance and steadfast courage that is done by these men.[26]

He returned to the theme in July 1942:

> I am always arguing that the members of Bomber Command do not get sufficient recognition. The conferring of decorations is not enough, for, to earn a decoration on Bomber Command, a man must not only be courageous and skilful in a high degree, but he must also have a large measure of good luck…… More than once I have proposed a special bomber decoration to be granted automatically when a person had completed a set number of successful sorties.[27]

Undoubtedly decorations were worn with pride by those who received them but some airmen displayed disdain: A decoration was a 'survivor's gong'. 'Most gongs are balls anyway. You've usually got to have bought it before you get the best ones,' wrote one veteran.[28] Jim Wright's objective was staying alive, whether he was decorated or not. 'Very nice if you were lucky enough to receive any but awards were seen to be largely a matter of luck. I would say that decorations were judged to be well-earned but we all knew that survival was the aim and that many, many aircrew deserved decorations but did not receive them ….. because they died.'[29]

A cynical attitude was displayed towards decorations. There was a taint of class bias in their award. Distinguished Flying Medals (DFM) were awarded to NCOs; Distinguished Flying Crosses (DFC) to officers. Flight Sergeant James Brown was a gunner whose Lancaster returned safely after an encounter with a night fighter: 'The four officers in the crew got DFCs but the three NCOs got nothing.'[30] The random distribution of awards devalued them; favourites could benefit at the expense of more worthy candidates. 'It all depended on the CO and some wing commanders only "gonged" the skipper and no-one else.'[31]

*

A more effective morale booster was perhaps verbal encouragement. Air Vice Marshal Symonds wrote in 1947, 'A bit of quiet praise from the squadron commander pushes morale right up.'[32] Commissioning policy directly affected morale; it was determined in light of operational needs and efficiency, which, in turn, impinged on morale. If the policy helped to prevent losses, then it helped to sustain morale. There could have been resentment at perceived inequities in commissioning, the award of decorations and pay. It is clear that, except for isolated cases, that this was not the case and that there was no threat to morale from these potentially harmful sources. Indeed, if the responses of the veterans are a guide, there was a certain insouciance toward both pay and decorations. Airmen carried out their duties to the best of their abilities; their only ambition – survival.

Chapter 8

Ringmasters: Leadership

'Whoever ran an air station successfully in time of war inevitably became an amateur psychologist.'[1]

Max Hastings believes that leadership was *the* decisive factor determining morale in the Service.[2] The obvious starting point for any discussion on leadership in Bomber Command begins with the most famous name connected with it. Air Marshal Sir Arthur Harris succeeded Air Marshal Sir Richard Peirse on 18 March 1942. According to *The Tatler* he was known as 'Ginger' to his friends.[3] This epithet did not catch on with the public, who much preferred 'Bomber'. To his crews he was 'Butch', an affectionate diminutive of Butcher, and to his friends he was Bert.

'I don't agree that there was any lack of morale when I took over,' Harris said, 'but there was, I think, amongst the crews a great feeling of disappointment, because they were doing their best under conditions when it couldn't be done.'[4] Harris was determined to transform the fortunes of Bomber Command after the lacklustre performance of his predecessor Peirse. There is scant evidence of crew admiration for Peirse, whereas Harris appeared to capture the attention of his men from the moment he took command. The public, too, was aware of his intention to prosecute the war relentlessly. This from the *Edinburgh Evening News*:

A Great Leadership

The RAF is fortunate, at this stage in the war, not only that we build bigger and better bombers than any other country, and have 'more beautiful' bombs than any other country, but that we have an air officer commanding-in-chief Bomber Command, Air Marshal A.T. Harris, who has shown more than once in the past that he is game to risk his Service career for the sake of doing his job as he thinks it ought to be done.⁵

After the first 1,000 raid 'The Harris Touch' was the headline in the *Belfast Newsletter*.⁶ Then he delivered his famous address, seen by millions in newsreels: 'They sowed the wind and now they are going to reap the whirlwind.' His crews knew he meant business. He was rarely seen by them, though. A remote figure who controlled the destiny of thousands, he somehow instilled in them the qualities inherent in his own uncompromising character. Hamish Mahaddie (q.v.), a Pathfinders group captain, himself an inspiring leader, said of Harris:

> He didn't, you know, come and see us and hand out cigarettes like Monty or pat us on the back, he was very seldom seen. I don't recall him ever for instance coming to the Pathfinders Group but he managed to give the impression that he knew what it was all about and we felt that everything he did was to our advantage and making us do our job better....... He sent the most amazing signals ...... something you read out to your crews at briefing ...⁷

In July 1942 it was reported that Harris had broadcast a warning to Germany:

> We'll scourge the Reich
> A message to the German people from Air Marshal Sir Arthur Harris, Chief of Bomber Command, was broadcast last night. 'We are going to scourge the Third Reich from end to end,' his message said. 'We shall be coming every night and every day, rain, blow or snow – we and the Americans. We are bombing Germany city by city, and ever more terribly in order to make it impossible for you to go on with the war ...... We prefer to hit factories, shipyards and railways ..... But those people who work in these plants live close to them. Therefore we hit your houses and you. We regret the necessity for this.'⁸

Of course, Harris did no such thing. He did not speak German. But for his crews the effect on morale was terrific. Similarly, they would probably have been wryly amused to hear that Harris had been deemed a war criminal by the Germans: 'Nazis name "War Criminals". Air Chief Marshal Harris and Dingle Foot, Parliamentary Secretary, Ministry of Economic Warfare [Liberal MP for Dundee] are on the Nazi register of war criminals which German Overseas Radio yesterday stated was being compiled.'[9] What Dingle Foot had done to incur Nazi wrath is unknown to this writer but Bomber Harris's mission was unlikely to endear him to many Germans. The German News Agency had him in its sights. 'It is significant that the British, having realised that they cannot win the war weapon for weapon have now resorted to the illusion that they can decide it by fighting against women and children. Sir Arthur Harris, who now speaks openly of murder, may be assured that he will one day be called to account for it.'[10]

Harris may have been a remote figure, rarely seen on bomber stations, but he was protective of his crews, always fighting for better aircraft, better equipment and better remuneration. He somehow conveyed to his crews the essential element of leadership, protection. They *believed* in him. Wing Commander Jim Wright was one who did:

> He was doing a difficult job in a resolute way. We did not enjoy our tours. We grumbled but got on with our respective jobs because we accepted that our leaders at all levels from Squadron through Groups Commands to Winston Churchill himself knew more than we (very young people) did and that our only hope of winning the war was to follow our leaders and their policies........ I think morale was good. Probably because, although we knew our losses were high and our chances of survival low, everyone was doing their best. Bomber Harris may have been Butch Harris but someone had to do his job and we respected that.[11]

Admiration was mutual. When asked in the 1970s why he thought morale was so high in Bomber Command, Harris replied, 'Because the boys we had were the pick. The pick of the litter and they were just full of guts and they deserved credit for what they did, and they get precious little credit for it.'[12]

*

During Richard Peirse's tenure as C-in-C he requested that senior officers be brought into his Command from other Commands. Arthur Harris, at that time Deputy Chief of Air Staff, recalling his incumbency as AOC 5 Group, disagreed, as was his wont. In his experience, he opined, such appointments were usually failures with, perhaps, one or two brilliant exceptions. These officers had often not flown for a long time or were just too old to manage administrative tasks and the demands of flying simultaneously. Harris wrote to CAS Portal:

> To expect some old war horse who has been sitting on his tail in an office for many years to skip through an OTU and then take command of such a unit [an operational squadron] is, from the physical and psychological points of view, too much to expect from the average individual......... I would assert most strongly that our best squadron and flight commanders today will be found from amongst the youngsters who themselves have done the job, and that was indeed my experience in No. 5 Group.[13]

It would also be easier for young commanders to bond with the young aircrews under their command. Much as they might show respect for an older man, the crews would share the same attitudes and argot as their younger commanders; older leaders would find it more difficult to find acceptance.

*

At group level men like Ralph Cochrane (5 Group) and Don Bennett (8 Group PFF) also commanded respect (though not always mutual). Their effective leadership had a trickle down effect, resulting in efficient bombing and good morale. At an Air Council meeting on 6 January 1944 Portal 'observed that in Operational Commands the results achieved reflected the effectiveness or otherwise of the work of Group Commanders and the state of morale in the groups........'[14]

Further down the scale of command strong leadership from the squadron commander was vital to morale. A former squadron leader, C.G.C. Rawlins, identified the reasons for successful leadership:

> To the young and eager pilots of those days, most brought up and accepting the British system of hierarchical leadership, it all seemed perfectly sound. There was, perhaps, more cameraderie between ranks than there would have been in pre-war days and consequently a little less automatic respect for higher ranks. It was a man's operational, rather than his service, record which marked him out as a respected leader in an operational squadron.[15]

Writing in 1942, Cecil Beaton appreciated the value of leading by example:

> The influence of the Commanding Officer seeps through the whole unit under his control. His personality and character can be of great moment. Confidence is inspired if the men know that he has excelled on operations and understands the potentialities of each raid. His assurance can raise temporarily lowered morale if weather has been bad, raids unsuccessful or casualties heavy.[16]

What were the qualities which made for a successful leader of men on squadrons and stations? He must have had operational experience; he must not avoid known tough targets; he should fly when morale was low; he should strive to know all his crews. A good leader would generate high morale; a poor leader would result in low morale and a potentially high incidence of wavering (q.v.).[17]

Sir Philip Joubert, as Inspector General, understood the importance of appointing station commanders adept at both flying *and* administration. He wrote, 'Our Group Captains are given responsibilities before which those of the average Army brigadier pale into insignificance ...... failure to attach proper importance to administrative matters cannot fail to react adversely on general efficiency, discipline and morale.'[18] Joubert recommended selection of commanding officers on the basis of maturity and length of service but this was not always possible given the alarmingly high casualty rate in aircrew. It appears that he failed to realise that skilled administrators with no operational experience – 'wingless wonders', as the derogatory euphemism had it – did not always command respect from the crews. A High Command out of touch with its fighting men and reliant on traditional class-based notions of leadership sometimes failed to take account of the bonds formed by those officers and men doing the actual fighting together. While administrative ability was necessary, the best results came from aircrews who had leaders of proven operational worth.

The two key elements of leadership are the sense of being protected by those being led and leading by example.[19] Lord Moran stressed the absolute importance of the latter: 'These pilots reach out instinctively to anything that increases their chances of survival …… the pilot must see his leader in action.'[20] Leaders who failed to fly regularly or who chose 'easy' operations on which to fly 'risked almost instant loss of credibility and social ostracism,'[21] states Mark Wells, author of the masterly study *Courage and Air Warfare*. Good leaders became equal to father figures to their men. Rank decreased in importance in combat situations and officers were drawn closer to their men than to those in ranks above them.[22] Officers in the RAF tended to have better relations with their enlisted men than in the other services and this encouraged a high degree of group identification.[23]

Miles Tripp remembered his new commanding officer, a man seen as a 'wingless wonder', who had never flown on operations before: '.... he intended to remedy the deficiency of being a wingless wonder and to fly operationally because he thought that the station commander should share the same dangers as his men.'[24] This won him the immediate respect of his crews.

It was policy to retain tour-expired aircrew but when they were promoted to senior rank – squadron leader, wing commander or group captain – young leaders who suddenly found themselves facing daily administrative tasks beyond their capabilities could not cope. During periods when losses were heavy wing commanders in their 20s and group captains in their early 30s were common. 'Many of them would not have been promoted on merit,' was the opinion of Wing Commander K.J. Newman.[25] Squadron Leader Rawlins pointed out that many commanding officers were lost because, although they lacked operational experience, they felt pressure to prove themselves and to win the respect of their men.[26] The resultant effect on morale of repeated losses of commanding officers on squadrons needs no elaboration.

When commanders who did survive to the end of their tours were stood down from flying, CAS Charles Portal realised the damage to morale which would result from preventing them from flying again. When he was ACAS Harris had requested 'an absolute embargo on such men flying.'[27] Portal strongly disagreed, believing that morale would be affected if aircrew did not see their leaders flying on operations. Harris eventually conceded the argument but, in reply, maintained that men *would* accept non-flying leaders who had proved themselves. He had…....

> ….… frequently stopped ….… operational flying by 'over-run' squadron and flight commanders in 5 Group [when Harris was C-in-C 5 Group] without ill-effects. The other crews recognised the fact that they had already 'done their stuff' and much preferred to retain their tried and trusted leaders even tho' they were not allowed to fly on operations any more than lose them in exchange for a pig in a poke.[28]

Leadership at squadron level was generally successful. Exceptional leaders like Guy Gibson and Leonard Cheshire were rare but other men, of lesser abilities, made good commanders. If they were able to balance firmness with fairness, if they were willing to fly on 'tough' ops and if they had good operational records, then aircrews would accord them respect. There were, though, as Harris had pointed out, instances of non-operational commanders winning the respect of their crews.

A final point must be made. '…..Much of the philosophy of the upper classes permeated the service ….… understatement, restraint and humility were virtues of leadership.'[29] Effective, often inspired, leadership in Bomber Command *was* achieved. In general, commanding officers demonstrated a flexibility to adapt to the exigencies of war. A combination of factors made this possible: deference to authority, leading from the front and a less rigid reliance on rank, which created strong bonds *between* ranks. As a result morale was never compromised; good leadership enhanced it.

Chapter 9

Bags of Bull:
Discipline

'Duty or Safety? Duty or Self Regard? You know which comes first! The driving force of high ideals and strong self-discipline will direct your conduct more worthily than the outward discipline imposed by King's Regulations and the parade ground. High morale.'[1]

On 11 August 1942 a meeting took place in the Air Council room of the Air Ministry. It was attended by the Cs-in-C of all Commands and the subject was discipline. It was agreed that every man in every branch of the Service should have a knowledge of the chain of command and who was responsible for his orders and his welfare. Suggestions for improvements in organisation of the disciplinary structure in the RAF were made. Arthur Harris was sceptical and the minutes of the meeting recorded his own suggestion: 'He did not think that aircrews could be expected to give much time and attention to disciplinary matters in view of the strain under which they lived and the short time which they spent at one station. He suggested that there ought to be a permanent disciplinary and defence staff at each station, leaving the relatively transient population of air crews and maintenance personnel free to devote all their energies to operations.'[2]

Harris had a point. In a crew concerned with survival, the last thing they needed was an officer fellow crew member admonishing them for having dirty buttons. On operational squadrons, too, the squadron or station commander was likely to be lenient with his men if disciplinary measures were required. The Air Ministry was well aware of this, as the following minute shows: there existed 'Avoidance by COs and subordinate commanders of adequate disciplinary action because it might result in the loss of the services of aircrew personnel.'[3]

Differences of rank were less significant in the RAF than in the other Services, but segregation of the ranks was still enforced, as the Mass Observation project discovered:

> The segregation, along with too much saluting of officers, with too great insistence on brightness of buttons and boots, with kit inspections, with pointless parades, in fact any irksome or unintelligible regulations, are lumped together under the term 'bullshit' ….. the average airman's conception of what is discipline and what is bullshit differs widely from the conception of the average officer ……. the average airman has little objection to saluting officers or polishing his buttons or his boots, but he resents it if he is 'ticked off' or punished for not doing so …… in general, the nearer one gets to action, the less bullshit is found.[4]

Discipline was inextricably linked with morale by the Air Ministry.[5] It is axiomatic that any organisation desirous of high morale will take measures to ensure compliance with the aims of that organisation. Yet, as Lord Moran realised, unnecessary discipline – the 'bullshit' of RAF parlance – caused men to rebel.[6] Disagreement led to friction, with resultant morale problems:

> Without discipline there is little chance of persuading men to stoically accept all the horrors of modern warfare. Deference to the commands of superiors has to be automatic and unquestioning, and any signs of democratic thinking or individualism that might threaten such a response must be ruthlessly stamped out.[7]

Sir Philip Joubert, whose report on discipline has been cited in the previous chapter (q.v.), acknowledged that the aircrews of Bomber Command were engaged in a highly dangerous occupation; it was recognised that disciplinary standards among them were poor. How could standards be raised without antagonising the crews and causing resentment?[8] Sutton, the AMP, commenting on Joubert's report, made his view clear in a minute of February 1944 that …..

> The powers of station commanders over aircrew must be exercised without hesitation and without regard to the breaking up of a crew. The loss of aircrew is as nothing compared with the general inefficiency arising from the knowledge that nobody dares disrate one member of a crew for fear of spoiling the team. Aircrew care nothing for reprimands or loss of pay. Today they know that they can get away with absence, drunkenness and theft or at least improper possession and they will still remain aircrew and get their promotion in due course. What incentive is there to maintain good discipline?[9]

There is a difference between discipline in the air and on the ground but 'if a man is slovenly on the ground, the odds are that he will be slovenly in flying.'[10] The post-war report by Dr. Stafford-Clark contended that....

> Such men (particularly NCO air gunners) provided the bulk of cases displaying low morale in a squadron, and they were fairly characteristic. They lacked the conscientiousness, integrity and responsibility of their more impressive colleagues ...... They lacked self-respect and so their discipline was bad and their standard of personal cleanliness was often indifferent. Their mental attitude was often surprisingly adolescent and immature.[11]

This assessment was also the view of Air Vice Marshal Sir Charles Symonds, who conducted a survey among senior officers. Some of these officers were prepared to tolerate indiscipline if the crews guilty of it performed satisfactorily in the air. Bomber crews imposed their own discipline in the air, backed up by regular discipline; this engendering a methodical approach, already instilled in them. 'You get far more cooperation in the air without it [discipline]. Besides, when a man's been shot at a few times, he is, in his own eyes, entitled to a bit of freedom.'[12]

ACAS Norman Bottomley was not a huge fan of NCOs, as his letter of 27 July 1942 to the VCAS Sir Wilfred Freeman on the subject of discipline demonstrates:

> When I joined the RFC 27 years ago as a Second Lt. I looked upon a sgt. or flt/-sgt. as being a hell of a chap, and so did the men. Today

every RAF station, and particularly heavy bomber stations, is lousy with sgts. and flt/sgts. – or rather men with three stripes on their sleeves, because every member of an aircrew has that rank. A great many of them are completely undisciplined and they definitely let the side down both in the sgts. Mess and out of it. They are very gallant chaps and do their job in the air well, but they are not sgts. or flt/sgts. except in name and have no idea of the disciplinary implications of their rank. One has got no power over these aircrew sgts. except not to recommend them for commissions. They don't care a hoot for reprimands or severe reprimands. REDUCE NUMBERS![13]

Bottomley continued:

In every group you will find a number of hardened criminals who spend their entire time popping in and out of detention, going AWOL and being put in prison by the civil power – then coming back and having another go at detention for being AWOL and so on. They are a perfect curse to the service and a burden on the taxpayer. I suggested that we should form one or two sorts of Penal Battalions or works companies in really unpleasant places overseas ….. but the suggestion was received with shocked disapproval. I still think it is sensible.[14]

Dr. Stafford-Clark would perhaps not have sent NCOs to penal battalions but he did recognise that they were more resistant to traditional discipline than officers. In the air it was different. One did not jeopardise the lives of one's comrades by behaving in an indisciplined manner. He maintained that: '…. there was a very small but definite proportion of Aircrew Sergeants who differed completely from their colleagues.'[15] Their motives were glamour and promotion; they had no regard for the risks of flying; they lacked self-respect. Their discipline was bad, they were dirty, behaved childishly and saw themselves as 'cinematograph heroes.'[16] They were mostly air gunners, whose educational standard was not as high as other crew members and their selection had been less rigorous.[17] It must be emphasised that this group of miscreants constituted a minority.

Those aircrew who did transgress found themselves not at penal colonies overseas but at punishment camps in England, euphemistically termed 'refresher courses'. It had been decided by the Air Ministry to open refresher schools at Brighton, Uxbridge and Blackpool in August 1942. The three-week courses would be for NCOs *and* Officers 'whose carelessness or disobedience had caused avoidable accidents.'[18] The courses would include drill, discipline, lectures, unarmed combat, hygiene instruction and games. 'The course will not be regarded as a punishment. Its object is to imbue those who undergo it with a proper appreciation of the importance of their contribution to the war effort.'[19]

Sir Edgar Ludlow-Hewitt, sharing Inspector General duties with Sir Philip Joubert, visited these 'Suspendair' disposal centres at Blackpool, Uxbridge and Brighton in December 1942. The course at Brighton drew criticism for too much 'bullshit' and an unawareness on the part of the instructors of aircrew mentality, i.e., a certain lax approach to discipline. This was true of '...... a certain type of NCO, who starts by treating the course with contempt [and] is liable to be affected adversely by the strict discipline.'[20]

Ludlow-Hewitt was also concerned that 'W' cases – waverers (q.v.) – were allowed to mix with students at the Initial Training Wing in Brighton. It was imperative to 'segregate the real "W's" and in particular prevent the association of young aircrews under training with depressed and demoralised ex-operational airmen.'[21] The Inspector General's conclusion from his visits was that defective organisation was causing delays in disposal of personnel and that this could have a serious effect on the morale of the course attendees and anyone coming into contact with them.[22]

Some attendees *did* regard the course as punishment. One, Sergeant Stevens, was invited to report on his experiences and he complained strongly of the harsh disciplinary nature of the course. One wonders if the sergeant suffered any reprimand for his report, for he does not hold back in his strong criticism of the regime he experienced. First he complained about the savage haircuts all endured. Then he resented the indignity and humiliation inflicted when NCOs were reprimanded in front of their peers, and he went on:

> What amazed me most of all was the attitude adopted by the officer commanding regarding flying and aircrew. Addressing a Warrant Officer DFM, who was on his third tour of operations, he said, 'Flying is a satellite to the real RAF, the real RAF is here...... Flying

and the bombing of Germany is only a temporary inconvenience......
[and] ..... No wonder this country is in the state it is in today.'.......
He is an officer of the 'Wingless Wonder' variety not fit to be a
commander and can therefore hold no sympathy or sense of true
fair play when dealing with aircrew ..... Many men [on the course]
have vowed never to fly again for the RAF .... Which will win the
war, parading smartly on a barrack square or bombing Germany?[23]

This response is confirmation that aircrews would tolerate discipline if its source was an officer with operational experience and one who held the respect of his men; they would be less inclined to comply when administrators without flying experience attempted to impose their authority. To balance the criticism, there was praise for the course from some who had been through it, as a minute from 91 Group HQ testified. Referring to the course at Brighton, it read: 'All units are agreed that the course is extremely good.'[24]

It appears that, in general, commanding officers *were* lenient with their men, because they had usually faced the hazards of operations themselves and were well aware that discipline in the air was vital, while petty restrictions on the ground were demeaning. The Air Ministry had to perform a delicate balancing act. Bertine Sutton, AMP, lamented that the high morale and discipline of pre-war days was long gone and it was decided at an Air Council meeting of 14 September 1943 to set up a committee to be headed by Ludlow-Hewitt to address slack disciplinary standards.[25]

Periodic reminders about behaviour and deportment of RAF personnel would be issued. An Air Ministry letter to all commands read:

The cumulative effect of irregularities in dress and slovenliness in deportment gives persons outside the Royal Air Force a bad impression of the discipline of the Service and the pride which its members take in it. The Royal Air Force has earned the admiration of the public and all ranks should strive to earn and maintain a reputation for smartness and behaviour equal to the reputation the Service has earned for efficiency.[26]

Another minute gave guidelines for potential disciplinary action: 'i) Walking in a slovenly manner, with hands in pockets. ii) walking in public linked with a female, when such action results in failure to observe saluting obligations.'[27] Other infringements of discipline included 'Flagrant departure from regular pattern uniform ….. top button of jacket left undone. …… field service caps worn at wrong angle …….' It is difficult to imagine Bomber Command operational aircrew complying with the following Air Ministry directive: 'Indifference to smartness within stations, such as strolling leisurely from one place to another during working hours instead of being marched in parties.'[28]

The Air Ministry did not hesitate to reprimand Bomber Command. A minute of August 1943 drew attention to the appalling behaviour of aircrew at Personnel Despatch Centres. At one of them 90% of airmen were guilty of insubordination, drunkenness and tomfoolery on parade. Public houses, cinemas and hotels frequented by airmen at other centres had experienced trouble. Mr. Richards of the Air Ministry, who had composed the missive, recommended harsh punishment, courts-martial and prison sentences, regardless of rank, if appropriate.[29] Most of these men were going overseas to the EATS, so it would be unfair to the majority of Bomber Command personnel who were *not* behaving in this manner to imply that it was commonplace. It was not.

As the war approached its end notes for talks to personnel were provided, reminding them that: 'Our discipline comes not from the parade ground but from each man and woman's common sense, loyalty and self-discipline. It is therefore the responsibility of each one of us to "preserve good order and Air Force discipline" when the German surrender comes.'[30] The majority of aircrew accepted the fact that a measure of military discipline was necessary, that a relaxed form of *self*-discipline had to be applied in the air and they carried on with the task for which they had volunteered.

Chapter 10

Are You Happy in Your Work?: Humour and Argot

Aircrews developed ways of coping with flying stress. They denied that the Grim Reaper was coming for them; it was always another crew 'for the chop'. The aphorism 'young men don't die' was clung to fervently. Flight Sergeant Charles Gale recalled in 1946: 'Other fellows are going to buy it. That chap and that chap and that chap may go for a Burton. But not me. It can't happen to me.'[1] The guilt of surviving while others had perished was present but mostly unspoken. Flight Lieutenant Wingham recalled: 'Often one saw a new crew come on the squadron who somehow had a smell of death about them …….. surprise was not expressed when the crew failed to return …….. publicly or with one's crew it was a matter of joking about the "chop rate" going up.'[2]

Black humour and massive understatement were features of life in Bomber Command and they contributed to the maintenance of morale. The ability to laugh off hardships and tragic events was employed as a defence mechanism against flying stress. Lord Moran wrote of the power of humour when he served as a medical officer on the Western Front in the First World War: 'Only humour helped …… humour that touched everything with ridicule and had taken the bite out of the last thing, death.'[3] A bomber station in 1943 was not so far removed from a 1917 Flanders trench; death stalked both on a daily basis. On one of those stations an airman went to the scene of a crash in which a fellow squadron member had been burnt to death. On seeing the charred skeleton he remarked, 'Well, I won't be playing cricket with *him* this evening.'[4]

*

In 1945 the linguist Eric Partridge wrote......

> ...... the Combatant Services have a far richer *new* slang than that used by civilians. Nor is the reason difficult to ascertain. In the Services the men live – or should live – a more exciting life; they deal with new equipment and various weapons; do things they've never done before – and pretend they never want to again; many of them visit strange countries; many become engaged in a service that is actually instead of nominally active; all of them mingle in such a companionship as they have never had before they enlisted and will never again, once they quit the Service.
>
> Such conditions inevitably lead to a rejuvenation of language – to vividness – to picturesqueness – to vigour; language becomes youthful, energetic adventurous. And slang is the easiest way to achieve those ends ......[5]

Slang usage was an important component of morale. The intrinsic morale of individuals, that is, for, if spirits were to be kept up, what better way than convivial relations with new friends – friends upon whom one's life may depend? Language is an important element in social interaction; each generation develops its own colloquialisms. The young men of Bomber Command were no different; the pressure to conform to certain norms exists in each generation. Non-conformity is neither desirable nor tolerated in a military organisation and rejection of the highly specialised argot which developed in Bomber Command would have led to ostracism. 'As the airman adjusted himself to the RAF he had to adapt to his role within this new society, and these roles were characterised by special language which he had to learn in order to become a full member of the society. The RAF argot was an exposition of the distinctive character of the RAF society and was an essential part of its culture.'[6]

RAF argot excluded outsiders; membership of an exclusive group provided not only comradeship but a feeling of security. The jargon was a symbol of belonging to the RAF and airmen did not like to hear it from the lips of others. Slang usually originated with officers but trickled down; sergeants, in close contact and on friendly terms with the officers in mixed crews, were particularly susceptible to adopting the argot. They would not, however, use slang in the presence of officers whom they did not know well.

Some RAF jargon has survived the passage of time. It has become entrenched in common usage – *cheesed off, gremlins (q.v.), carry the can, bang on, go like the clappers, flap,* as in *get into a,* for example; other slang phrases are relics of the past, quaint and sometimes faintly ridiculous to modern ears. In this category could be placed: *popsie* (girlfriend), *wizard prang* (excellent bombing results), *pukka gen* (reliable information) and *duff gen* (unreliable information). *Split-arse* (daring) is not a phrase heard much nowadays; neither is *a soggy type* (a weak, stupid person). *Gone for a Burton* (killed) and *a piece of cake* (an easy task) are still understood by Baby Boomers but perhaps not by Gen Z.[7]

In an article in the *Daily Mirror* on 26 January 1940 by 'A Special Correspondent', its readers were informed that the 'RAF have their own "slanguage". The vocabulary of the last war has gone into history but new words and phrases are being invented every day to form a new "dictionary". …… When something does not please the airman of today he takes a "poor view" of it. A job properly done is "buttoned up", something badly done a "black". If an airman is fed up he is "browned off".'[8]

The provincial newspaper the *Lincolnshire Echo* felt it was its duty to alert its readers to this strange new language, although it may not have been so unfamiliar to readers in Lincolnshire, living as they did surrounded by Bomber Command airfields:

> Three ropey types, all sprogs, pranged a cheesey kite on bumps and circuits. One bought it; the other two went for a Burton. The station-master took a dim view and tore them off a strip. They'd taken a shagbat wofficer, who was browned off, along, and the Queen Bee was hopping mad.
>
> Translation: three unpopular individuals, all brand new pilot officers, crashed a worn-out aircraft while making practice circuits and landings. One was killed; the other two were severely reprimanded [although *Gone for a Burton* usually meant *killed*]. The station commander disapproved and roundly rated them. They had

taken along a somewhat plain WAAF officer, who was bored, and the WAAF commandant was very angry.⁹

Pull your finger out (get a move on) attained legendary status in the RAF and can, of course, still be heard today. The phrase almost took on a life of its own. Accident reports were used by *Tee Emm* to highlight flying safety. An award was given to any airman who had *put up a black* (committed a blunder). This dubious accolade was *The Most Highly Derogatory Order of the Irremovable Finger*. When nominations for the award were requested, hundreds were sent in. The *Tee Emm* reports were anonymous, so that all were kept guessing as to the identity of the 'culprit'. The relevance of this to morale was that no-one was ever quite sure who had been nominated and the award acted as an incentive to make improvements in one's tasks. Replicas of the MHDOIF medal were cast at many air stations and the unfortunate recipient of the award was obliged to wear it for a short period. *Pull your finger out* had widespread use in Bomber Command, its variant *dedigitate* confined to officers.¹⁰ The word *finger* alone signified a problem of some kind, as exemplified here in a *Tee Emm* poem:

> When the Court of Enquiry assembles
> Please tell them the reason I died
> Was because of an irremovable finger
> Which mucked up my angle of glide.¹¹

*

Mess banter, almost incomprehensible to contemporary outsiders, was a feature of Bomber Command life. The ultimate transgression was line-shooting. Boasting, the antithesis of understatement, was frowned upon and persistent offenders were stigmatised as 'line-shooters'. Flight Lieutenant D. Hawker maintained:

> I'm sure there must have been many true stories which were never told because of the 'line book' which was kept in the bar of the Mess.

Perhaps someone would be telling some friends of a hair-raising experience he had managed to survive ('a dicey do') and if someone thought the story had a few embellishments, he would shout 'line!'. The story teller then had to buy drinks all round. It was much cheaper to keep one's experiences to oneself![12]

Lexicographer Eric Partridge provides another example of how to silence a 'line-shooter'. Absurd exaggeration from the assembled listeners would do the trick: 'There we were, upside-down in cloud, f***-all on the clock and still climbing.'[13] The transgressor would sheepishly fall silent.

Chapter 11

Bus Drivers:
The Tour

No man could be expected to fly indefinitely and a limit was imposed on the number of operations to be completed. This was termed the *datum line*. Originally gauged in hours (200), the limit was finally set at 2 'tours' of 30 and 20 operations respectively.[1] When the heavies and Mosquitoes were later introduced a tour would be gauged in sorties rather than hours, as the increased speed of the new aircraft enabled more sorties to be completed in the same number of hours, and it would have been unfair for crews of older, slower types of aircraft to remain on the hours basis.[2] The total of fifty sorties was the maximum a man was obliged to carry out, although he could volunteer for a third tour if he wished.[3] A flyer would have a goal to be attained. As Lord Moran put it: 'There is a point on the horizon. Something to hope for.'[4] 'They [crews] must feel at the outset that they have a sporting chance of doing their job and surviving. If they know their period of operations is limited, they will exert their utmost efforts to make that period a successful one. If they feel it is unlimited, they will tend to operate at lower tempo', wrote Sidney Bufton, Director of Bombing Operations, in February 1943.[5] An Air Ministry minute of 27 September 1944 provided a summary of how the tour lengths had been decided:

> The policy on which operational tours in Bomber Command are founded is based partly on experience gained in operations over a long period related to the capacity of the individual to stand up to the strain, and partly on the capacity of the Manning and Training organisations to meet requirements in complete crews.[6]

The imposition of a limit was a clear indication that the Air Ministry linked flying stress (q.v.) with morale.

Dr. Stafford-Clark made a correlation between the various stages of the tour, the onset of flying stress and its effect on the morale of the individual. When a man joins an operational squadron he is busy absorbing his new environment and is excited about the prospect of beginning his tour. He is perhaps a little apprehensive but keen to 'do his bit'. Morale is high. After five to eight operations he has had a few hair-raising experiences, perhaps seen aircraft explode or crash – and he still has twenty-five more trips to complete.[7] Now anxiety accompanies each sortie. D.J. Gill remembered: 'One soon realised, after watching other aircraft being shot down, that the doomed aircrews in those aircraft also believed that they were immortal.'[8] Fear creeps in. He must marshal all his resources of bravery and resolve to climb into his aircraft, battling to stave off the exhaustion of continual emotional strain. Trust in his crew and in his aircraft is absolute. Without it he feels he is doomed. By the twelfth to fifteenth operation his fear is now fully realised – and there are still fifteen ops to go. It seems an impossibility to get to the end. He can only think of the present, surrounded by reminders of death – the empty tables in the canteen, the empty beds in the Nissen Huts. In the argot of Bomber Command, 'there's no future in it'. 'How long was our luck going to last, we all thought from time to time, wrote F/Lt. T.W. Fox.'[9] Then, with only five trips to go, perhaps he *will* survive. His morale rises. Experience *might* keep him alive until the tour's end.[10] Stafford-Clark's analysis will be examined in a later chapter (Flying Stress).

*

Crews bore the strain but only if they had some hope of survival. The Air Ministry believed that 'The maintenance of morale requires an adequate survival rate. This should certainly not be less than 50%, i.e., an even chance throughout.'[11] It was estimated in November 1942, and noted in an Air Ministry minute, that the chance of surviving two tours was 19%, one crew in every five.[12] At one stage of the war, in early 1943, 2.5% of men would survive a second tour, an unbelievable and sobering statistic.[13] And this before the gruelling Battle of Berlin, in which many crews perished, had begun. Such statistics had to remain secret. 'It would do infinite harm if any details regarding the subject were to get round any of the squadrons,'[14] wrote the AMT, Air Marshal Sir Guy Garrod, to Portal on 21 December 1942. The result would be a disastrous decline in morale.[15] Garrod disputed the assertion that aircrew had a one in five chance of survival on a second tour: 'It can be argued that a crew doing a second tour is so much more skilled than the average crew doing a first tour that it has a far higher percentage chance of survival during its second tour than during its first tour, but we have not sufficient data one way or the other on this point.'[16] For clarity, survival meant avoiding being wounded, reported missing, taken prisoner or killed in action.

Portal replied to Garrod on 24 December:

> I am extremely anxious that statistical information relating to the 'chances of survival' of aircrews in the various types of operational employment should be confined to the smallest possible number of people. It is of course essential that these matters should be studied in relation to the proposed length of operational tours but the information can be so easily distorted, and is then so dangerous to morale, that all possible steps must be taken to safeguard it. On the other hand, it is undesirable to issue general instructions on safeguarding this information since it would be dangerous to spread the knowledge that the subject is regarded as being of great secrecy..........
>
> .... I also suggest that correspondence on the subject should be personal between heads of departments and Commanders-in-Chief and should not be conducted through the usual channels.[17]

Two weeks later, at an Air Council meeting (7 January 1943), chaired by Portal, survival rates were discussed at great length.[18] While those in High Command discussed statistics, those at the sharp end could see with their own eyes the losses in their squadrons but knowledge of the statistics of tour survival would obviously have a serious impact on morale. They rationalised their feelings according to the stage of the tour they had reached and this corresponded roughly with Stafford-Clark's observations. Pilot Officer Rowling reflected: 'At first one was inclined to think it was all luck, and although you've certainly got to be lucky doing your first few trips experience is everything.'[19] George Hull, in a letter to a friend, wrote: 'When I think back to what happened there last night, I am sure that this morning we are living on borrowed time.'[20] If one survived the first five operations, morale rose; around the twelfth survival seemed impossible. As the end of the tour approached morale rose again.[21]

*

The first tour took an average of six months to complete. Crews preferred several trips in a short space of time in order to get the job over and done with; tours which became long drawn out affairs were demoralising, which explains why 'scrubs' were so hated. When one was all set to notch up another sortie, only to have it cancelled at the last minute, it sapped morale. In effect, despite the careful calculations of the Air Ministry, the weather and the moon dictated the temporal length of tours.

When the sortie became the unit of measurement rather than hours, a definition of a sortie was required: it would be an operation which the squadron commander believed had been carried out successfully – i.e., the aircraft had actually bombed the intended target. ACAS Norman Bottomley minuted CAS Portal, asking for a more sympathetic line to be taken, to give crews the benefit of the doubt. 'They [crews] would certainly have a warranted grievance if they believed that higher authority was not concerned in a fair and general interpretation of an operational sortie.'[22] The courage and determination of the crews should also be considered alongside bombing results.

The first tour of thirty operations was never to be exceeded but the second could be, by up to five more if one crew member needed to make up his twenty trips and the others had already done twenty.[23] The tours were tinkered with over the next four years of the war, with variations in the Pathfinder Force and Mosquito squadrons, who would do longer tours. When the Pathfinder Force was formed forty-five operations would constitute the first tour in a PFF Squadron, but any crew suffering fatigue after a minimum of thirty operations could be withdrawn. When this was the case the crew would do an OTU course as instructors and then a second tour, either in the Main Force or in the PFF, of no more than twenty operations.[24]

The loss of experienced airmen engaged in their second tour unnerved new crews. If such men were lost, then training and experience offered no protection, reasoned the newcomers. Such apprehension was acknowledged at the highest level of command. At an informal meeting between Sir Charles Portal and a selection of commanders, including Pathfinder Hamish Mahaddie and 'Willie' Tait, both wing commanders at the time of this meeting, it was believed by those present that: 'The loss of experienced crews towards the end of their second operational tour has a lowering effect [on morale] throughout the whole squadron.'[25] D.G. Simmons, of the Air Ministry, an airman who had first hand experience of operations, wrote to Wilfred Freeman, VCAS, in November 1942, expressing his opinion that two short tours would safeguard aircrew morale:

> …. the average aircrew personnel are simple ….. A large number of them boost up their morale by the simple but often effective saying 'It won't happen to me'. I must admit my own personal experience was that this somewhat unintelligent outlook was far more comforting while on the job than the rather saner course of taking a mathematical view of one's chances……. from the morale point of view I am convinced that two or more short tours are preferable to 'flogging the horse till he drops'.[26]

Opposing this view, an Air Ministry minute to Freeman in January 1943, argued against a second tour for *some* men who had come to the end of their first tour. These would become flight and squadron commanders, some would be decorated, and none should go on operations, '…. as the good they can do to the morale of their squadron by carrying out one or two trips a month would not outweigh the loss to the Service if they did not return.'[27] Aircrew did not usually respond favourably to their leaders who did not fly, but, argued the minute, the undoubted bravery and resolve which had been demonstrated by those leaders would earn them the respect of their crews and stifle criticism. Arthur Harris was against any change, asserting that there was a long list of enthusiastic volunteers for second tours. He stated, 'I think that these discussions on the possibility of doing away with the second tour can only have the effect of gravely lowering morale.'[28] Others within the RAF agreed. Sir Charles Symonds believed that second tour men had lost their enthusiasm but this was more than compensated for by their experience. Second tour crews were always welcomed on squadrons.[29]

It was not the first time Harris had resisted any tampering with second tour policy. He had previously reacted strongly to an Air Ministry paper with the title 'Operational employment of aircrews, 24 November 1942', in which the abolition of the second tour had been suggested. In a 'most secret' memorandum Harris stated: 'The only serious argument which might be produced in support of this proposal .... is that the rate of casualties imposed by enemy defences .... is so high that morale cannot be expected to survive a second tour of 30 sorties without cracking.' Experienced crews, he reasoned, had a better chance of survival, experience being *the* major factor in returning from operations. They also gave confidence to the less experienced. Furthermore, he declared, '....there is no indication that a majority or even a substantial proportion of the crews concerned is unequal to the strain.'[30] Harris also argued that if a man who had completed one tour and had proceeded to an OTU as an instructor, with nothing to look forward to when he had completed the course, he would feel permanently 'on the shelf', resulting in poor instructing and low morale among trainees.[31]

Harris wrote to Portal:

> [scrapping the second tour] can only have the effect of gravely lowering morale .... and any idea that those who have fought in part of the war and escaped unscathed should not be called upon to take any further part in active operations, can only be described as disastrous .... I therefore hope that the second tour may be accepted as a necessity to the limited extent for which it will be required and that we should now consider the question closed and get on with the war.[32]

Edgar Ludlow-Hewitt wrote to Norman Bottomley in January 1943, supporting Harris's view.[33] The second tour was essential and would remain policy.

On completion of the first tour, the airman would instruct his own speciality at an OTU for six to nine months and then proceed to his second tour of twenty operations. It was inevitable that some would feel hard done by. Certain squadrons may have borne heavier losses than others and their crews considered that they had a rightful grievance, as expressed in an Air Ministry memorandum: 'You will appreciate that there is an inequality of sacrifices which is causing a considerable degree of restiveness, with a consequent lowering of morale.'[34] A Canadian officer offered this observation: 'After the first tour of operations in Bomber Command personnel are "rested" by going to instructional work at an OTU. But this is no rest. The men know very well what percentage of aircrew finish 1st tour operations; they also know what percentage will finish the second tour.' He suggested leave in Canada for RCAF personnel who had completed their first tour: 'Men would come back as refreshed in mind and spirit that they would conceive of themselves as going into operations for the first time – but with a fighting ability which in their first sortie they never knew...... This...... would give a tremendous impetus to morale and the war effort generally.'[35]

In 1944, Assistant Under Secretary of State Folliott Sandford sent a memorandum to all Commands, reminding personnel that they were still obliged to do a second tour, although, 'Aircrew personnel who are relieved from operational duties on account of excessive operational strain before expiry of the normal operational period should not be sent immediately to training units where their temporary lack of zeal and zest might have a depressing effect on the personnel under training.'[36] Those who did complete their two tours, and who had been instructors at OTUs or HCUs, were not required to do another training tour. They could be employed as non-flying station commanders, instructors in central schools or flying in Transport Command.[37] Station commanders who remained on the ground were not popular, although, as stated elsewhere in this chapter, they were often admired as men who had proved themselves and needed no more to demonstrate the fact. The commander of 4 Group, AVM Roderick Carr, did not approve of the suggestion. He complained to Bomber Command HQ that retaining non-flying flight and squadron commanders after their tours had finished had a negative impact on morale.[38]

That same year second tours again came under scrutiny; consideration was given to making them voluntary. Bertine Sutton, the AMP, was wary: 'Even if we could rely upon men being asked carefully and tactfully whether they wished to volunteer for a second tour, very many would feel unable to demur for fear that they would be classified as "windy".'[39] CAS Charles Portal minuted Archibald Sinclair: 'In general I am in agreement with AMP and AMT that the adoption of the principle of "second tours for volunteers only" would be wrong ......'[40] He added as an afterthought: 'It would be extremely damaging to the RAF if our policy on operational tours were allowed to become a topic of public discussion.'[41]

*

In May 1943 Arthur Harris asked the Air Ministry for an extension to the PFF tour, citing operational needs as the reason. In its reply the Ministry gave permission but 'Should it become necessary to extend for certain Pathfinder crews the maxima stipulated for operational tours, such crews should be carefully watched and should be withdrawn from operations directly they exhibit signs of undue fatigue.'[42] It was agreed by all that Mosquito crews were far less at risk than the Main Force 'and it is considered,' wrote SASO Robert Saundby to the Under Secretary of State for Air in March 1944, 'that 50 sorties in a Mosquito are less dangerous and less strain than 30 sorties in a heavy bomber.' He asked the under secretary for permission to fix Mosquito crew tours to fifty for the first and thirty for the second.[43] This was approved.[44]

There were exceptions. Nos. 138 and 161 (Special Duties) Squadrons, transporting SOE agents and supplies to resistance groups, did not have to follow the thirty sortie rule. Saundby informed the Under Secretary of State for Air Balfour on 30 July 1943 that, as crews on these squadrons did not fly the same perilous routes as regular squadrons, they could either do 30 trips or 250 hours, whichever was the longer.[45]

*

Arthur Harris wrote to Sir Archibald Sinclair on 8 March 1944. He referred to the ruling on the datum line made on 8 May 1943. In March 1944, Harris wrote,

'The risk fatigue and strain in respect of operations carried out against short range and lightly defended targets in France and short range mining operations ("gardening") where fighter defence is practically nil, is nowadays in no way comparable to those associated with long range targets in Germany.'[46] At this time the Stirling and Halifax crews were employed on easier sorties such as French targets and 'gardening'; the Lancaster crews were sent to Germany. The risk to the latter was far greater than that to the former and it was unfair to them that a 'gardening' trip should have exactly the same value as an operation to Berlin. Harris's suggestion was that 'gardening' represented one third of an operation.[47] Rulings were made. Group commanders and station COs would decide whether an easy target would be classed as half, or a third of, a sortie.[48] And in the later stages nickelling operations, the dropping of propaganda leaflets, did not even count as a third of an operation. They counted for nothing.[49] U-Boat patrols, searches and sweeps were judged to count as one operation, wrote Bomber Command HQ, in reply to a query from the PFF.[50]

An Air Ministry minute to Portal on 15 March 1945, with hostilities nearly at an end, addressed the contentious issue of half and third sorties:

> It may be true that Bomber Command crews prefer to get through their operational tour of 30 sorties without the complication of counting points or fractions of a sortie for attacks upon targets which require little penetration. I cannot help thinking, however, that once it was decided to lengthen the tour on the grounds that ...... the risks in completing an operational tour are now much smaller than they were, the crews would appreciate a system which means that the length of the tour will correspond roughly with the risks incurred subject to an overriding maximum of 30 sorties.[51]

*

As the war drew to a close AMP Bertine Sutton suggested to the VCAS Wilfred Freeman that first tours should be extended, operations now being far less stressful. ACAS Thomas Williams was in complete agreement: '... Bomber Command sorties of today are nothing like so exacting as they were a year ago and therefore an extension of the length of tour is fully justified. Curtailment of operational effort is the alternative.'[52] An Aircrew State Committee meeting of 25 January 1945 had decided on thirty-six sorties instead of thirty for the first tour in the Main Force. Second tour lengths would remain the same; it would be unfair to those engaged in it, as it was they who had borne the brunt of the Battle of Berlin, with its attendant heavy loss rate. No. 3 Group crews, on mainly daylight operations, would have forty trips in the first tour and twenty-five on the second. No. 8 Group Pathfinders would see no change.[53]

Harris agreed to the extension. Robert Saundby, writing for Harris to the Under Secretary of State for Air Balfour, insisted that, in the interest of fairness, group commanders 'should exercise their discretion in removing from operations [on extended tours] at any time personnel who, in their opinion, have had an exceptionally hard tour of operations involving greater strain than has been common to the general run of aircrews.'[54] It may have been the case that the Air Ministry brought about the tour extension *after* Harris had already initiated the change without consulting the Ministry for approval. It was hinted in various minutes to and from the AHMS and the AMP Bertine Sutton that Harris was guilty of deliberate disobedience.[55]

Extended tours did not apply to Canadian aircrew. Harris was not happy. He gave his reasons in a letter to the AMP on 12 March 1945: There were 1,757 Canadian aircrew in non-RCAF squadrons, dispersed among 553 crews. When the 30 sortie limit was reached each of these crews would have to lose its Canadians. This would have an impact on morale. It would also create operational problems. With six extra operations, who would replace the Canadians who had been removed from crews? In his usual blunt manner, Harris wrote: 'I submit that the Canadian authorities have no constitutional right to adopt their existing attitude in this matter and that if they persist it should be brought to a showdown in the highest quarters.'[56] And he could not resist another barb directed at the Air Ministry: 'The deplorable state of affairs that has thus arisen is of course the result of the wholesale "alienisation" of the Royal Air Force, against the dangers of which I repeatedly and long ago warned the Air Ministry. We now have the tail wagging the dog ......' He signed off by stating that he would have to disband some squadrons and impose a forty-sortie tour on those that remained until the matter was resolved.[57] Harris received support from Thomas Williams, ACAS, who himself wrote to Sinclair pleading for an approach to Canada at ministerial level in an attempt to resolve the situation.[58] It was academic anyway. The war would be over in two months.

The problem of tour lengths and the six month rest period in between was addressed throughout the war.[59] Sinclair, sensitive to the potential damage to morale of fluctuating tour lengths, wrote in 1944:

> A tour in Bomber Command is a pretty grim and hazardous undertaking for a young man ...... He settles down to do his thirty sorties. It must be very upsetting for him if he finds that in March it is lengthened and in April it is shortened again and must give to him and his family a feeling that we don't know our own minds on a matter which is probably life and death to him.[60]

....

And the men who were finding out first hand how 'grim and hazardous' was a tour, what of them? Flying Officer R.J. Fairhead described his first trip: 'As we approached the target, Bremen, the sky in front of us over it was full of bursting anti-aircraft shell explosions (flak) to such an extent that it didn't seem possible that any aircraft could get through it without being hit...At this point I became very scared – stiff, in fact! This horrid apprehension lasted only a few minutes however ....'[61]

Limiting tour lengths did not necessarily compensate, in the eyes of the aircrews, for losses sustained. In the first two years of the war the squadrons of Bomber Command suffered severe losses. The survivors had lost their friends – for the early squadrons were cohesive units of pre-war regulars – but had been able to carry on. There had been depression but no demoralisation. As Bomber Command expanded it became easier, but no less distressing, to accept the heavy losses which regularly accompanied the much larger raids of the later years of the conflict. The turnover of aircrews was so rapid that a crew might arrive on a squadron one day, go missing the next and no-one on the squadron would have any idea of who they were. The deaths of strangers were regrettable but could be endured. George Hull realised that:

'….. it happens so many times [yet] if we want to retain our sanity ……
we must forget it – nobody on the squadron even remembers O-Oboe this
morning.'[62] J. Bormann recorded in his diary his sadness at the loss of a
friend: 'Certainly a black day. Mac is missing; have lost the greatest pal I've
ever had ………. Scotty's crew also, Sqdn/Ldr Smith last trip, second tour,
Sqdn/Ldr Powell, P/O Hislop and P/O Filstead. Has placed a gloom on the
whole station.'[63] A later diary entry, 24 June 1944, by Bormann reveals that
he, too, was approaching the limit of endurance: 'Feeling am losing my grip.
First Mac gone then Max and now Paul. Can't get the sight of that burning
plane out of my mind.'[64] Happily, he survived his tour.

Flight Lieutenant T.W. Fox recalled a trip to Montorgueil, France, on 24
June 1944: 'Approaching the target we saw an aircraft above release his stick
of bombs and very sad to say they landed on a Halifax which was flying at our
height just a few hundred yards in front of us. The aircraft disintegrated into
very small fragments with no sign of life at all. We flew through the smoke
and debris and on to the target; after "bombs away" we turned for home
feeling quite sick. The aircraft in question was one from our own squadron
and the crew we knew very well indeed.'[65]

P/O. Byrne's tour progressed. Flying through heavy flak on a daylight
raid to Dortmund on 29 November 1944, Byrne witnessed a collision: 'One
could see ugly black puffs burst as if from nowhere. Just before we reached
the target another kite flown by P/O. Summers of this squadron knocked the
fin and rudder off another kite and seven chaps met a horrible death. The
kite fell away from the stream slowly at first. Then spun down bursting into
flames and falling in two pieces. We saw no-one jump out of the aircraft.'[66]
On 6 December 1944, Byrne had to miss an operation to Merseburg near
Leipzig. His crew was reported missing. 'The hand of fate proved that I had
not to take my 11th trip with them….. Quite possibly my life was saved by a
mere chance.' The Wop/Ag. who flew in his place was on his first trip. 'I pray
to God that my crew are not killed.'[67]

Byrne's new crew flew to Ludwigshafen on 15 December. 'I was very
pleased to be going on another op. I know now that I have really something
to fly and fight for. No matter how long or dangerous the trip. My heart, body
and soul are striving for one supreme purpose. That purpose being to avenge
my crew…… I will not fail in my duty. My life is given now to my job. I must

and will have German blood.' When his aircraft was over the target, 'I cursed the Hun and inwardly wept for my [first] crew...... I called the Jerry so much shit! I sincerely hoped our bombs would smack his wicked filthy skull clean open. I have no mercy. My heart is cold now. I am only out for revenge!'[68]

*

A contemporary observation of the perception of tour survival by aircrew revealed:

> Most people start off on aircrew with the idea that 'At any rate I shan't be killed.' But, in general, the more trips they do the more vivid does the possibility of their being killed become to them, although you sometimes do hear people say, 'I was getting as nervous as hell but suddenly everything seems all right again.' Most people who go on aircrew are eager to go on their first trip. Perhaps there is 1 in 50 who is not ...... but by the 7th or 8th trip are rather the other way round. I have estimated that out of 10 airmen who have done 7 or 8 bombing trips 2 are definitely looking forward to going again; 7 would (largely from boredom) rather not go and feel more or less anxious, but feel that after all it's their job and they might as well get it over, and 1 definitely dreads the idea of going and would give anything not to go - these latter eventually develop diseases of some kind and are taken off aircrew.[69]

The final comments of the Mass Observation contributor regarding 'diseases of some kind' of course is a reference to flying stress.

Happily Flight-Lieutenant Fox and his crew finished their tour without a scratch. It was possible:

> This was the end of our tour of operations over enemy territory after completing 43 missions, to all of us in the crew we had finished what we had intended to do without being harmed in any way at all. All these raids were dangerous, whether by day or by night, and we just happened to have luck on our side. We had discipline in the crew

and when flying we were dedicated to the task and always wanted to achieve the aim we had been set. There was a very extraordinarily high proportion of flying personnel in Bomber Command who had these qualities.[70]

All aircrew realised that sooner or later, however well trained, chance determined whether they survived or not. They also knew that assiduous team work, assisted by unflagging morale, *might* keep them alive.

Chapter 12

There's No Future in It: Combat

Flying itself in the 1940s was dangerous. Crews which survived training had already been exposed to the formidable hazards of flying an aeroplane. Add combat to the multitude of other problems which one may encounter and most airmen faced their first operational flight with a degree of apprehension. Combat, in the context of Bomber Command meant one thing: an encounter with a fighter. Anti-aircraft fire, flak, was a one-sided affair. A bomber crew could not usually retaliate to flak, although there were certainly exceptional occasions, when they were at a low enough altitude, to do so.

A strong motivating factor in a man's decision to volunteer for flying service was the desire to 'prove oneself'. Leonard Cheshire, who flew over 100 operations, wrote during the war: 'It is difficult to imagine yourself being fired at and not feeling afraid. Perhaps that is why I am so glad of this war, because I must know whether or not I am a coward.'[1] For some, the realisation that imminent violent death was statistically possible had a sobering effect. The confidence instilled in training could evaporate with alarming speed. J. Bormann wrote: 'First op and certainly had some mixed feelings on take-off with full bomb load. Funny a chap may be on his last few days but one doesn't realise.'[2]

It is true, though, that some men did not feel fear and that many craved excitement, presumably following the axiom that they were young and that young men did not die. One rear gunner told his wireless audience in October 1940: '.... the highlights of aerial combat .... came only now and then. At the end of seven and a half hours in the tail turret, one rather sighs for them.'[3] Whether that particular gunner's excitement for action was shared by all is debatable but it was true that a gunner's role consisted of hours of boredom and eye strain, occasionally punctuated by a few seconds of mayhem. The Air Ministry was well aware that the feeling of helplessness in a crew once it had been located by a night-fighter 'must have an adverse effect upon the morale of the crews.'[4] Consequently it was thought that reports on the personal experiences of aircrew personnel would serve to promote a spirit of competition and boost morale, although it may have been better not to publicise some of the more harrowing experiences. As examined in the chapter *The Crew*, 3 Group suggested personal experience reports.[5]

The amazing courage of Sergeant Norman Jackson, who climbed onto the wing of his aircraft to put out an engine fire, is well-documented, as is the unbelievable escape by Nicholas Alkemade, who fell 18,000 feet without a parachute, and lived to tell the tale. The reader will find extensive coverage of both stories in print. Another exploit would have been a sure-fire winner as a morale booster. Flying Officer Reg Lewis was posted to 138 (Special Duties) Squadron on 11 September 1943. As a member of Squadron Leader Cooke's crew he flew to France and Norway, delivering and collecting SOE personnel and dropping supplies to resistance groups. On the evening of 7 February 1944 Reg's Halifax Mark II took off from Tempsford. The crew as usual, was pilot Squadron Leader Cooke, with F/O. Gornall as flight engineer, F/O. J.S. Reed, wireless operator, F/O. R.L. Beattie, rear gunner, F/O. Withecombe, despatcher and P/O. Ernest Bell, bomb aimer. Flying through cloud, the aircraft iced up and one of the starboard engines caught fire. The whole crew managed to bale out at 23.00. Here follows Reg's own account, as recorded in a top secret report, 'Evaded Capture in France'.

> I came down at about 23.00 hour within a yard of a house in a very small village. As I could hear somebody moving about nearby I ran for about 400 yards, leaving my parachute for the time being. The person moving about eventually made off, so I returned and hid it in a ditch.
>
> I walked about for an hour to try and discover my whereabouts, and eventually knocked at the door of a small cluster of houses. A woman opened a window at the top of a house and after some discussion, during which she fetched her 14-year-old daughter, I was admitted. With the help of drawings I made them understand that I was a British airman. Another daughter of about 24 joined us and it was decided that I should stay the night and that they would try and obtain help for me in the

morning. I discovered that I was near and south of CHATEAUNEUF D'ISERE. In the morning at about 09.30 hrs another girl turned up who explained that the mother had gone off on a bicycle to get help.

At 11.30 hrs a man arrived with a Dutch lad, who was also in hiding, and I was taken to a house in the neighbourhood of S. MARCEL, where I eventually linked up with BELL, BEATTIE and REED.

From this point on Reg's means of evading capture are unknown but in Pilot Officer Bell's statement he makes reference to 'an organisation'. The official record states that he was captured at Châteauneuf-de-Galaure on 7 February, the night of the aborted mission. There is no mention of capture in Reg's own report. All four arrived in Gibraltar on 11 April 1944, from where they all travelled to RAF Lyneham, arriving on 12 April. At the time the report was written Squadron Leader Cooke, the pilot, Flight Engineer Gornall and Flying Officer Withecombe were still 'evading in France'. Beattie, Reed and Bell all reached Gibraltar and then home. No. 138 Squadron operations record book contains this terse entry on 7/8 February 1944: 'Missing on Operations.'[6]

Reg Lewis's aircraft had not been brought down as a result of combat, though. Those which had, and on which at least one crew member had lived to tell the tale, were assiduously chronicled in combat reports, compiled by squadron gunnery officers. Some crews, of course, emerged unscathed from combat. The Air Ministry promoted personal experience reports; squadron operations record books detailed combat incidents. Here is a random sample, collated from these three sources.

When returning from a raid on Essen on the night of 1/2 June 1942 a Stirling of 15 Squadron, was hit in the tailplane by fire from a twin-engined fighter over Ghent while flying at 7,000 feet. The rear gunner opened up without effect. The German disappeared. Then another attack, possibly by the same aircraft, was made and one of the starboard engines was hit. The squadron combat report continued: 'Both rear and mid-upper gunners opened fire with long bursts and saw their shots strike the belly of the E/A right along the fuselage. Enemy's port engine caught fire. A large sheet of flame and black smoke poured from the machine which turned on its back and was last seen falling rapidly. E/A is claimed as probably destroyed.' There were no casualties and the aircraft landed safely, despite the outer starboard propeller flying off and only three engines operating.[7]

Another Stirling crew was attacked:

> I am bomb aimer in a Stirling aircraft which left at approximately 1800 hours on the 28th November 1942 to bomb TURIN. I do not know the names or fate of the rear gunner and mid-upper gunner but I think that the rear gunner may have been killed as the tail of the a/c was damaged and I heard a scream on the intercom for the rear turret. While on our return flight we were hit by flak somewhere N. of PARIS. The aircraft was damaged and set on fire and the Captain ordered us to bale out. The navigator and I baled out at about midnight 28/29th Nov. I did not see what happened to the others.[8]

On 6 December 1942 a Stirling of 7 Squadron from Oakington was attacked by a night fighter after being hit by flak over Mannheim. The only survivor of that crew, Sergeant McLean, told the story of its demise; the gunnery officer reported:

> The rear gunner got out of his turret into the after-part of the fuselage, and with the aid of a torch, which he fortunately carried, was able to clip on his parachute quickly, pull the handle on the jettisonable door and baled out. This, he states took him less than 30 seconds and he fears that the rest of the crew did not have much chance of jumping as the aircraft immediately went into a steep dive and crashed about a mile away. He himself was only about halfway down when he saw the aircraft explode on the ground and start to burn fiercely. Sgt. McLean came down safely in a ploughed field ......[9]

P/O. Freberg, another member of 7 Squadron as a navigator, baled out at 7,000 feet after his aircraft was hit by flak. The pilot and air bomber were still on the Stirling as it went down.[10] There was a happier outcome for yet another Stirling of 7 Squadron, which was attacked by three fighters while returning from a trip to Genoa on the night of 23/24 October 1942. First by

Flight Sergeant Cadet J. Manton after his first flight, in an Oxford Trainer, at an OTU. 'The training process was long and arduous, and lasted from eighteen months to two years.' (Courtesy of Imperial War Museum CH13877)

Halifax crews of 35 Squadron await transport to their aircraft at Linton-on-Ouse, Yorkshire. (Courtesy of Imperial War Museum D6034)

Bomber crews mount the flatbed of a dispersal truck to be transported to their aircraft for an operation. (Courtesy of Imperial War Museum D4751)

A Lancaster crew. (Courtesy of Imperial War Museum CH7487)

Aircrew relaxing in the mess. 'The homely schoolboyish atmosphere seemed fantastically unwarlike.' (Courtesy of Imperial War Museum CH5654)

In the sergeants' mess. 'Piss-ups were very frequent. In addition to flight piss-ups, there were squadron piss-ups, stand-down piss-ups and, as good as any, gong list piss-ups. Inter-squadron drinking matches were a highlight.' (Courtesy of Imperial War Museum CH7378)

On a Halifax bomber station. F/O. Pierre Richard believed that, 'Rather heavy social drinking had been encouraged in Bomber Command. Take their minds off the carnage, was the idea, I think.' (Source: Alamy)

'Eating, drinking, dancing, women and the pictures are the five main activities, (possibly in conjunction with each other).' Hammersmith Palais de Danse, London, 1941. (Courtesy of Imperial War Museum D2975)

P/O. Wilkerson of No. 35 Squadron with a WAAF officer at an all ranks dance at Linton-on-Ouse, Yorkshire. 'There was a lack of partners at segregated dances and it might be good for morale if officers and NCOs, and WAAFs of all ranks, were given the chance to mingle.' (Courtesy Imperial War Museum D6057)

Above: 'Scrubbed'. The last minute cancellation of an operation. (Courtesy of the 50 and 61 Squadrons Association)

Below left: Sgt. G. Cameron, the pilot of Handley Page Halifax B Mark II, HR837 'NP-F' of No. 158 Squadron RAF, poses with two of his crew amidst the damage caused when it was hit by a falling bomb from another aircraft while raiding Cologne on the night of 28/29 June 1943. In spite of the severe damage to the fuselage, none of the crew were injured and Cameron managed to fly HR837 back to the squadron's base at Lisset, Yorkshire. HR837 was repaired and flew a further eleven operations with the squadron before being turned over to No. 1656 Heavy Conversion Unit. (Courtesy of Imperial War Museum CE84)

Below right: East Wretham, Norfolk. Two crew members examine the rear of their aircraft, a Lancaster of 115 Squadron, where the rear turret, complete with its unfortunate gunner, was sheared off by bombs dropped from an aircraft above during a raid on Cologne on the night of 28/29 June 1943. (Courtesy of Imperial War Museum CE79)

Above: Sergeant J.B. Mallett, Sergeant H.H. Turkentine and Sergeant R.H.P. Roberts, flight engineer, bomb aimer and rear gunner respectively of a Lancaster of 57 Squadron at breakfast in the canteen at Scampton after an operation. All three were killed with the rest of the crew of Lancaster T-Tommy when it collided with high-tension cables near Scampton after a raid on Berlin, 2 March 1943. (Courtesy of Imperial War Museum CH8806)

Below: F/O. R.G. Hayes (left) and Flight Lieutenant J. Gordon, navigator and pilot respectively of a de Havilland Mosquito B Mark IV of No. 105 Squadron RAF, listen intently during a briefing for a night raid on Berlin in the Operations Room at Marham, Norfolk. Both men were killed on 5 November 1943, when their Mosquito, DZ587 'GB-B', crashed at Hempnall, Norfolk, while returning from an evening raid on Bochum. (Courtesy of Imperial War Museum CH18010)

A WAAF intelligence officer, Section Officer P. Duncalfe, questions the pilot, Warrant Officer H. Blunt (to her left), and crew of Avro Lancaster B Mark III, JB362 'EA-D' ('D' for 'Donald') of No. 49 Squadron RAF, on their return to Fiskerton, Lincolnshire, from a bombing raid on Berlin. On their next sortie to Berlin five days later, Blunt and his crew were shot down in 'D' for Donald and killed. (Courtesy of Imperial War Museum CH18658)

Above left: Flight Lieutenant William Reid VC. Bill Reid was awarded the Victoria Cross after pressing on with his attack on Dusseldorf on the night of 3 /4 November 1943. His aircraft had been attacked by a fighter and his navigator, Flight Sergeant Jefferies, killed. Reid was wounded. After bombing, he brought the aircraft back and crash landed at Shipdham, Norfolk. (Courtesy of Imperial War Museum CHP794)

Above middle: Flying Officer Michael Seamer Allen DFC. F/O. Allen was a Beaufighter navigator with 141 Squadron. (Courtesy of Imperial War Museum CH11449)

Above right: Wing Commander A.J. (Jim) Wright DFC. No. 61 Squadron and 630 Squadron Lancaster navigator. (Courtesy of 50 and 61 Squadrons Association)

Above left: Flying Officer Pierre Richard DFC. F/O. Richard was a Mosquito navigator with 571 Squadron. 'It took a long time to adjust to home life but at least you could lie in your bed and no-one could say to you, "You're on ops to Berlin tonight". It was over. Finished.' (Courtesy of Stephen Richard)

Above middle: George 'Johnny' Johnson MBE, DFM. Bomb aimer. Dambuster. 'I can honestly say that I never once felt I wasn't going to come back.' (Courtesy of Sue Bartlam)

Above right: George Vandekerckhove DFC. (Courtesy of Canadian Warplane Heritage Museum)

Below: Wing Commander Dudley Burnside and his Wellington crew of 427 (RCAF) Squadron at Croft, Lincolnshire. Pilot Officer Heather, the navigator, was killed and Sergeant Geoffrey Keen, the wireless operator, lost his foot when their aircraft was hit by flak on 13 March 1943. W/Cdr. Burnside became a Group Captain with 195 Squadron. (Courtesy of RAF Memorial Flight Club)

Above: Pilot Officer George Vandekerckhove DFC with crew and ground crew. Rear left to right: Sgt. A.D. Rothwell, Sgt. Edward Bartlett, P/O. George Vandekerckhove DFC, pilot, Sgt. William Williamson; Centre left to right: four unknown ground crew, F/Sgt. John Albert, Front left to right: P/O. Alan Young, unknown ground crew, unknown ground crew, F/Sgt John McLean. Sgts. Rothwell and Williamson were the only survivors when their Halifax was shot down during a raid on Berlin on the night of 30 August 1943. Also on board, and killed, was Sgt. Cyril Campbell Gofton, second pilot. (Courtesy of Michel Becker, *Aircrew Remembered*)

Below: Per Ardua ad Astra. Another op done. A Lancaster crew of 50 Squadron at RAF Swinderby. (Courtesy of 50 and 61 Squadrons Association)

a Breda, which inflicted slight damage to the fuselage, then by a Macchi 200, which made four attacks without effect and disappeared after the Stirling's gunners opened fire. It was claimed as damaged. To round off an eventful night for this 7 Squadron crew an Italian biplane joined the party. It too was forced to retire and was also claimed as damaged.[11]

The gunners of this crew had been lucky. Not so Sergeant Glazzard, a member of F/O. Andrews's Lancaster crew of 115 Squadron. Returning from Wuppertal on the night of 29/30 May 1943, a night fighter struck.

> The first indication of attack which the crew received was a burst of cannon fire which stopped the port outer engine, put the hydraulics out of action, caused the bomb doors to open and also damaged the starboard rudder. This burst also damaged the tail turret and fatally injured the tail gunner [Sgt. Glazzard], who died without regaining consciousness after the aircraft had landed at base........The M.U. gunner, whose turret was u/s, fired a two second burst using the rear gear release at a range of 90 to 200 yards. The E/A replied and scored hits on the starboard side of the fuselage of our aircraft. Our aircraft then climbed to starboard and the E/A, which was still following at a range of 100 yards, fired another burst of cannon and machine gun fire, which passed well beneath our aircraft. The M.U. gunner replied with a three second burst and scored hits on the starboard side of the fuselage of the E/A. The E/A then broke away in a diving turn to starboard and was not seen again. Our aircraft then resumed its course to base and made a successful crash landing.[12]

The standard manoeuvre for a heavy bomber to shake off night fighters was the corkscrew, a jinking movement from port to starboard. A lumbering heavy bomber could not outpace a single or twin-engined fighter and the corkscrew was its only hope of survival. Which is how this crew escaped. The rear gunner of a Lancaster of 61 Squadron spotted a Focke Wolf 190 at 18,000 feet near Schiphol, on return from Dusseldorf on the night of 11/12 June 1943. At the same moment the Lancaster was coned by a searchlight and the pilot took the aeroplane into a steep dive, shaking off the searchlight and losing the Focke Wolf into the bargain.[13]

Encounters could be fleeting. A Halifax of 10 Squadron was on its way home from Gelsenkirchen on the night of 25/26 June 1943. The bomb aimer saw an ME 109 approaching head on. Its tracer fire passed underneath the Halifax, followed by the ME 109. Before the rear gunner knew what was happening the German aircraft disappeared into the night. There was no damage and there were no casualties.[14]

There was a sadder outcome from the following combat. F/Lt. Grieg's crew, of 57 Squadron, was attacked several times by a fighter over the target, Cologne, on the night of 8/9 July 1943, 'during which attacks the Mid-Upper Gunner, F/Sgt. Nutt, was badly wounded. The aircraft was brought back to England by the most direct route and landed at the first available airfield, Manston, in an attempt to save the life of the wounded gunner, who had survived despite intensive wounds to his face and eyes. This desperate attempt was in vain, however, as F/Sgt. Nutt died the following day.'[15]

Michael Allen, navigator on 141 Squadron, does not fit the stereotype of Bomber Command aircrew, lumbering in a 'heavy' towards Germany every other night, although he *was* a member of Bomber Command. With his pilot Harry White, they patrolled the skies in their Beaufighter, in a night intruder role. One entry in 141 Squadron's Operational Record Book gives a flavour of Michael Allen's war:

> 15 July 1943. F/O/ White; F/O/ Allen. At 00.15 on the 16th July 1943 we took off from West Malling in a Beaufighter VI on an Intruder patrol to JUVINCOURT. We flew over Rye at 00.22 hrs and made landfall over the French coast at AULT 00.50 hrs. On the way in we saw an orange coloured fire on the ground at ARRAS accompanied by a good deal of smoke. After patrolling JUVINCOURT without any sign of activity from 01.33 hrs until 01.55 hrs we flew south-east. When we were about 8 miles S.E. of RHEIMS at 02.00 hrs we saw an ME110 3,000 ft. ahead of us flying straight and level at 10,000 ft. We were 2,000 ft. above flying S.E. in the same direction as the E/A, so we at once dived down to get dead astern and slightly below. Opening fire at 750 ft. we slowly closed to 600 ft. in a two second burst of cannon and machine gun. There were strikes on both engines and on the fuselage and a moment later the whole aircraft exploded in flames, splitting into two burning pieces, one

of which was blown right behind us. We watched both pieces strike the ground, where they continued to burn, and then, as we were not to [sic] well off for fuel, made for the French coast. As we flew over DREUX a searchlight came on and tried unsuccessfully to pick us up, and there was a good deal of heavy flak, far to [sic] accurate for comfort. We recrossed the coast at OISTREHAM [sic] at 02.45 hrs flew over Beachy Head at 03.05 hrs. and landed Wittering 03.50 hrs. Enemy casualties: 1 ME110 destroyed. Our casualties: nil.[16]

The next combat resulted in one of Bomber Command's Victoria Crosses. The operations record book of 61 Squadron gave the basic facts of the incident in question, which occurred on the night of 3/4 November 1943: 'F/L. Reid was attacked by enemy night fighters on the way out [to Dusseldorf] but although he and Flight Engineer were wounded and the Navigator killed outright he proceeded on to bomb the target. On returning, a crash landing was made at Shipdham.' The navigator was Flight Sergeant Jefferies, the flight engineer Sergeant Norris and the other crew members were Sergeant Rolton (air bomber), Flight Sergeants Mann (Wop/Ag.), Baldwin (air gunner) and Emerson (air gunner). Pilot Bill Reid received the VC.[17]

When combat did occur it was not always easy to confirm the result. A 103 Squadron crew had a narrow escape, while unable to claim a 'kill': 'There was one combat when W/O Frost was attacked by a twin-engined aircraft, which fired, wounding both Mid-Upper and Rear Gunners, both being seriously hurt, and damaged the starboard engine, in addition to other fuselage and turret damage. The Rear Gunner fired a burst at the enemy aircraft, which caught fire and went into a dive. A burning mass seen on the ground was believed to be this aircraft, which is claimed as a probable. He belly landed at the emergency airfield at WOODBRIDGE.'[18]

A Lancaster of 97 Squadron was attacked by a twin-engined fighter on the night of 3/4 September 1943. The mid-upper gunner gave the order to corkscrew and managed to loose off a burst, 'tracer was seen to enter the nose of the enemy aircraft.' Another fighter hove into sight, this time the rear gunner coming into action. A duel ensued between both gunners and the two fighters. Simultaneously 'great searchlight activity appeared. Fifty to sixty searchlights lit up the sky in order to assist the fighters. These searchlights were about a mile in front, thus giving a great amount of light.' They were also of assistance to the Lancaster gunners, who were able to see quite clearly their opponents. During the combat another Lancaster was weaving nearby, hampering the efforts of the gunners, anxious not to hit it accidentally. The crew of the Lancaster which had been attacked arrived back at base with slight damage and a fund of stories for the mess.[19]

There are many combat reports pertaining to Bomber Command's worst night, the Nuremberg Raid of 30/31 March 1944, but these reports, of course, are the ones made by crews which survived the fighter onslaught of that night. Lancaster 'R' of 61 Squadron was one of many. It was attacked by three fighters. The rear gunner spotted a JU 88 at 400 yards astern. The pilot corkscrewed to port, being hit by cannon shells from the German aircraft. The starboard inner engine was struck. Both gunners fired bursts as the JU 88 pulled away. 'Hits were made. No claim made.'[20] Another JU 88 materialised. The rear gunner opened fire from 400 yards, the German opened fire from 350 yards and the mid-upper gunner from 250 yards. This time the starboard outer engine was hit. The Lancaster gunners continued firing and hit the JU 88's port engine. It was seen falling rapidly and the gunners claimed it as damaged. Meanwhile, another JU 88 had crept up unobtrusively. Still corkscrewing, the pilot, F/O. Paul, succeeded in shaking off the fighter, with the mid-upper gunner Sergeant Billington and rear gunner Sergeant McGibney continuing to fire, joined in the front turret by Wop/Ag. Sergeant Brazzier. The JU 88 disappeared. 1,500 rounds, 1,000 rounds and 50 rounds respectively were loosed off by the 3 gunners. There is no mention in the report of how the Lancaster managed to return on two engines, but it did, as the combat report testifies.[21]

On this eventful night three fighters were also awaiting the arrival of another Lancaster – 'G' – of 61 Squadron. The first attack failed. In the second the mid-upper gunner, the wireless operator and the navigator were all hit and 'put out of action'. The rear gunner fired a long burst but had to break away to engage another enemy aircraft, a JU 88, from which cannon fire made multiple hits on the Lancaster and wounded the flight engineer. Throughout, the pilot, F/O. Freeman, had been corkscrewing. 'As soon as the attacks were shaken off the Lancaster jettisoned its bomb load and turned for home with only three members of its crew uninjured.' That would have been the rear gunner, the bomb aimer and the pilot.[22] Two of the aircraft were claimed as damaged and one probably destroyed. Violent hail and sleet storms were encountered by one aircraft and an electrical explosion which struck the aircraft caused the pilot to lose control. The crew were ordered to abandon the aircraft; the wireless operator and mid-upper gunner did so successfully, while the remaining members were too stunned to carry out this order. At 1,000 feet the pilot regained control of the aircraft. Two other crews of 61 Squadron were lost that night.[23]

No. 427 (RCAF) Squadron's adjutant wrote the morning after Nuremberg, 'The squadron suffered a heavy loss this night........ Returning crews reported numerous night fighters that were aided by the bright moon...... P/O. Weicker in "N" Nuts attacked by fighter. No fire and no casualties. A number of the pilots actually saw the night fighters shooting down our aircraft and tracers filled the air...... Target was well pranged but believed a costly "do".'[24] It certainly was.

....

If one avoided the night-fighter, then there was flak, heavy and light. Flying through a flak barrage tested men's resolve to the utmost. In 1942 a new type of flak was reported, the 'scarecrow'. 'These are believed to be used as morale killers.'[25] Not flak at all, it was, in fact, an exploding British bomber hit by cannon fire from a night-fighter, not visible to any nearby crews, which had crept up underneath.[26] Crews preferred to believe that the spectacular aftermath of one of these attacks was caused by a new type of ordnance and not by the destruction of a machine and seven men.

Wing Commander K.J. Newman, writing many years later, held to the belief that a scarecrow was not an exploding aircraft:

> In training we had been warned that the Germans occasionally put up a pyrotechnic called a 'scarecrow' to explode within the bomber stream. It was intended to resemble the destruction of a Pathfinder aircraft, with red and green markers cascading from it, in order to distract the bomb-aimer's concentration. The thing exploded right in front of the nose of our aircraft and I did not have time to take

avoiding action. It did not look quite right for a Pathfinder as the colours were slightly different and I wondered – and fervently hoped – that it was a scarecrow. We passed right through it and there was a strong 'firework' smell in the cockpit; if it had been an aircraft we would have hit at least some of the debris as it was so near. So I have no doubt whatsoever that the Germans did deploy such devices to try to put us off our aim, although considerable doubt about their existence has been expressed since the War.[27]

The myth persisted. In 1946 a wing commander wrote: '...... it was on this trip [to Essen] that I first saw a "scarecrow". This was a weird and wonderful contraption fired up by the Germans which burst in the air and floated for a time with streamers of flame dripping off it. It was supposed to look like an aircraft on fire .... this was supposed to be extremely frightening to the British Air Huns.'[28] In 1977 former pilot Jack Currie recalled the words of a briefing officer before a raid on which Currie flew. The officer was describing a raid of five nights before: 'A considerable number of scarecrow flares were employed by the enemy, but I don't believe anyone is going to be worried by these rather amateurish attempts at psychological warfare.'[29] Currie went on:

> I remember Buzz Marshall telling me that he had been severely shaken by his first sight of a scarecrow flare which had burst a few feet above and in front of him. It had looked for all the world like a PFF [Pathfinder] kite receiving a direct hit with TIs [target indicators] and marker flares igniting in a multi-coloured blaze of light. I had asked Buzz how he knew it wasn't an aircraft, and he had said he didn't know - the IO [interrogation officer] had told him it was a scarecrow at interrogation.[30]

Whether the myth was propagated deliberately by the higher echelons of Bomber Command in the interests of morale or whether they genuinely had no idea what the scarecrow was is not known. It was convenient, though, to perpetuate the belief that it was a flak burst and not an exploding aeroplane. In 'A note on recent enemy pyrotechnic activity over Germany' the RAF Operational Research Section concluded that:

> At a distance they are supposed to look very similar to an aircraft falling in flames ...... intended to give crews the impression that ...... the defences are stronger than they really are .... they are used purely as a deterrent and are not intended to be lethal .... the Germans have always placed great value on horrific devices ...... the phenomenon is purely probably a 'scarecrow'.[31]

*

A reliable indicator of the state of morale was the incidence of 'early returns' from raids, particularly noticeable during the winter of 1943/44 when Berlin was the main target. Mechanical failure of some kind was often the reason but those crews who regularly abandoned their flights aroused suspicion.

> It is seen that some aircraft have bad records and these are being specially investigated ...... there is undoubtedly a tendency for some pilots to return early quite frequently. In this respect there have been cases where pilots have received promotion despite a poor record of early returns. It is suggested that this is most undesirable, as nothing so quickly reduces morale on a squadron ....It is possible that some crews carry on when defects in the aircraft are discovered in the early stages of an operation and may be lost, whereas others return early.[32]

Crews were put in an invidious position if they suffered genuine problems en route to targets. To return early invited suspicion; to press on in a malfunctioning aircraft could mean death. Many crews did press on when they should have returned, so strong was the deterrent effect of cowardice allegations.[33] An early return did not count as a sortie but avoidance of a particularly well-defended target was preferable for some crews. One airman admitted that he and his crew sabotaged the turrets of their aircraft to avoid a raid on a known tough target.[34] F/O. Fairhead described, in his memoir, one occasion when he was unhappy with the performance of an engine on his Lancaster and was absolutely certain that the aircraft would not have sufficient power to take off. His sortie was abandoned. Fearing that he would be suspected of 'getting the wind up' and deliberately sabotaging the sortie, he was interviewed by the squadron commander and exonerated. Commenting on his CO, he wrote, 'I always had a genuine respect for senior officers in the RAF. They always treated those below them with courtesy....' A tribute to the bond which existed between men who had a mutual respect for the dangers of their occupation.[35]

Those who did return early could expect a thorough grilling by the squadron commander. His crews would scrutinise his handling of the situation, for if he was perceived to be too lenient with a guilty crew – or too harsh with an innocent one - morale on the squadron could dip. Raid abort rates tended to be highest on squadrons with rigid leadership and poor equipment.[36]

Another indicator of declining morale was 'creepback', when crews unloaded their bombs too early in order to avoid heavily defended targets. As successive crews bombed, their loads gradually crept back from the aiming point. Pathfinders Commander Donald Bennett was scathing in his criticism of Main Force crews which released their bombs too early, referring to them as 'fringe merchants'. He also accused them of dumping some of their bombs in the North Sea on the way to the target so that they could gain extra height and thus extra protection against flak.[37] The formation of 8 (Pathfinder Force) Group in January 1943 theoretically meant a degree of elimination of creepback and more accurate bombing but, of course, there were times when the target markers of the PFF went down too early, then the Main Force would bomb too early on the markers.

*

Bomber Command needed to know how casualties could be avoided, or, at least, reduced. With this in mind, the Operational Research Section of the Command investigated the incidence of crew casualties caused by enemy action on night operations. Data collected during the period April to November 1942 provided answers and recommendations. Wellingtons suffered twice as many fighter attacks as the new heavies, no doubt as a result of its slower speed and lower ceiling. After analysis of data over a certain period it was found, perhaps unsurprisingly, that the two gunners and the bomb aimer were the most vulnerable crew members while over the target area. On the question of second pilots, it was rare that another crew member had to take over from an incapacitated pilot. Pilots were protected to a certain degree by armour and were less likely to be hit by fighters. The gunners only had perspex between them, flak and fighters. Of the three, the rear gunner was the most vulnerable, with fighters attacking from the rear. In the period studied only six aircraft were lost due to injury or death of the pilot. The report concluded that very few of the crews of bombers were hit by the enemy.[38] Aircrew were more likely to be injured in flying accidents than in combat. Another report, in July 1943, gave answers to questions from AMP Bertine Sutton regarding crew wastage. It was found, again unsurprisingly, that the rear gunner was the most likely member of the crew to be wounded on return from a raid. Data showed that 1 rear gunner in every 500 sorties would be wounded, a light casualty rate, easily borne.[39] Except for that one unfortunate gunner.

As the Battles of the Ruhr and Berlin unfolded, data would have to be amended to reflect the increasing numbers of casualties. Could experience help a crew survive? In a report on 'The effect of experience on operational efficiency' it was found that experience had little effect on the chance of becoming a casualty. If one's luck had run out, the Grim Reaper could claim an experienced, as well as an inexperienced, crew, although the latter were the worst affected. All raids from December 1943 to March 1944 were studied. This amounted to 17,000 sorties, in which 300 aircraft were lost. Training was no substitute for real operational experience but increased and more effective training would help.[40]

*

It would be platitudinous to state that the results of combat could have an effect on morale. If a rear gunner has shot down an ME 110, his morale is going to be sky high; if a crew arrives back at base with a dying rear gunner who has to be prised from his turret, its remaining members are not going to be living it up in the mess. Two powerful factors could mitigate fear in combat: absorption in one's duties and the cloak of darkness. After his first operation to Germany Pilot Officer Rowling wrote: 'I wondered if I might be a bit windy when it all started but was too busy locating the target to try and disentangle any different feelings. I don't think fear entered into the picture at all.'[41] Individual morale could be sustained in this way and it depended upon one's crew position. Johnny Johnson: 'I was there. I was doing a job and I had to do that job properly. I was concentrating on that, regardless of what was going on outside. I didn't worry in the least what was going on. I was concentrating on the bomb sight. That was the job I had trained for. As soon as I said "bombs gone", head up, get the hell out of here.'[42] Jim Wright said, 'As a navigator I was lucky enough to be busy before, during and after every flight. No time to dwell on anything other than the navigation task in hand.'[43] A navigator could shield himself from the activity outside by retreating behind his curtain; a rear gunner, on the other hand, was on constant alert in a very vulnerable place and was consequently more prone to anxiety.

When it became apparent that bombers could not defend themselves in daylight and night operations began, the blanket of darkness provided a measure of protection. It also shielded crews from the demoralising effect of witnessing the destruction of their comrades' aircraft. True, at night they did see planes hit, exploding, going down in flames but regularly witnessing crashes in daylight would have had a far more serious effect on morale. 'The deleterious effects of crashes are caused almost entirely by the man himself anticipating a similar catastrophe, so that the more unavoidable, distressing or personally related it seems to him, the worse are the repercussions on his morale.'[44] Which could be sustained for longer if one was protected by darkness. Bernard Dye recorded in his diary: 'Saw a Lancaster blow up, poor devils didn't have a chance.'[45] Distressing as this was, Dye would have resumed his duties, the distance and remoteness of what he had witnessed providing a degree of protection. Airmen became inured to sights they would have preferred not to have seen. Don Charlwood wrote: 'After a time the most timid of men can become accustomed to the most threatened of lives. We became accustomed to seeing planes disintegrate beside us.'[46] It is not difficult to imagine the intense relief when the wheels touched down on one's home airfield after an operation. Naturally, an individual's morale was at a high level on every landing.

Overall losses of Bomber Command as a whole were known to crews almost immediately. Bernard Dye recorded the loss of 72 aircraft in a raid on Berlin on the night of 23/24 March 1944 in his diary, lamenting: 'It was a hard blow for us. Nobby and crew went down over the target. Nobby was a great skipper – is missed by all – it was a bad day for Bomber Command.'[47] Until the even worse night exactly one week later, Bomber Command's biggest loss of the entire war.

*

Most crews did press on, even in the Command's severest test, the sustained attack on Berlin. 'What Bomber Command suffered from in the Battle of Berlin was not a widespread drop in morale but a deterioration in efficiency caused by adverse weather conditions …….. and steadily increasing casualties which led to an ever greater reliance on inexperienced crews.'[48] Many optimistic reports appeared in the national and provincial press. It was acknowledged that losses had been severe but optimism was the order of the day. This from the *Midlothian Advertiser*:

> Bombers Crews' courage
> Despite the fact that we lose so many of our bomber crews over Germany every week the high morale is wonderfully maintained. The heavier ground and air defences in Germany seem to carry no fear for them. When crews are chosen for operational duties, the 'lucky' ones are always envied by those left behind, and some novel excuses are advanced by those who, due for a rest period, do their best to wangle their continuance on operational flights.[49]

Five months later, at the height of the Battle of Berlin, Air Commodore E.L. Howard Williams enthused in the *Ballymena Weekly Telegraph*:

> An air force is as strong as its morale and fighting morale at any time varies in direct ratio to the quality of fighting equipment.…... Of the air crews I should like to say that their morale, even to an old hand like myself, was something to marvel at. Thousands of them were eagerly awaiting their turn to strike at Berlin. …… How high was the appreciation of air crew and ground crew alike for the quality of

our aircraft and their ancillary gear? They had only one complaint. It was that they wanted more of it. Give them quantity as well as quality and the world is theirs.[50]

And a further five months on, an anonymous air marshal, waxed lyrical in the *Daily News* about morale and praised particularly the qualities of the product of the secondary schools, who were now making up the majority of aircrews:

> A few days ago I asked one of our invasion Air Marshals …… about the morale of British airmen. 'It has never been higher', he replied. These boys will do anything you ask them to do. They know they are on top of the world; and though there have been grievous losses of personnel their spirit is unaffected. He added that there is a great reservoir of trained pilots and crews….. When I enquired about their technical fitness and other qualifications, he said at once, 'Thank God for our State system of education. Without it we could not have built up this great service. The public schoolboys are fine fellows with special aptitudes for leadership. But their number is relatively small. In any case, give me the secondary school boy. He has a better technical education than the average public schoolboy and is easy to train.'[51]

Afterword. All twenty-one aircraft of 195 Squadron returned from a raid on Scholven on 22 February 1945. Even when none were lost and morale should have received a boost, death stalked Bomber Command crews. In one of the aircraft Sergeant C.S. Ford, was slumped in his rear turret. He had been killed by flak over the target. A lonely death but he was not destined to lie in a grave far from home, as were so many of his comrades.[52]

Chapter 13

Newton Got Him: Occupational Hazards

'*There was no single moment of security from take-off to touchdown.*'[1]

Ten Little Bomber Boys

Ten little bomber boys off to strafe the Rhine
One went to Hamburg and then there were nine

Ten aircraft were reduced to none by a variety of careless mistakes ....

And ten expensive aircraft will never fly again
With their ten expensive aircrews who took so long to train[2]

Flak and night fighters were not the only enemies of Bomber Command. The weather, the intense cold, lightning strikes, bombs dropped from aircraft above, 'friendly fire' from 'trigger-happy' gunners in other aircraft, take-off and landing accidents and collision all conspired to affect morale. In 1939 flying itself, independent of any combat danger, was not a safe pursuit. 'It still resembled at best driving a badly-suspended heavy lorry fast through traffic on bad roads in winter, while conversing with the traffic police through megaphones.'[3] With a full bomb load take-off was perilous and engine failure could spell disaster.[4]

In Training at OTUs and HCUs

The moment a man volunteered for aircrew in Bomber Command was the moment he put his life at risk. 5,327 of them never even got to an operational unit. They were killed in training. Here follows a random sample of accidents which cost some of those lives.

Sergeants William Bray and Arthur Broadbent of No.2 OTU died when their Beaufighter flew through low cloud into the side of a hill on 13 April 1942.[5] Sergeant Taylor, a Canadian trainee rear gunner of an OTU in 92 Group at Hinton-in-the-Hedges, Oxfordshire, emerged from his turret on 16 February to stretch his legs before resuming training. He walked into a revolving propeller.[6]

Wing Commander K.J. Newman recalled his time at Lindholme HCU. There were, he said, regular crashes involving trainees, usually on take-off or landing. One of Newman's friends lost his life because an instructor, whom Newman referred to as 'dangerous', ordered his friend to continue an exercise in an aircraft which could not reach the required height. It flew into a Scottish mountain. Newman was of the opinion that many accidents at his OTU were caused by ruthless instructors, who ordered trainees, fearful of accusations of cowardice, to fly in poorly maintained, old aircraft. 'Even if you had doubts about a/c airworthiness, you flew rather than be labelled LMF........ it went against the grain to ignore minor faults which could easily become major ones, particularly as I was responsible for the lives of six other young men as well as myself.'[7]

At Hemswell HCU Flight Lieutenant D. Steiner remembered: 'An horrific accident occurred whilst we were there. A Hurricane collided with a Lancaster [on a fighter affiliation exercise] over the centre of the aerodrome and cut off the Lancaster's tail, both aircraft dived straight into the ground killing all on board. It was said that there were two crews on the bomber...... The Hurricane crashed into a small wood nearby ...... the rear turret landed some yards away on the cricket pitch. It was complete and upright but the interior was not a pretty sight.'[8] P/O. J.R. Byrne recalled a similar horror at another OTU:

> This is the most horrible incident I have to relate...... A Wimpey bomber has pranged and burst into flames. God! How bloody terrible. I walk across to the scene of the crash and there I see this 'prang' – my very first. ...... Poor buggers [sic] in the front. Didn't [have] a chance. Burnt to almost nothing...... It can be horrible for

aircrew to die. That of being burned to death. ..... I found some of the dead crews [sic] shoes against the wreck also one chaps' [sic] flying helmet and intercom system. The pilot's body was found burned to a very small size in a ditch. God knows where the Air Bomber's body was. Probably underneath the blazing wreakage [sic]. God! What an awful sight. How really bloody terrible. ..... They died an airman's death..... They that lived and talked with us are now no more.[9]

P/O. Byrne was not spared further ghastliness. On 15 July 1944 five members of a crew on his OTU were: 'blown to pieces and burned to death' on their last OTU flight before proceeding to leave and then to an HCU. A short circuit had caused a fire at 10,000 feet:

When the Navigator left the machine he jumped to a terrible death. He pulled the ripcord of a blazing parachute 9,000 feet above the Earth. Poor lad. He wouldn't know much about it, thank God ...... One chap pulled his ripcord a little too soon. The result – hung up on the blazing geodets of a diving Wimpey ..... The skipper was the only person alive last night. So badly burned that he could not even speak. He will probably die.[10]

On Operational Stations

On the squadrons, before aircraft even set off on operations, one had to develop a resigned acceptance of the frequent accidents which occurred. Take-off and landing mishaps, mid-air collisions, prematurely exploding bombs, all had a demoralising effect on those who witnessed such events. Jack Currie recalled.....

A ground crew flight-sergeant, cycling along the perimeter track on his way back from a far-off dispersal, was neatly decapitated by a prop-blade of the port outer engine. Oblivious of this misfortune, the crew wiped their brows as their bomber staggered into the air, and went on their eastward way. Next day, news of the headless NCO was passed to the pilot, and he took it badly. The incident seemed to shatter his already shaken confidence and he could be observed, white faced and hollow-eyed, standing alone in the mess or crew room for several days, before disappearing from the squadron scene.[11]

Wing Commander Newman recalled a similar horrific incident on his station: 'One night a member of a friend's crew walked into one [a prop] and was cut to pieces.'[12] Many more tragic incidents as appalling as this would have severely dented the morale of anyone unlucky enough to witness them, as it obviously did to the unfortunate pilot remembered by Currie.

By the time crews reached an operational squadron they had few illusions about the dangers awaiting them. An Air Council meeting on 9 September 1941 recorded that there were 60-70 accidents per day.[13] The Council sought to encourage a spirit of competition to reduce aircraft wastage during training and on operational squadrons. It was believed that avoidable accidents were caused by lack of discipline. Offenders were to be punished.[14] Harris was in no mood to tolerate this slackening of discipline. The ability to hit Germany hard, he wrote, was hindered by the high rate of avoidable accidents, caused by lack of flying discipline or poor and inefficient control by aircrews.[15] He went on, 'The losses in aircraft and aircrew personnel attributable to avoidable accidents is far in excess of losses due to enemy action.'[16] He was determined to act severely against officers who failed to bring avoidable accident levels down. He threatened, 'Station commanders, squadron COs, flight commanders and captains of aircraft who are not up to that job or who fail in their duty in this respect must be removed and downgraded.'[17] A letter from HQ 5 Group to all pilots in the Group stressed the importance of conserving aircraft:

> A word about this low flying business. I know what fun it is, and we've all got to be able to handle our aircraft easily at low levels. But do it in the proper place and in the proper way and that is *not* over your girlfriend's house. There has been an appalling loss of life and valuable aircraft through this sort of senseless showing off. Remember you are trained and your aircraft is built to kill Huns and help win the war.[18]

Sergeant pilots were again the subject of criticism (q.v.). The Group letter goes on to berate them: 'Of course, one of the troubles, as you know, is the very little disciplinary hold squadron commanders have over these sergeant pilots.'[19]

On 30 September 1940 a Blenheim of 107 Squadron, RAF Wattisham crashed on landing, killing Sergeants Jack Merritt and Sidney Walters. 'Airframe complete write off scattered in pieces over a wide area due to explosion of four 250 lb bombs.'[20] 20 February 1944. As the aircraft of 630 Squadron made their way from East Kirkby to Stuttgart, one Lancaster crashed on take-off. All its bombs, including a 4,000 pounder, exploded. 'Comparatively little damage was caused tho' a good deal of glass was broken. It is understood that this also occurred as far away as Skegness & Boston [approximately 20 miles]. 6 of the crew were killed and the rear gunner escaped with shock and abrasions.'[21]

Another bomb incident demonstrates just how tenuous was the hold on life of a Bomber Command crew man. He did not need to be in the air over Germany for death to visit. Aircraft of 103 Squadron were lined up ready for take-off to Berlin on 23 August 1943:

> All of a sudden there was an enormous CLANG from the next dispersal …… the bomb doors of a Lanc had not been closed and its bombs had fallen to the ground ……. the incendiaries were now burning with the Cookie and 1000 pound bombs ……. We threw ourselves to the ground and waited for the bang ….. Nothing happened ….. then the Wingco tore up in his car and yelled, 'Get your aircraft away!' All seven of us scrambled into the Lanc. …… just as we were nearest to the fire, the whole lot exploded. Large lumps of exploding bombs came hurtling past and through our aircraft ………. We had a full bomb load and were scared that our bombs would also explode, so we jumped out of the front hatch and stopped running several hundred yards away ……. Unfortunately, Harry, the wireless op had been hit in the head by a large chunk of metal and was past all help.[22]

Sergeant Early, a Wellington crew member of 149 Squadron, Mildenhall was killed when his aircraft flew through low cloud, hit the ground and caught fire on 12 February 1941. His pilot, R. Warren, survived.[23] Sergeant Williams and Sergeant Earnshaw, pilot and navigator of a Hampden of 50 Squadron, were killed when, on returning from an operation, their aircraft ran out of fuel and crashed near Brampton, Cumberland on 10 January 1942.[24] 'We his parents are anxious to know how our boy met his end,' wrote Sergeant Earnshaw's father to the squadron.[25]

On 26 February 1942 a Stirling of 15 Squadron at Mildenhall ran out of fuel after an operation and crashed on a farm close to the airfield. On this occasion no aircrew were killed but an unfortunate soldier, 2nd Lieutenant L.B. Murray, on attachment to the squadron, and on board, lost his life.[26] A Hampden of 144 Squadron hit a wireless caravan parked on the airfield, killing two aircraftsmen and seriously injuring another. Not aircrew but valuable ground crew; the effect of the mishap on the Hampden crew can be imagined.[27] A similar accident occurred at Linton-on-Ouse on 11 September 1940, when a Whitley of 77 Squadron ran into a tent, killing three ground crew.[28]

Barrage Balloons

Barrage balloon cables were a hazard. AVM William Foster MacNeece Foster, AOC 6 Group, felt it necessary to inform Bomber Command HQ of the alarming number of accidents involving OTU trainees and barrage balloon cables. Cross-country flights had to be limited because of the barrage above Coventry. From August 1940 to June 1941, when Foster contacted HQ, there had been nine accidents concerning five OTUs. Three of these were fatal, with nineteen deaths and three injuries. During the same period forty-three RAF aircraft had struck cables; only nine Luftwaffe aircraft did.[29] If there were more effective control of the balloon barrage, suggested Foster, 'the risk of fatal and demoralising accidents will be considerably lessened.'[30]

Here are two cases of fatal accidents caused by collisions with cables. A Hampden returning from a raid on 13 June 1940 hit a cable at Felixstowe, Suffolk. The impact tore off the port wing and the aircraft crashed into a flour mill on the docks. The entire crew perished.[31] Eighteen months later, 3 miles across the River Orwell, the captain of a 3 Group aircraft suffered the same fate when he flew into a cable near Harwich on the night of 18/19

December 1941. He managed to land on Thorney Bay, Canvey Island but died of exposure.[32]

One distinguished airman was spared on the night of 17/18 May 1940. F/O. Guy Gibson reported that he had hit a balloon cable, not in Britain, but near Hamburg. He was flying an aircraft of 83 Squadron when he felt an impact. Thinking it was flak, he flew on but, having returned home safely, he inspected the wing tip and found that the cable had sliced through it 'like a knife through butter'.[33]

On Operations

In 1941, to discover why there were so many crashes of aircraft on operations which were not caused by enemy action, VCAS Wilfred Freeman ordered Peirse to set up a committee of inquiry and to report to the Air Ministry.[34] Among its findings was pre-flight negligence. Before an aircraft was even in the air, its crew could have been endangered by comrades. Form 700, which had to be completed after a flight to record any faults, was often dismissed by pilots as yet more 'bumph' – unnecessary bureaucratic form filling – and problems would be passed on verbally to ground crew, then forgotten by them, with potentially fatal results for the next occupants of the aircraft.

Once airborne, a myriad of problems could occur: icing up, lack of oxygen, fatigue, frostbite, fog, hail and electrical storms, quite apart from frequent mechanical failure or sheer exhaustion.[35] 'We can never know how many aircrew were lost because at the end of a long sortie the men were simply worn out with noise and vibration and cold and smell and stuffiness and too exhausted to find the airfield or to land on it.'[36]

Setting off from North Luffenham airfield on a 'gardening' operation on the night of 9 March 1942, a Hampden of 408 (RCAF) Squadron stalled at 50 feet. It crashed into a pillbox and caught fire. Two Sergeants, F. McKinnon and W. Morris were killed. The squadron wing commander reported to the Under Secretary of State for Air:

> The pilot managed to get away from the aircraft and saw someone blindly groping amongst flames. This person turned out to be the navigator [Sgt. Ball]. As the pilot went to extricate this other

person the mine exploded blowing the navigator onto barbed wire entanglements some ten to twelve feet away.... [petrol tanks and ammunition were exploding] .....and it was found impossible to extricate the other two members of the crew who were trapped in the fuselage. Medical evidence pointed to the fact, however, that these two aircrew must have been killed on impact.

Sergeant Ball died of injuries and shock. The pilot, D. Hunter, was the sole survivor.[37]

There was a happier outcome for another crew, of 193 Squadron, Elsham Wolds. 'F/O Russell-Fry broke cloud at 3 /4,000 ft. over base but visibility was very bad and he suddenly saw the ground 50 ft. below. He opened up the throttles but the aircraft touched down in a ploughed field near BARTON. None of the crew were injured.'[38]

Aircraft Collision

D.J. Gill feared mid-flight collision. 'I feared this more than enemy action,' he wrote. One was braced for fighters or flak but collision was unexpected. With aircraft turning back early, or from an incorrect location, into the bomber stream, the chance of collision was very real. 'Nobody knows how many aircraft and their aircrews were lost due to collision ...... the number was probably very high ..... it was a genuine reason to be fearful', he wrote.[39]

A Beaufort of 42 Squadron, Leuchars was practising torpedo attacks close to the Isle of May, in the Firth of Forth, on 11 May 1942. It collided with another aircraft, broke in two, caught fire and hit the water. The bodies of the pilot and navigator were recovered dead but Sergeants Douglas MacDonald and S. Counsell were trapped in the aircraft. A pathetic letter arrived at the squadron from Sergeant Counsell's mother: 'Could anything be done to recover my son's body, which I gather is still in the plane?' In reply she was told that: 'it is unlikely that any attempt will be made in the future to recover the bodies as the sea where the aircraft crashed is deep with strong currents, thus rendering it inaccessible.'[40] 16 December 1943. The Battle of Berlin. An aircraft of 103 Squadron met with a violent end. 'F/S. Richter crashed at ULCEBY soon after take-off [from Elsham Wolds], after a believed crash in cloud with aircraft B2 of 576 Squadron. All the crew were killed and the aircraft completely destroyed.[41]

Max Hastings related the scene at the 50 Squadron briefing for the thousand bomber raid on Cologne:

> 50 Squadron put up seventeen aircraft that night. At briefing, when the CO announced that there would be more than a thousand aircraft over the target, there was a moment of awed silence. They were alarmed by the prospect of collision, but they were told that Bomber Command's operational research scientists had computed that statistically there should be no more than two aircraft colliding in the target area. Somebody piped up: 'That's fine, but do they know which two?'[42]

The scientists were spot on. Of the 41 aircraft lost that night, sure enough, two had collided.[43] It is not known if the comedian was in one of them. Jack Currie also dreaded mid-air collision.......

> …….. not only when circling over base in cloud, but later, when converging on a rendezvous or target, our aircraft rocked and trembled, and I wondered whether turbulent air was moving us, or perhaps the slipstream of another bomber which I might see too late to miss. Such demons often perched on my shoulder, prodding me with chilly fingers, stilling the lullaby of over-confidence.[44]

On the first night of 1944 421 Lancasters set off for Berlin. 'A violent multi-coloured explosion was seen while the bombers were flying over the North Sea and it was presumed that a Pathfinder had exploded, possibly after colliding with another Lancaster.'[45] Another collision with a happier outcome occurred on the night of 3/4 November 1944. Flying Officer Elwyn Fieldson's 76 Squadron Halifax made its way to Dusseldorf, unloaded its bombs and was promptly hit by another Halifax. 'Then there was a God awful thump on our rear end, which knocked us into a near vertical dive with the whole aircraft vibrating madly.'[46] No-one in the crew had been killed or wounded and Fieldson nursed the 'Halibag' home. 'Three days later we were back on ops.'[47]

'Friendly' Bombs

Rogue bombs could induce terror *after* the target had been hit. On a daylight raid to Duisburg a loose bomb was rolling around in the bomb bay of one aircraft, having avoided release. Navigator Miles Tripp was able to report half a century later: 'Had its detonator jarred we would within seconds have become scraps of skin floating in the wind above Duisburg.'[48]

As the bomber force grew, the large number of aircraft setting out on operations increased the possibility not only of collision, but of being the unfortunate recipient of a bomb load from colleagues flying above. One rear gunner, identity unknown, was minding his own business when a bomb from above sheared off his turret, taking the poor man with it.[49] Miles Tripp recalled: '... on the second Solingen trip the Lancasters were bunched so close that at least three were bombed out of the sky by their fellows flying directly above.'[50]

Bill Reid was the victim of one such 'friendly' incident. On 31 July 1944, as a pilot of 617 Squadron, he set off for the target, Rilly-la-Montagne near Rheims. A 1,000 lb bomb from an aircraft above smashed into Bill's Lancaster, killing five of the crew. The plane's nose broke off in the impact and he and his wireless operator plummeted earthwards with it, becoming the only survivors of the crew and the latest additions to the Stalag Luft reception centre.[51]

The problem of 'friendly bombs' received attention from the Air Ministry but no action was taken. The risks, it was felt, were real but not significant enough to warrant action.[52] Harris wrote to Portal on the subject and both believed that the small losses incurred in this way did not merit special attention.[53]

'Friendly' Fire

Anti-aircraft gunners could be responsible for 'friendly fire'. On D-Day J.S.A. Marshall recorded in his log book: 'the navy, ours, shot down a plane (Lanc) about 200 yards on our port. Trigger happy b******s.'[54] Miles Tripp remembered being the subject of attention of an anti-aircraft battery while over Stratford-upon-Avon on a training flight.[55] Sergeant Morrison revealed his unease: 'Flying over Holland and Belgium is less thrilling and dangerous than doing ditto over England, where someone always tries to take a crack at us.'[56] Fighter Command, too, sometimes latched onto the wrong target. Guy Gibson fulminated: 'A few loose-fingered fighter boys would shoot down the odd bomber, and feelings began to run high again.'[57]

Another source of potential danger was fire from gunners in other aircraft. Constantly scouring the night sky for potential danger, a jittery gunner could easily mistake a 'friendly' aircraft for the enemy. Or a navigator, in this case Miles Tripp, could accidentally let rip while returning from a sortie. Tripp's pilot was not amused. 'Bloody good job you didn't shoot down a Lancaster.'[58]

Gunners rarely fired. If they did, it was as good as announcing their presence to prowling night fighters. This caution prompted an order from 5 Group HQ for gunners to show more aggression. They should 'seek out fighters rather than being frightened of them.'[59] When they obeyed the order the result was increased indiscriminate firing at 'friendlies'. The order was swiftly rescinded.

In Germany

In the later stages of the war, if an airman was unlucky enough to be shot down, but lucky enough to survive, a rather unpleasant prospect potentially awaited him – a lynch mob. The very first war crimes trial of German personnel had begun in Kharkov, Ukraine. On 19 December 1943, one day after they were found guilty, the four defendants were publicly hanged. It was realised that German reprisals could be a result of the trial's outcome. The Air Ministry was fearful of the effect on aircrew morale if German reprisal threats were made. A letter from Air Marshal Sir Richard Peck of the Ministry to the ACAS made clear its position:

> It is through what they read in the Press and hear on the radio that the morale of our crews will be reached......I think what is wanted is a letter from the Air Ministry to the Ministry of Information drawing attention to the possible effect upon the morale of aircrews of publicity regarding any threats of reprisal which may be made by the Germans, and asking them to use their influence with the Press

to ignore, or at least reduce to the minimum, any publicity on this aspect of the trials and to play down any comment upon it.[60]

The Ministry of Information was in agreement with Peck: 'I fully appreciate the wish of the Air Staff that the morale of our aircrews should not be subjected to the strain of dwelling upon the German threats.'[61] The Ministry of Information would keep an eye on the outcome of the trial. Its letter was sent on 22 January 1944, by which time the German defendants had already been hanged.[62] Sure enough, the threats soon materialised. An Air Ministry minute headed 'Survey of enemy propaganda' cited an article by Joseph Goebbels in the *Völkischer Beobachter*, containing thinly veiled incitement to violence. 'The Anglo-U.S. terror airmen have embarked on systematic murder "putting themselves outside all internationally recognised rules of war" ……. it would be asking too much if we were expected to employ German soldiers to defend the murderers of children against these children's parents.'[63]

A minute from the Controller, Press and Censorship, Ministry of Information with the heading 'Lynching of aircrews' on 30 May 1944 issued guidance to the press designed to suppress any reference to Goebbels's remarks. 'It is evident that Dr. Goebbels and the enemy propaganda machine have launched a propaganda campaign deliberately designed to undermine the morale of our aircrews …. It is of the highest importance that this campaign should receive no assistance by its reproduction in the British Press, which of course, is widely read by our aircrews.'[64]

Further apprehension was generated by the Great Escape of 24 March 1944. Aircrew preferred to believe that if they were shot down, they would become prisoners of war and not another name on the list of 'killed in action'. That is exactly what P/O Byrne confided to his diary: 'God, it is not your will that I be killed in this war. But be taken a POW'[65] The fate of fifty of the escapees, murdered by the Gestapo, was well known among aircrews. The ACAS wrote to the Under Secretary of State for Air on 6 June 1944: 'There is no doubt that these shootings [of the participants in The Great Escape] had, and still have, an effect upon the morale of our aircrews.' It was vital to maintain the pressure on the press to combat German propaganda.[66]

Aircraft Types

All these threats to safety could be accepted if aircrews had confidence in their aircraft. 'Since you were stuck with the type of aircraft you were given, you soon convinced yourself that it was a jolly good one.'[67] Sir Charles Symonds considered that loss of confidence in an airman's aircraft was a major factor in the deterioration of morale: 'The men are faddy about their aircraft and if something goes wrong which they can't understand [see Gremlins, this chapter], they get very depressed and anxious.'[68] Furthermore, 'Besides confidence in a type, they have *confidence in one aircraft* and always like to fly that one, however "ropey" it is.'[69] The Lancaster emerged as the outstanding bomber of the war but Bomber Command had been engaged in two and a half years of war before the 'Lanc' came into service. One contemporary commentator, the Great War pilot Oliver Stewart, made clear his affection for the new heavy bomber:

> As we learn more about the behaviour of the Avro Lancaster on operations, so we learn to admire it more. A sight of the Lancaster is a tonic to tired minds and tired hands. Nobody has ever discovered what makes an aeroplane look good; but it is established and known to all pilots that very few aeroplanes that have looked good have ever proved less than good in their behaviour in the air.[70]

The early types used, the Blenheims, Whitleys, Hampdens and Wellingtons, were regarded with affection by the crews who flew them, the aeroplanes' defects and weaknesses conveniently ignored as their crews convinced themselves, for their own peace of mind, that *their* aircraft was the best. The Whitley was known to the crews who flew in it as the 'flying coffin', a soubriquet conferred on it because of its shape and its peculiar nose down attitude in the air.[71] Its vulnerability soon gave its nickname a grim truth.

The first of the 'heavies', the Stirling, engendered affection from its crews. Sergeant C.N. Searle remembered that, 'The RAF were very good at morale boosting, and, as I remember, we on the Stirling squadrons were always made to feel that we were the only ones that mattered.'[72] Ron Dixon was another fan of the Stirling: 'The old Stirling would take a hell of a lot of punishment but the engines were no good. It was a real old bus of an aircraft but I used to love it.'[73] George Hull eulogised about the Lancaster in which he flew: 'She's a lovely creature. To other people she's A-Able, a nice kite; to us, however, she's a beautiful woman to be taken care of and treated with respect.'[74] But morale in squadrons equipped with the Halifax and the Stirling was as high as those with Lancasters.

Not many bettered Arthur Harris in argument. VCAS Sir Wilfred Freeman was an exception. He tolerated no nonsense from the renowned belligerent. Warning Portal that they could expect intransigence from Harris on the matter of providing extra armour for 100 Lancasters, to then be used in daylight operations, he insisted that Harris must be ordered to accept the decision.[75] Of course, Harris never gave up without a fight and offended Freeman when he complained about the possible removal of these Lancasters for use in, as Harris interpreted it, an experiment which he described thus: 'The object of putting these special aircraft on to day bombing is apparently to attempt assessment of their vulnerability as compared with the ordinary Lancaster by exposing them to the attacks of enemy fighters and recording the result.'[76] Freeman would not tolerate this insubordination. In his reply, on 3 June 1942, he wrote:

> Dear Bert,
> I thought that over a period of one and a half years I had got accustomed to your truculent style, loose expression and flamboyant hyperbole, but I am not used to being told – for such is the implication of Paragraph 5 of your letter – that I am deliberately proposing to risk human lives in order to test out an idea of my own, which in your opinion is wrong…………..Instructions have been given for the armour to be made as far as possible detachable and I should now be glad if you would carry out the order given to you in the letter dated 26th May.[77]

Given that daylight operations in 1942 were still laden with risk, the outcome of this squabble in the upper echelons of power is unknown.

Harris was not a fan of Handley-Page, a fact revealed in correspondence with Freeman in October 1942. After high losses on squadrons equipped with the Handley-Page Halifax, he told Freeman: 'I am convinced that, as usual, Handley Page is covering up behind a mass of verbiage and a lot of pettifogging minor modifications, by which he hopes to postpone either the full realisation of the hopelessness of the Halifax or the necessity to switch as far as possible to something better.'[78] Harris wanted all effort to be put into Lancaster production, while 'whatever production of this deplorable type [the Halifax] remains can, as necessary, be relegated to softer jobs, such as mining, bombing the French and possibly eventually to overseas theatres.'[79]

Flight Lieutenant T.W. Fox was almost certainly oblivious to Harris's opinion but he waxed lyrical about the Halifax Mark III: 'What a difference [to previous Halifax Marks], and with a full bomb load too; much more power, a better rate of climb and a much more comfortable flight. At least we were faster than the Lancaster bombers but still unable to carry an equivalent bomb load...... on the return journey we could always leave the Lancasters behind.'[80]

The Harris/Freeman feud had begun with the introduction of the Mosquito in April 1942. Harris wrote to Freeman: 'The Mosquito is now so delayed that it must inevitably suffer a still grimmer fate than has always been the lot of such naive attempts to produce an aeroplane so much faster than anything the enemy possesses that it requires no armament. It will go down in history in consequence as a second "Battle", as far as its bombing role is concerned.'[81] The astute Freeman was a sounder judge than Harris. He replied: 'I have received your unhelpful letter dated 10th April....... I note what you say about the Mosquito. You will prove to be wrong.'[82] He was.

Those men who flew Mosquitoes must have felt they were the chosen few. Flying high and fast provided a sense of invulnerability. True, Mossies were not invincible, as the loss of two illustrious Mosquito pilots Gibson and Pickard demonstrates, but it was surely with a greater sense of protection that the crews of Mossies set off on their missions. Morale must have been high on Mosquito squadrons. On examining the operations record book of one Mossie squadron, 571, it was found that in the entire month of November 1944, there was not a single loss.[83] This contrasts markedly with the almost daily losses of the 'heavies' in this period.

The short-lived, two-engined Avro Manchester, plagued with faults, did not endear itself to its crews, who soon realised that flying in one was likely to guarantee a very brief career as an airman. Morale was low on Manchester squadrons but it was a brief interlude and forgotten when the Manchester evolved into the Lancaster.

Weather

Aircraft type was of no consequence to the weather, a formidable enemy. 'Many brave crews perished in attempting to land in impossible conditions.'[84] All raids were dependent on weather conditions and the unexpected often occurred. Fog and ice accounted for many losses; electrical storms occasionally caused havoc. On one raid to Hamburg several crews abandoned their sorties after encountering a violent electrical storm and one bomb-laden Lancaster exploded, probably after being struck by lightning.'[85] The log book of J.S.A. Marshall indicates, in typically understated fashion, the fear such conditions could induce: 'I had to take off on instruments as there was violent thunder and lightning which was blinding ...... it was dicey.'[86] Johnny Johnson also had an encounter with lightning:

> The only near experience I had was before I joined Joe [McCarthy]. I was flying with an NCO crew and we'd been to Wiesbaden, which was one of the long trips. It was the second time we'd been up there. 10/10ths cloud, it was a question of sky markers rather than ground markers. Coming back, we'd just dropped our load, suddenly there was a blinding flash. 'Colin, Colin, are you all right, Colin?' He was fighting so much to get the aircraft back under control..... we'd been struck by lightning, of course. You see this Elmo's Fire creeping up the aerial. We'd dropped about 2,000 feet before Colin got control. That was the closest I ever got to not coming back. My first thought was, oh, this is what it's like to be dead, then my eyesight came back.[87]

On 16 December 1943, the weather was at its most malevolent. Fog enveloped many airfields; 'thirty-two Lancasters were lost and 127 men killed. The night became known as Black Thursday.'[88] 24 March 1944. Berlin. 'Stronger winds were encountered than were forecast, causing overshooting of target and also causing aircraft to fly south of track, many encountering the Ruhr defences,' recorded the adjutant of 15 Squadron. Two crews were lost as a result.[89] 'Facing fog, icing and thunderstorms, crews often wondered who their real enemy was [but] ..... they cheerfully took it all in their stride. However, periodically, even *their* mantle of youth and confidence could not hide a temporary drop in morale.'[90]

Icing posed a threat but could be countered by either climbing to shake off the ice or diving to melt it. Running the engines at different speeds was another method. It would shake off the ice. There were occasions when condensation would form inside the cockpit. One could rub alcohol to disperse it but to do so meant removing one's glove. Frostbite could be the result.[91] 2 December 1943. The Battle of Berlin. 'F/S. Rathbone bombed the markers from 21,500 ft. at 20.16 hrs. His Rear Gunner's hands were frostbitten,' read the 103 Squadron ops book.[92] 20 January 1944, Berlin again. 'There were no casualties but the M.U.G. [mid-upper gunner] of R- Robert died of anoxia & exposure.'[93]

The constant uncertainty brought about by the weather was demoralising. 'Scrubs' – cancelled operations – caused a sharp decline in morale on the stations.[94] 'There was nothing worse than being briefed and then delayed interminably at the dispersal. Every contact with ordinary existence had been severed but no connection had been made with the potential death sequence.'[95] Symonds and Williams cited an experienced squadron commander, who thought that:

> Last minute scrubbing was the most demoralising factor with which he had to contend in managing an operational squadron. He would much rather send his squadron on a raid even with ten-tenths cloud over the target, than subject them to the disappointments, frustration and demoralisation of last minute cancellation due to weather conditions on the continent.[96]

Any euphoria experienced as a result of the temporary reprieve was soon dispelled by the knowledge that they would have to go through the agony of waiting, always the tensest of times, before attempting the scrubbed op again.

An examination of one squadron's (15) operations record book for just one month reveals the extent to which frustration caused by scrubs could have on morale. '1 July 1943: 3 a/c for mining op – cancelled; 2 July 2 a/c for mining op – cancelled; 3 July: 16 a/c to Koln, 1 failed to take off, 2 returned early, 1 lost. Target clear. Concentrated fires east of Rhine. Fires seen 100 miles away, 2 a/c on mining, 1 lost; 4 July: 12 a/c for ops. Cancelled, bad weather; 5 July 3 a/c for mining. Only one took off. 6 July: 3 a/c for mining. 1 returned early – captain sick; 7 July: Stand down. 8 July: 3 a/c for mining. 1 returned early – rear turret not working; 9-12 July: no ops; 13 July: 8 a/c to Aachen. 1 returned early, 8/10 cloud, fires concentrated; 14 -18 July: no ops; 19 July: 10 a/c for ops. Cancelled; 20 July: 9 a/c for ops. Cancelled; 21 July: No ops; 22 July: 18 a/c for ops. Cancelled; 23 July: 18 a/c for ops. Cancelled.'[97] Two raids – Cologne and Aachen, a spot of 'gardening' and seven scrubbed operations, every one a delay for a crew's tour length. If they were not scrubbed and made it to the target, they often encountered cloud which prevented them from observing the accuracy of their bombing. Naturally, good visibility worked wonders for morale, when the results could be seen.[98] A successful raid would dissipate the dejection felt on scrubbed ops.

An interesting observation was made in an Air Ministry report on the effectiveness or otherwise of meteorology forecasts during the war. Smoke from factory chimneys caused the formation of fog, a serious threat to aircraft either taking off or returning from operations. '...... but for the amount of industrial smoke in this country the bombing effort against the enemy would have been greater than it was.' The introduction of FIDO alleviated the operational problems caused by fog.[99]

Gremlins

Repeated unexplained mechanical failures caused anxiety and a drop in morale.[100] Enter the gremlin, a mischievous creature which sabotages aircraft for the fun of it. Closely related to the gremlins were the *Marcolins*. These malevolent creatures confined their mischief to wireless telegraphy activity by inserting themselves into the H/T lead and migrating into the radio transmitter.[101] Their name was derived from the Marconi Wireless Telegraphy equipment in use. R.J. Fayers wrote, on 1 August 1942, 'Two gremlins bounced on our nose the other night.' His aircraft refused to lift and the flight was abandoned, 'the gremlins triumphant.'[102] Gremlins and Marcolins frustrated aircrews but it was preferable to blame some non-existent being for problems which may have arisen than a fellow crew member or other unfortunate on the squadron.

*

Avoiding the 'chop' took many forms. Pierre Richard had faith to see him through. 'I was fortified by my Crusader connections and the faith that had always been with me. I never flew an operation without carrying my Crusader badge in my breast pocket and I always found a way of having a brief prayer, on my knees, in quiet seclusion, before each bombing raid. Those words I had with my Maker gave me comfort, strength and fortitude to go forward in faith to do what I believed, and had prayed, was the right thing to do.'[103] Others put faith in good luck charms. Fighting men are disposed to carry talismans, which they imagine give protection.[104] With its alarmingly high casualty rate, many Bomber Command men carried lucky charms. For these men it helped to combat stress.[105] Dr. Stafford-Clark was bemused: 'This wide acceptance of a primitive system of magical ideas by men whose duties made them familiar with some of the most highly developed scientific apparatus at that time in use was an ironic comment upon the materialistic illusion of inevitable progress.'[106] He listed hare's feet and girlfriends' stockings and noted one captain who forbade his men from taking out a chop girl, an unfortunate WAAF whose previous aircrew paramours had met a sad end.[107] J. Walsh 'saw many young aircrew marrying young girls and the husband getting the Chop shortly after. It happened to our Wireless Operator.…….. My explanation was that they became more careful and tried to avoid danger and that I believe is not the way to fight a war.'[108]

Most of the lucky charms carried by aircrew were gifts or mementoes of civilian life. A girlfriend's stocking or a watch given by the wearer's father were evidence that the owner's 'existence had a reality beyond his own physical body' and that, therefore, he was 'too important to die'.[109] Sometimes the simplest of actions became ritualised: crews urinated on the tail wheel before take-off; others had a final cigarette before boarding; some had to put charms in exactly the right place in the aircraft. Any deviation from routine unsettled the superstitious.

All but two of Miles Tripp's crew mates took talismans on operations. His pilot, 'Dig', had to have his hat behind him in the correct position; the wireless operator took his girlfriend's brassiere; rear gunner Harry McCalla refused to fly without his red and blue scarf and Tripp himself always took a plethora of charms: a silk stocking, a Land Army brooch, a scarf and a small bone elephant. When his first tour began he dreaded the approaching third sortie because a friend had been killed on his third op.[110]

The possession of talismans was by no means universal. For those men who did not carry one aircraft serviceability and concentration on their tasks in the air were far more important for survival.

Chapter 14

Bang On!:
Bombing Results

Each man needed to feel that his own contribution mattered directly in the attainment of the goal.[1]

> The PFF had marked the spot
> It really looked a show
> With reds and greens cascading
> So clearly there below
> But wasn't it a pity -
> Through carelessness in aiming bombs
> They didn't hit the city.[2]
>
> *Tee Emm*

Whether at the very beginning of the war, during the Battle of the Ruhr, throughout the Battle of Berlin or in the final days, crews would respond differently to bombing results. Some took pride in accuracy, others were unconcerned as long as they got back in one piece. Crews on daylight raids were pleased when they could actually see the results of their efforts; those on night attacks perhaps caught an occasional glimpse of success. They dropped their bombs, took their photographs and made for home. One operations record book entry, that of 103 Squadron in December 1943, encapsulates the difficulties facing all squadrons throughout the war. 'This attack was apparently quite successful, but owing to the cloud, results were not too visible.'[3] In other words, the squadron was oblivious to the results of the raid. What was clear, at any stage of the war, was that poor results plus heavy losses equalled poor morale.[4]

The obvious indicator of success in Bomber Command was the destruction of targets. The more proof aircrews had of success, the higher would be their morale. 'Air crews feel a great satisfaction in seeing their targets "go up". Big fires delight them especially.'[5] It was even possible to accept high losses if good bombing results were observed to be effective. 'If the crews feel the losses have been balanced by success, it doesn't worry them,' was the reflection of one medical officer.[6] Another believed that morale actually *improved* when losses were high, as long as success balanced out the losses.[7] Evaluating success proved more difficult for bomber crews than for fighter pilots. There was tangible evidence of success when a fighter pilot shot down a bomber. Not so for bomber crews who, more often than not, were unable to see their targets.[8] *Evidence* was the key to good morale.

*

Charles Portal was C-in-C Bomber Command in May 1940. He would soon become CAS. In a letter to the then CAS, Sir Cyril Newall, he bemoaned the long periods of stand-to, which sapped morale. This was the period of Blitzkrieg in France, Holland and Belgium when, if Bomber Command did go into action, it suffered horrendously high losses, particularly in squadrons equipped with Fairey Battles. A 50% casualty rate, Portal wrote......

> .... is to raise the crews to the highest possible degree of nervous tension. ...... To imagine that this can be done again and again whenever the enemy chooses to pretend to march, without seriously and profoundly affecting the morale of all the units concerned ..... would be a grave mistake. .... The strain on morale becomes even worse when ...... it is not possible to give the crews any detailed information about when or where they would have to go or what they would have to do.[9]

He added that a serious mistake in policy had been made which should be rectified before it became too late to avoid the destruction of the bomber force. Instead of being used tactically, in support of the retreating British

Army, it should be attacking industrial targets. One week later, now CAS, Portal wrote to the new C-in-C Bomber Command, Sir Richard Peirse:

> May I ask that as far as possible I may have a general directif for the Heavy Bombers and then be left to get on with it? This would mean one control of the day-to-day operations, fewer changes of plan and consequently better morale in groups and units. .... We want clear directions on policy and all the information and Intelligence that you can give us, and then be told to get on with the job. ..... I know you will not take this as a complaint. You have always been so helpful and understanding that I am sure you will do all that you can.[10]

Two days earlier Portal had also written to Peirse with the bizarre plan to swamp Germany with the colorado beetle, a pest of the potato crop. This idea was seriously considered.[11] And then quietly forgotten.

It is, perhaps, understandable that morale was at a low point during the 'Phoney War'. The occasional raid with small numbers of aircraft, minelaying and scattering leaflets over Germany were hardly conducive to fostering morale; rather the opposite, in fact, demoralising inactivity. 'Bomber Command feel themselves futile .... once the fungus of futility was allowed to eat into the Royal Air Force it would be all up with its offensive spirit. And it is difficult to keep up the offensive spirit in men who are not allowed to hit back.'[12] The reduction in the number of 'nickelling' raids and the increase in bombing activity had a dramatic positive effect on the crews; they began to feel that they had some purpose in the overall scheme. The optimism of the early days is reflected in the correspondence of Sergeant Morrison. On 18 December 1940 he wrote to his sister:

> From midnight on Sunday to six a.m. on Tuesday we did 1,700 miles and did two raids, one to Frankfurt the other to Mannheim. We saw the fires and A.A fire at Mannheim from ninety miles away and did a bit to increasing them. To quote Harry [fellow crew member], 'it was a piece of cake' and almost the whole town was on fire when we left after snooping around for twenty-five minutes.[13]

Morrison was describing the first area raid, on Mannheim, on the night of 16/17 December 1940. Before the policy became official, this was nevertheless the first time a city centre had been deliberately targeted.

On 23 December 1940 Winston Churchill asked Sir Richard Peirse, 'What is your policy on attacks?' To which Peirse replied, 'Oil and North Italy', then concentrated attacks on industrial cities 'to burn up the town and destroy public services and the like.'[14] That was all very well but did the aircrews know what the policy was? Peirse was adamant that his crews *did* know and defended himself from criticism by blaming Groups for poor crew briefings before raids.[15] In a letter to one of his group commanders, AVM James Robb, of 2 Group, Peirse emphasised the need to brief crews *in detail*. 'This should enable each individual to realise the important part which he plays in the plan and the vital importance of making the best use of favourable weather conditions, by accurate navigation and bomb aiming, to achieve the destruction of the target.'[16] Another of his group commanders, Air Marshal Jack Baldwin (3 Group), believed that morale rose when his crews read the fortnightly summaries of raids, which had recently been introduced. They took pride in their part in particular raids.[17] Despite Baldwin's optimistic comment, there remained deep concern over crews' ignorance of their role. Air Ministry minutes abounded. '….the ignorance of crews in the purpose behind their operations is at present quite lamentable and must have a very serious effect on the success of our operations.'[18]

The VCAS, Wilfred Freeman, wrote to Sir Richard Peirse on 31 August 1941 to inform him that Churchill was aware that crews often had no clear idea of their objectives and were going into battle not knowing why. The fact that some crews were lost without knowing what or why they were bombing was an unacceptable state of affairs. If crews were informed about the importance of their targets within the overall policy of Bomber Command, '….. it would stimulate interest and enable them to do their job more intelligently,' wrote the I.G., Sir Edgar Ludlow-Hewitt, in March 1941.[19] He contended that the crews had no concept of the broader bombing plan:

> I attended a briefing the other day in which crews were being briefed for an attack on the centre of COLOGNE. As regards operational detail it was admirably done. But nothing was said about the general

policy involved in the attack on a new kind of target. I do not know what the crews thought about it, but in the absence of an explanation one would, I suppose, be liable to assume that the sole object of the raid was one of frightfulness against the civilian population.[20]

Baldwin, minuted, 'At the present moment I do agree that both groups and stations are a little in the dark as to details of the major plans and that any information we can hand on to crews will tend to increase their interest and keenness.'[21] One factor which prevented crews receiving all information about a coming raid was security. A suggested solution, from Mr. Elwood of Bombing Operations, was that only captains and navigators should be given the relevant information. 'They are quite intelligent and reliable enough to be trusted not to broadcast anything about which they were specifically told to keep their mouths shut.'[22]

*

If there were any in Bomber Command who felt that it was achieving results in those early years, they suffered a severe shock when the Butt Report of 1941 revealed the inaccuracy of bombing efforts. Bomb aiming errors were made clear by ever-improving photographic technology and they could not be expected to carry on indefinitely with no obvious success.[23] The camera was the sole reliable means of judging accuracy. Before the advent of reliable photo reconnaissance, crews' reports had to be relied upon. When the true picture was revealed morale certainly dipped.[24] 'Some of the crews who were told of their errors frankly disbelieved the photographs; while others took them very seriously and got worried and depressed.'[25]

'During 1941, when 700 aircraft failed to return from operations, Bomber Command's crews in short were dying largely in order to crater the German countryside.'[26] The aircrews of 1940 and 1941 would have been appalled to know that more of their number were killed in their attacks than the enemy were killed by their bombs.[27] How to resolve the equation of results and aircrew losses became a matter of absolute urgency. One flying officer wrote of a raid in 1942, 'We lost 55 a/c and I should say at least 350 aircrew, which for the conditions and the damage done was rather more costly than it was worth.'[28] Yet the resilience of the aircrews is demonstrated in a further missive from F/O. Rowling: 'It's quite a good life now that we are into it. We feel as if we are at last doing something to make Jerry sit up and take notice.'[29]

At debriefings after raids the only evidence available came from the aircrews' own impressions. It was unreliable. After a stressful operation with adrenalin still high, some men exaggerated; others understated. An Air Ministry minute to Peirse on 17 September 1941 pointed out that misleading raid reports could lead to errors in policy.[30] The national press compounded the misinformation. A *Daily Mirror* headline on 3 August 1940 read, 'RAF lays Hamburg in ruins.' Patently untrue in 1940. It went on, 'wrecked by repeated raids by the RAF.... All these attacks have been carefully planned to avoid damage, if possible, to towns and cities which are non-military objectives.'[31]

Portal admonished Peirse on 23 November 1941 for inaccuracies and inconsistencies. Peirse had blamed inexperienced pilots for heavy losses of one raid, on the night of 7/8 November, to which Portal replied that the average number of operations carried out by the aircrew on the raid was sixteen and they were therefore not inexperienced. He demanded a revised report to 'include information which would provide satisfactory answers to the questions I have put, and which I am sure the Prime Minister will ask.'[32] The 7/8 November raid was the last straw for Portal. Peirse was dismissed.

*

Harris did not escape criticism when he became C-in-C. On one occasion, in April 1942, he was reprimanded by the VCAS, Sir Wilfred Freeman, for issuing wildly exaggerated claims of bombing results in a routine press communique:

> This account is grossly and dangerously exaggerated. It reminds me of the worst statements produced in the October 1940 – June 1941 period. Bombast is entirely contrary to our policy. It is bound, in the long run, to have an effect opposite to that which you aim at, and it will give valuable material for German propaganda. Moreover, I cannot believe that it is calculated to inspire confidence in the many

people in Bomber Command who are in a position to know the truth about current operations ……. Will you please ensure in future that your communiques bear a closer resemblance to the facts.[33]

The raid to which Freeman referred was 'to Germany', with eleven Hampdens and six Wellingtons despatched. Ten Hampdens returned with their bombs; one of them machine-gunned an airfield in Holland and bombed a railway line. Five Wellingtons bombed a target they could not identify; four more Wellingtons were sent and two did not attack. The other two bombed but had no idea of what they had bombed. The communique released by Bomber Command was, to say the least, economical with the truth: 'Throughout the hours of daylight yesterday and darkness last night individual aircraft of Bomber Command were making widespread attacks on objectives in the Ruhr and elsewhere in Germany.'[34] It was not an auspicious beginning for Harris's tenure as C-in-C but as the bomber offensive increased in strength it became easier to report on actual success – there was more of it.

Five days later Freeman, in a more emollient tone, assured Harris that he would make efforts to ensure publicity for the results of successful raids but that the process took time and when the information did get to press it had often been overtaken by events and ceased to have a positive effect on the public.[35] At the same time, efforts had to be made to ensure that all Air Force personnel were aware of successes. A memorandum was circulated to all RAF commands making suggestions for the provision of news to personnel:

> All ranks should be encouraged to take a greater interest in the performance of the Royal Air Force and to feel pride in its achievements ……. At present it is a matter of chance ……. and it is not unnatural that they should regard with casual interest, or even indifference, matters which are of high value in creating and maintaining morale.[36]

Cecil Beaton observed in 1942 that 'These men listen keenly to the radio news bulletins each day to hear if their operations have been mentioned, for this is the one sure indication that they have done something of value.'[37] There was scepticism, though, and even derision from those very airmen: 'Perhaps the most frequently heard grouse of an intelligent serious nature is "duff gen" from the BBC and the Press. Few airmen nowadays believe anything they read in a newspaper and laugh out loud at improbable statements from the BBC.'[38]

Harris was fortunate in taking up his post as Commander-in-Chief at the same time as the increasing number of available 'heavies' and improved navigation devices. Successful raids on Lubeck and Rostock, followed by the '1,000 Raid' on Cologne on the night of 30/31 May 1942 had a dramatic effect on the morale of the aircrews and public alike. Harris reflected in his memoir .....

> There is also no doubt that these two successes had a marked effect on the general morale of Bomber Command itself; throughout 1941 both aircrew and ground staff had been getting more and more depressed by the obvious failure of their attacks and they, as well as the country at large, needed the stimulus of some special achievement.[39]

Harris was satisfied with the result of the Lubeck raid but less so with Rostock. The former, with many wooden buildings, burned easily; Rostock did not. In a letter to the VCAS, on 20 April 1942, he extolled the power of high explosive bombs, as opposed to fire-inducing incendiaries:

> The moral effect of H.E. is vast. People can escape from fires and the casualties on a solely fire raising raid would be as nothing. What we want to do in addition to the horrors of fire is to bring the masonry toppling down on top of the Boche, to kill Boche and to terrify Boche; hence the proportion of H.E. .... We must not expect any more Lubecks, because there ain't no such places; we blotted the only one that was. Lubeck was easy money.[40]

Newsreels of the 1,000 Raid, accompanied by footage of Bomber Harris urging his crews to 'let him [the enemy] have it, right on the chin', provided marvellous propaganda for the British public. Seemingly endless streams of bombers thundering into the night, towards Germany, carrying retribution to the enemy, worked wonders on cinema audiences; adulation of the RAF reached new heights. Aircrew morale had received a significant boost. However, the assembly of 1,000 (it was actually 1,047 [41]) aircraft could only be repeated in the immediate future on 2 more occasions, in raids on Essen (1/2 June) and Bremen (25/26 June). Harris drew on aircraft from OTUs as well as operational squadrons to achieve the magical figure of one thousand but he was unable to do this regularly. Bomber Command did not yet have sufficient aircraft.

There followed unsuccessful raids on various Ruhr cities, reversing the feelgood factor which had resulted from the Cologne success. Martin Middlebrook asserted that, '…….. twice in the war it is recognized that morale sagged and this period, the middle and later months of 1942, was the first of those occasions.'[42] A loss rate of more than 4% would be unsustainable. During the summer and autumn of 1942 the loss rate was 4.6%.

The introduction of photographs had led to some improvement in bombing accuracy but 'Night photographs have revealed that a large number who have claimed to have hit the target have been a considerable distance away from it when they actually made their attack.'[43] 'There was little evidence either that this was in any way a successful attack [on Clermont-Ferrand]. Most crews brought back excellent photographs of undamaged buildings,' read the operations record book of 630 Squadron on 10 March 1944.[44] Crews thought they had done a successful job but interrogation revealed otherwise. They had to be debriefed by intelligence officers, who knew every detail of the operation, so that they could separate fact from fiction.[45] One wing commander stressed the need for crews to be debriefed as quickly as possible in order to prevent contact with other crews. Facts became distorted when crews compared their experiences. He also recommended verbal interrogation, as exhausted aircrews baulked at the laborious process of writing down detailed raid information on questionnaires. '….they are naturally more interested in bacon and eggs and bed.'[46]

*

1942. To address the problem of poor bombing results the idea of a special marking group, to be known as the Target Finding Force, was put forward. In a letter from Jack Baldwin to Arthur Harris on 16 May 1942 Baldwin outlined his reason for the rejection of this idea. It would be better, he said, just to raise the standard of Main Force crews.[47] Harris replied on 3 June. He was in agreement. He resisted the idea of a TFF, stating that OTUs were now producing good quality crews, obviating the need for a special marking force.[48] The plan was not shelved, though. The Target Finding Force was given a new name in an Air Ministry minute of 9 June 1942. What was proposed was a 'Commando Bombing Force', consisting of crews with more than average ability which would be picked from the various existing squadrons. Greater accuracy and surprise would achieve results. 'The existence of the Force would have an excellent effect on the morale of Bomber Command as a whole.'[49]

There were still objections on the grounds that squadrons would lose their best crews and an 'elite' force would be resented.[50] To no avail. The Pathfinder Force came into being on 15 August 1942. It consisted of volunteers, either as individuals or as a whole crew, together with the best available from OTUs. One incentive designed to boost morale was the award of a Target Markers Badge.[51] The PFF squadrons were distributed throughout the groups: 1 Group received one Wellington squadron, 8 Group one Stirling squadron and half a Wellington squadron, and 5 Group a Lancaster squadron.[52] The creation of the Pathfinder Force would lead to improved accuracy but, on its first operation, to Flensburg on 18/19 August, PFF crews succeeded in marking targets in Denmark 25 miles from Flensburg.[53] There was a long way to go before anything near pinpoint accuracy would be achieved.

The Air Ministry kept a wary eye on the Main Force. It was still believed that crews were not given all the facts and were therefore indifferent to the results of raids. One Ministry minute of September 1942 put it succinctly: '...... the best could only be extracted from crews if they were taken into our confidence and made aware of the policy behind each and every operation.'[54]

When the Battle of the Ruhr began in March 1943 the new navigation aids *Oboe*, *Gee* and *H2S* enabled far more accurate bombing but strengthened German defences in the shape of flak and numbers of night fighters took a grim toll of the crews, sustaining heavy losses over a long period. Despite those losses, Martin Middlebrook maintained that, 'Their morale never wavered and the old dictum was proved that heavy casualties can be sustained by a force as long as successful results are being visibly achieved.'[55]

Saturation of the target by a large force would become, and remain, the major tactic employed for the duration of the war. The bomber stream kept enemy defences busy; this had psychological benefit, as it reassured crews that an over-worked German flak crew or night-fighter pilot deprived of information from his radar team was less likely to locate them.

Morale rose when crews could see the effect of bomb concentration. Pilot Officer D.A. Duncan remembered, 'When you saw a couple of thousand tons going down on a Ruhr city in half an hour – that was fantastic!'[56] The devastation of Hamburg in July 1943 had the same effect on aircrews who peered into the furnace below them. 'The aircrew do feel that they are, at last, really achieving something vital towards ending this war, and their spirit and press-on attitude is at a peak,' recorded 83 Squadron operations record book.[57] Sergeant O.E. Burger of 77 Squadron put into words what many fellow aircrews must have felt when they returned from the Hamburg raids of July 1943:

> The first two raids on Hamburg were so *obviously* successful to those of us who took part in them ...... one returned from most trips in what I would call a neutral frame of mind. Relief to be back and glad that one more was under your belt – and that was about all. But, with these two on Hamburg, there was an added exhilaration which came from the absolute conviction – actually on the night – that we had pulled off something special.[58]

Relaying news of this achievement to the public, the national press did so with a certain amount of euphoria:

> Salute to the RAF
> .... we are definitely beginning to win this war .... Great Britain's air effort has been prodigious, unparalleled, miraculous ..... this glorious chapter of our national story .... Today we see the RAF effort at its peak ...... We salute its gallant members ...... and thank them ..... for the splendid work they are doing .... The triumphs of our airmen have not been achieved without grievous loss – grievous not on account of numbers, which have been

relatively small – but on account of the quality of lives which have been sacrificed ……. The RAF has *got it down*…… The RAF is unbeatable.[59]

Harris spurred his crews on: 'Air Chief Marshal Sir Arthur Harris yesterday sent the following message to all his crews: In 1939 Goering promised that not a single bomb would reach the Ruhr. Congratulations on having delivered the first 100,000 tons of bombs on Germany to refute him. The next 100,000, if he waits for them, will be even bigger and better bombs, delivered even more accurately and in a much shorter time.'[60]

In the attacks on the Ruhr in the spring of 1943 losses did begin to mount but general morale was not tested. That threat came in the winter of 1943/44, the Battle of Berlin. During this period Harris pushed his men to the extremes of endurance. From 18/19 November 1943 to the end of March 1944 sixteen major raids were mounted on Germany's capital and sixteen on other cities in the Reich. Between 400 and 800 aircraft, with Lancasters and Halifaxes now the mainstay of the force, made the interminable trip to Berlin on long, cold winter nights. The print media relished the opportunity to report apparent success and its reports did not now exaggerate results; they were scrupulous in revealing losses, while dramatising the headlines to create the impression of wholesale destruction. 'Berlin's heaviest raid yet: well over 2,000 bomb tons shower on Nazi capital: our loss is lighter even than last time.'[61] 'Fierce Berlin air battles as RAF again sweep in to stoke smouldering fires.….. Fighters, mass flak defied. 41 missing.'[62] 'Second smashing for Berlin: 800 "Heavies" hammer Frankfort [sic] ….. RAF loses 50 aircraft in widespread missions.'[63]

Berlin was a *big* city. It would not burn as Lubeck and, to a lesser extent, Rostock had burnt. A large force of night fighters took its toll. Crew trepidation grew with every trip to the 'Big City'. 'The story of the Battle of Berlin is of a steady deterioration of effectiveness by the bomber force at increasing cost.'[64]

The raid which could be called the last of the Battle of Berlin was on Nuremberg on the night of 30/31 March 1944. If the losses sustained in *any* raid were to break Bomber Command morale, this would be it. 795 aircraft – 572 Lancasters, 214 Halifaxes and 9 Mosquitoes – took part. Little damage was caused to Nuremberg; 69 people were killed in the city and another two in Schweinfurt, which was bombed by aircraft of the Nuremberg force by mistake. In Bomber Command's worst night of the entire war 95 aircraft – 64 Lancasters and 31 Halifaxes - were lost, 11.9% of the force.[65] In human terms this represented 545 men killed, more than in the entire Battle of Britain in 1940. 545 families grieved.

Martin Middlebrook, the assiduous chronicler of Bomber Command's fortunes, believed:

> The main strain fell on the men who flew Lancasters and Halifax IIIs, the latter having the most severe test to face because, when the fighter struck and bomber pilots made for altitude, whatever their orders, the Halifax IIIs were now left at the lower altitudes and the Germans found them first. There were no 'freshman' raids for the Lancaster and Halifax men; a new crew could arrive at a squadron from a training unit and a flight to Berlin could be their first operation. Aircrew morale was undoubtedly put to a severe test.[66]

One pilot recalled:

> The Battle of Berlin did cause morale to sag. Crews were weary and angry, strained and more fearful of their next trip than usual, cursing 'Butch' Harris for his unrelenting demands and his apparently uncaring attitude towards his men. The results didn't appear to come anywhere near justifying the losses and the hardship.[67]

This had been the Commands second severe test, which was met with fortitude. Morale dipped but did *not* break.

No. 195 Squadron took part in the raid on Dresden on the night of 13/14 February 1945. By this late stage of the war there was precious little the Germans could do to prevent utter devastation. For the inhabitants of Dresden it was an indescribable nightmare; for the crews of Bomber Command it was just another op, obviously successful and with minimum risk to their lives. Squadron Leader Farquarson, of 195, recorded his assessment of the raid with satisfaction: 'Very good attack. PFF excellent. Master Bomber and

Deputy directing attack well. No flak. Already alight when we got there. Could see target from 80 miles away. Saw Dresden from 150 miles away on return.'[68] F/O. Armstrong agreed. 'Bombed on fires and red TIs. Everything seemed to be on fire. Early attack must have been successful. One attack showed cookies bursting in midst of fires. Town seemed one mass of flames and billows of smoke. Reflection on clouds seen from Stuttgart.'[69]

Overwhelming superiority had finally given the crews of Bomber Command what they had lacked in the early years – evidence of success. Morale now could not have been higher.

Chapter 15

Sex-Appeal Bombing: Ethics

The majority of aircrews did not spend too much time agonising over the morality of bombing. They were too busy trying to stay alive. Their war was against flak, night fighters and the weather; predominant in their thoughts when stepping on board their aircraft was the conquering of fear. They were not fighting the civilians far below in the cities gradually being pulverised. Bringing about the end of the war as quickly as possible and by any means possible was the only ethos of any worth in the achievement of that aim. If flattening a city helped, then, by all means, do it. It was regrettable that people had to die as a result but – that is what happens in war. Soul searching on a large scale about dropping bombs on people rather than on industrial targets would have led to a dampening of enthusiasm for the task and a weakening of resolve, with resultant collapse in morale.

When airmen volunteered they did so for a variety of reasons; none volunteered to be agents of a policy deliberately designed to kill civilians. That policy, in the form of the area bombing directive, did not evolve until late 1941. Once in the Air Force it was, of course, impossible to question the ethics of area bombing; it was their duty to implement it. A Pathfinder navigator remembered: 'If we believed it morally wrong, should we have spoken out to our squadron commanders and refused to participate?'[1] Obviously, to question the policy was unthinkable. Dissent was impossible. There is a danger, viewed from the safety of eighty intervening years and not from the cockpit of a Halifax, Stirling or Lancaster in 1942, to assume that the morality of area bombing was even an issue while the war was in progress. True, dissenting voices were heard, but from a very small number of people. 'The ethical issues raised by bombing were never clearly in focus during the war years. What criticism there was came from the belief that western states should maintain the values of liberal decency in the way they conducted the war.'[2]

Those engaged in the actual bombing must be convinced of the rectitude of their cause. 'In wartime men find it particularly easy to believe that a nation whose policies are immoral is made up of immoral individuals. Germans were "Huns"; the only good German was a dead German.'[3] The first issue of *Tee Emm*, the RAF training manual, contained this uncompromising remark: 'They [the Germans] are all tough, hand-picked gangsters out to kill and destroy.'[4] If an airman adopted this conviction, dropping bombs on such degenerates became wholly justified. In any case, when airborne, consideration of ethics was the last thing on the minds of aircrew as they battled to stay alive.[5]

The experience of the German bombing of British cities brought the idea of reprisals sharply into focus. Interestingly, those who suffered most from the effects of bombing, i.e., those in cities, were those who least desired retaliation; those most vociferously in favour were inhabitants of rural areas and those belonging to the upper and middle classes.[6] Unease about retaliation bombing lingered, even after the attacks on London. 'If it's wrong for them to bomb us, it's wrong for us to bomb them.' was one response to a Mass Observation query and another agreed, 'No, they are human just the same as we are.'[7] One respondent, an upper-middle class girl, aged 17, had an ingenious suggestion which was unlikely to be accepted by anyone in the Air Ministry: 'It would be far quicker and save petrol if the RAF bombed London systematically and accurately and the Germans bombed their own country. To have reprisals is insane but all war is insanity. So what?'[8]

When the Luftwaffe turned its attention to provincial cities and towns reprisal raids gained favour. 'Bomb 'em out, I say! Give them some of their own medicine.'[9]

> Even the smallest towns managed to squeeze a Spitfire or Hurricane into their main streets and to display large bombs on which the public were invited to stick and sign savings stamps which, it was

promised, would be faithfully delivered by the RAF. Mild old ladies would be heard remarking ……. that they hoped it would help to smash some German town, and mothers watched proudly as small children signed their names on a bomb destined to kill or maim German families.[10]

Reflecting the mood of the public, an RAF gunner displayed no qualms and responded to Mass Observation: 'Reprisals is a dirty game but it's war anyway.'[11] Politicians and bishops who criticised bombing policy received short shrift from two 'bomb-droppers' who wrote to the *Daily Mirror*: 'Re the Bishop of Wakefield's sentiments on RAF bombing policy: may we humbly suggest that the said policy be left in the very capable hands of our leaders, who have already proved their worth; and the Church attend to things they know something about.'[12]

*

It required no great effort on the part of propagandists to persuade the British people that the bombing of Germany was necessary. An ardent enthusiast of bombing, J.M. Spaight wrote in 1944: 'It was he [Hitler] who really began the battle of the towns. He is probably very sorry now that he ever did so.'[13] One year before an anonymous wing commander had written,

> ……. it [the 1,000 Raid on Cologne] was a terrible thing and it ought not to have had to happen. But equally no-one can doubt that it did have to happen sooner or later and the sooner the better. If innocent Germans suffered in Cologne, the attack brought nearer the day when many more innocent people will cease to suffer in Europe. In war the only choice is between evils; the only possible good is to choose the least of the evils.[14]

These two contemporary comments provide evidence of the prevailing mood of retribution and righteousness. Another contemporary commentator, Cecil Beaton, wrote in 1942:

> These men [aircrew] set about their task with quite an objective feeling. They have no real hatred of the individual enemy ..... they are given incentive for revenge when a submarine sinks a ship without warning, or the enemy shoots down a friend on a parachute, but in most cases their assault is an impersonal one.[15]

There were exceptions to Beaton's assertion that it was an impersonal war for the aircrews. Some did desire revenge. It was personal for George Hull, who wrote in his diary in 1944, 'Our cookie [a 4,000 lb bomb] is always dedicated to someone or something. There was the first on Berlin, reprisals for John, with an extra on Frankfurt for both John and his Dad, there have been cookies from the people in Australia, the people of Manchester, the people of London.'[16] Airman Bernard Dye, in a eulogy to a friend, wrote: 'I will hit the Huns, but hard too, I will get my revenge for my dear pal Nick, who was buried today 11/4/43.'[17] And Pilot Officer J.R. Byrne's diary entries in November 1944 reveal his hatred for the enemy. His first operation, to Dusseldorf, was on 2 November, in a Lancaster with the name 'Press on Regardless'. 'I now felt frightened. I wondered just how I would react to the coming flak, s/lights, fighters, etc.' He was in no mood to show mercy: 'filthy Hun. Let the bastards die like the rats they are..... really a wizard show.'[18]

Hitting back at Germany is a constant in airmen's diaries and correspondence of the time. F/O. F.H.B. Lackman wrote: 'There is no doubt that a point is coming when tremendous air armadas will operate day and night ..... with an effect that may finish the war without invasion ...... and God help the Hun.'[19] His belief that bombing alone could end the war was consistent with the view taken by Arthur Harris. Lackman was killed in a raid on Leipzig in February 1944, part of the prolonged assault on Berlin which failed to realise that aim.

Evidence of unease and guilt does exist in airmen's correspondence. Alec Cranswick wrote to his mother: 'I don't like what I have to do, but I think of you and my country and know I must carry on and do all I can. I must do what my pals who have not returned would have done. I shall try to forget the horrors we are committing.'[20] Cranswick did not survive his tour. Duty and retribution overrode guilt. George Hull wrote of '...... the ultimate futility of all this slaughter ..... of course, I hate the job but I am fighting for the people

I love, and the boys who have already paid the full price. To give in to matters on ideological grounds is to let them all down.'[21] Expressing his feelings after experiencing a Luftwaffe raid, Robert Raymond, an American serving in Bomber Command, wrote: 'The blast effect .... was considerable and made me appreciate what we were doing to enemy targets ...... verily, it is better to send than to receive in this racket.'[22]

In his memoir, *No Moon Tonight,* Don Charlwood included a letter he received from a friend, Johnnie Gordon, who wrote: 'Sometimes my conscience troubles me about the blind mass-murdering of the Main Force. I think Bomber Command's policy is fixed too relentlessly on mere victory by annihilation.'[23] Many others may have had similar misgivings but believed that it was a military necessity to continue.

Cranswick, Hull, Raymond and Gordon must be regarded as typical. Most aircrew would have felt distaste at their task, ameliorated by its necessity. But Leonard Cheshire was *not* typical. 'I rather enjoyed it.'[24] He was not alone. A Mass Observation report of 1941 included the comment: 'There is no doubt that flying generates a sort of sadistic "hunting" instinct and I have no doubt that given favourable circumstances most airmen would machine-gun civilians in an enemy town just for the fun of doing it.'[25] 'Technology was a factor in rendering the killing process more mechanical.'[26] The bomber became emotionally detached from the bombed. It was even possible to be untroubled by remorse, with the complex tasks allotted to each crew member absorbing all their attention, little thought was given to the effects of their efforts thousands of feet below. When Guy Gibson took the BBC reporter Richard Dimbleby to Berlin in 1943 he wrote gleefully in his log book that 'The residential quarters got it!'[27] Sergeant Morrison wrote, with evident satisfaction, 'I think it's pretty safe to say that Mannheim got a bigger beating up than any English town has had.'[28]

Individual crewmen may have had revenge on their minds but most crews just got on with their job dispassionately. Emotions could cloud judgement. A Mass Observation report of June 1941 states:

> I have arrived at no very satisfactory generalisation about their [aircrews] attitude to 'reprisals'. At the time of the heavy bombing of London there was a considerable amount of talk about bombing

Berlin. I heard a number of enthusiastic descriptions of 'fantasy' raids on Berlin by the whole Air Force, with the object of laying it in ruins. Taking air crews as a whole, I should say that there is slightly less 'reprisal feeling' than amongst civilians ...... the advantage of bombing military targets is more appreciated.[29]

Forty-five years after his career as a Mosquito navigator came to an end, Pierre Richard gave voice to an opinion with which every one of his fellow aircrew comrades would have agreed: 'I can understand how to many the bombing campaign may be distasteful, but, as our commander-in-chief Butch Harris said, many times, "It was an essential part of winning the war against an evil foe".'[30]

The morale of Bomber Command aircrews did not suffer as a result of ethical considerations. With a few isolated exceptions they 'pressed on', convinced of the rectitude of their cause. The impersonal nature of aerial warfare enabled them to ignore the mayhem they had unleashed beneath them. In the air all thoughts were concentrated on surviving. Whether men were troubled by their task is immaterial. They were part of a military machine in which they were required to obey orders; private misgivings had to remain as such.

Chapter 16

Teased Out: Flying Stress

Flying stress is the conflict between duty and desire, self-respect and self-preservation.[1]

Flying stress was the greatest threat to morale in Bomber Command. In 1940 the Air Ministry produced guidelines on 'Flying Stress and Neuroses'. It attempted a definition of psychoneurosis: an illness which had both mental and physical symptoms with no complete explanation. It was psychological in origin, caused by an unresolved mental conflict.[2] If the number of men suffering flying stress reached a critical mass, the Command would collapse as a fighting force. A report to a senior medical officer early in the war highlighted the urgency which was required to ensure that flying stress did not take hold among aircrews, many of whom had fatalistic forebodings. 'There is a feeling of inevitability of death or a period of invalidism due to wounds or fatigue.'[3]

The contagion of flying stress had to be controlled if morale were to be protected and the men charged with that control were the COs and MOs of bomber stations.[4] A secret memorandum provided the template for future action regarding flying stress: 'The supervision of aircrews has to be directed to ensure that they do not reach the limit of their endurance and the threshold of breakdown which will result in lowered efficiency, wastage of highly skilled and trained personnel and lowering of morale.'[5]

Medical officers were advised to monitor the aircrews of their units constantly for any signs which might indicate the onset of flying stress. An MO should 'think squadron and live squadron every minute of the day.'[6] 'A Medical Officer' was quoted in the *Portsmouth Evening News* on 19 November 1941:

The time came when they were faced with the cold reality of losses. Everyone had been drilled to expect these in the abstract, but when friends and companions were lost it was none the less a shock. With the passage of time the mood of numb sorrow changed to a tempered realisation of the difficult part of their duty and an inflexible determination to follow it. Many of those who had been mourned as lost were found in the lists of prisoner of war and it was not long before the crews had adapted their minds to the psychological needs of war.[7]

Prevention rather than treatment was the preferred path. When treatment was necessary it should occur as soon as possible for, when an individual reached the end of his tolerance, deterioration was rapid. Insomnia, lack of appetite, palpitations, giddiness and a noticeable increase in alcohol consumption were the more easily recognisable physical symptoms; more difficult to detect were the mental signs: restless behaviour, anxiety, depression and lack of concentration. It would also help to know of any recent trauma, such as witnessing the death of a friend in combat, a terrible accident or, more mundanely, but equally important, domestic trouble.

Domestic strife or relationship problems were severe distractions, which is why the 'living in' policy was employed in Bomber Command; enforced separation of aircrew and their families was designed to remove anxiety and improve efficiency.[8] The policy was not universal but it was preferred. Hence: '..... in the squadron the man is ..... cut off from his family life and is so involved with the squadron and crew spirit and is so preoccupied with the job in hand that the anxiety and cares of his private life are relatively unimportant. Thus, during his period of greatest hazard he is protected from many of the stress factors of civil life.'[9] Wives were often not keen on supporting their husbands' flying careers. Air Marshal Symonds, the co-author, with Wing Commander Denis Williams of the major, influential report (see below) which produced these findings, believed that the wives of NCOs exerted a strong influence on their husbands, whereas officers put duty before family.[10]

When an airman experienced personal problems it could affect his capability to fly. Distraction in any shape or form spelled disaster. 'The secret armour of a quiet mind' was a phrase utilised by the novelist Neville Shute in his 1944 work *Pastoral*.[11] An airman untroubled by emotional turmoil will be an effective combatant; an airman dwelling on personal problems will not be focussed on his task and will become a danger to himself and to his crew. It seems probable that married airmen, or men in relationships, carried an extra burden which could have affected their efficiency in the air and ultimately would encroach on the morale of their crews. When a pilot was seen brooding over a girl, he was widely regarded as a candidate for the 'chop list'.[12]

Identifying cases of flying stress was made more difficult by the fact that even men who were aware they had passed the limit of endurance would not admit it for fear of being seen as a coward. Getting a few operations under his belt might alleviate his torment temporarily; the fear of being proved a coward fades with experience but, unfortunately, *actual* fear increases with experience.[13]

*

In 1942 Air Vice Marshal Sir Charles P. Symonds and Wing Commander Denis J. Williams carried out an exhaustive study of 'psychological disorders in flying personnel of Bomber Command'.[14] They visited several stations and interviewed forty-four duty officers and thirty-seven medical officers. Their research led to a report with recommendations and suggestions on how to deal with cases of flying stress.[15] They found that men could withstand much. This they termed 'the load':

> The present investigation reveals …….. that picked men under certain conditions may carry a load of physical and mental strain far greater than could have been predicted, and this without complaint or surprise to themselves. The load is relative. There are natural sources of strength and endurance to support it, together with the advantages of training, discipline, leadership and morale, and the confidence born of first-rate equipment.[16]

It was threatened by a number of factors, as outlined above. When a man could no longer bear the load, he was suffering from flying stress. Almost all aircrew suffered some degree of fear; only a few 'cracked'. The conventional wisdom, as the reader will recall, was that certain men were predisposed to stress and should be 'weeded out' at the selection stage. Future problems would thus be avoided.[17] This belief followed Lord Moran's axiom that '...... a man of character in peace becomes a man of courage in war .... the experience of war cannot change; it exposes.'[18]

When a man did slip though the selection process it was the role of the medical officer, in close liaison with the station commanding officer, to come to a decision, based on both men's knowledge of the airman concerned. The input from the CO was important, in that the medical officer did not mix with NCOs, other than at briefings and debriefings, and consequently had limited opportunity to make observations of them; the CO, having knowledge of both officers *and* NCOs in his unit, was often able to provide useful information on the sergeants to the MO. One squadron commander told Symonds, 'You can usually tell when a man has had enough, you can tell by the results of his trips.'[19]

Other comments made by COs to Symonds and Williams demonstrate their empathy with the men under their command: one honest commander said, 'If they are as afraid as I am they know what wind up is. They are scared stiff and I don't blame them either.'[20] Another, a wing commander, knew what action to take if a man showed any sign of stress: 'If ever I hear a man say "this is my last trip" either I don't send him on the trip or I tell him he has another dozen to do, then send him twice more and unexpectedly take him off.'[21]

Anticipation was a major source of anxiety in aircrew. They wanted to get on with operations as quickly as possible and any delay caused great agitation. Morale dipped if there was any uncertainty due to the weather and cancellations, especially last minute scrubs, were met with groans of dismay. Prolonged periods of inactivity or repeated cancellations had a serious impact on crew morale. An MO was quoted in a report: 'One freshman was scrubbed 17 times before he got his first trip. He only lasted three trips after this and then said he had had it.'[22] Attempts to combat anticipatory anxiety were made by some COs, who held late briefings so that their crews had less time to ruminate on their fate in the coming raid. Once in the air the crew member would be absorbed in his task and anticipatory anxiety evaporated. When nothing disastrous occurred morale was boosted. The relief felt was in inverse proportion to the total indifference to other crews which may have 'got the chop'.[23]

*

Was the airman refusing to continue flying for genuine medical reasons or was he temperamentally unsuitable for flying duties and was looking for an escape? This was the dilemma facing MOs and COs. It was extremely difficult to distinguish between genuine cases of flying stress and those men who, although medically fit, did not wish to continue flying. An official RAF pamphlet of 1939 for medical officers had laid down the guidelines: 'For practical purposes of disposal it is necessary to draw a clear line of distinction between those who are medically unfit to fly on account of nervous disorder and those whose unfitness or unwillingness to fly is due to temperamental defect.'[24]

A man who has made no attempt to overcome his fears is clearly less deserving than the man who has flown many sorties and has *tried* to overcome his fears. Why should they be treated with equal consideration? 'Nevertheless I do not think it necessary or wise in the interests of aircrew morale to attempt to discriminate more closely in disposal,' wrote the Director General for Personnel and Supply to the Air Member for Personnel in 1944.[25]

The MO should be able to distinguish between a man who has made an effort to overcome fear but has broken down and a man who has made no effort. 'This distinction is important and may well decide the balance of judgment between sickness on the one hand and defective morale on the other.'[26] 'By discouraging the belief that weakening or loss of mental control provides an honourable escape from unpleasant duties, he [the MO] will be contributing in no small measure to the prevention of neurosis and the preservation of morale.'[27]

Dr. Stafford-Clark praised Symonds for his provision of a 'definition' of flying stress, which had previously been erroneously associated with shell shock: it was the stresses to which a man is liable, rather than the reactions brought about by the stresses, which the medical officer should address.[28] Given the extreme nature of their work, it was no surprise that some aircrew were unable to cope. Stafford-Clark divided these into two categories: those whose inability to continue flying was not, in essence, due to a medical condition and those whose ability to continue was 'impaired by the conflict between excessive fear and sense of duty.'[29] Anxiety was the most common observable state among those who could bear the load no longer. Hysterical reactions were more likely to be displayed by men whose refusal to fly was due to lack of will.

On turning his attention to the effect of flying stress on morale, Stafford-Clark, in his time with aircrews, looked for.....

> ...the influences of the cumulative stresses of operational flying upon the morale of the individual concerned, and the extent to which this might be offset by the increasing skill and confidence of experience on the one hand, or reinforced by the mounting fatigue of continual emotional tension on the other; finally, the degree to which morale could be sustained despite these depredations by any means at the disposal of the unit medical officer or squadron commander.[30]

Stafford-Clark had seen, in his four years on bomber stations, depressed airmen who believed they were cowards. If such a man had unfeeling superior officers who did not know him well, this was how the officers perceived him: as a coward. Removing him from the station and posting him to another unit only served to reinforce the man's opinion of himself; it became a self-fulfilling prophecy.[31]

Stafford-Clark realised that flying stress could occur at any time in a flyer's career, but he saw a pattern, based on the stage of a man's progress through his tour of operations. (See Chapter 11: The Tour). He found that men who suffered a mid-tour reaction or those near the end of the tour had a good chance of a return to flying. He had respect for these men, who broke down and wished to continue flying despite their fears, but were unable to do so. The doctor gave a tragic example of a mid-tour man treated by him: a sergeant wireless operator who had completed eight sorties, after which his plane had crashed on take-off. Intensely happy that he had escaped, he then refused to fly on the grounds that he had a duty to his pregnant wife. He was persuaded to return to flying and his morale was restored. He was killed on his tenth trip.[32]

Men who were unsuitable for flying and had had a reaction from the beginning should not return to flying. This group, believed Stafford-Clark, were malingerers, or, to use RAF parlance of the day, waverers (q.v.). They should, of course, have been weeded out at the training stage.[33] It was these men who posed the biggest threat to morale in any unit. Stafford-Clark's remedy? 'There can be no compromise about their disposal; it must be immediate and decisive, and the first step is their prompt removal from the operational unit.'[34] He saw this as the paramount duty of an efficient MO, the need to protect the morale of the unit at all costs, as, '…. indifferent morale can rot the fittest body of men. There are few epidemics as formidable.'[35] Symonds was impressed by Stafford-Clark's analysis: 'This is the best contribution to the problem of flying stress I have yet seen…… A unit MO of this type is bound to make an occasional mistake in diagnosis for lack of psychiatric experience but this is offset by his contribution to unit morale.'[36]

In the final analysis, the MO, assisted by the CO of the station, had to distinguish between genuine cases of flying stress and those who feigned nervous reaction in order to escape from flying and, as perceived by them, certain death. The latter were classified as 'waverers'.

Chapter 17

Frozen on the Stick: Waverers

Modern sensibilities would judge the policy termed *Lacking in Moral Fibre*, initialised to LMF, as a brutal form of discipline. Immediate removal from a unit, loss of rank and flying badge, demotion to aircraftman 2nd class and detailed to menial work were the results when an airman was deemed a waverer. The deterrent value of the policy was powerful and a strong incentive to carry on flying. For most, continuing to fly and risking death on every operation was preferable to the dreadful stigma a man would suffer if he admitted that he could no longer continue. The fear of LMF trumped the fear of death.

Lacking in Moral Fibre, was predicated on the belief that mental breakdowns were suffered by weaklings. It was known that stress was cumulative and, as suggested by Lord Moran, every man has a store of courage which is finite. However, it was believed that behaviour in combat was determined by education, breeding and character. As has been previously noted, if weak characters could be spotted at the selection stage, the number of 'lack of moral fibre' cases could be reduced to a minimum.[1] This belief took no account of the many courageous airmen who would find the 'load' unbearable when they were engaged on their tours. They were *not* weak men who had slipped through the selection net.

Before he became C-in-C Bomber Command, Arthur Harris, as AOC 5 Group, was in no mood to give waverers an easy ride. For Harris, they were weaklings, eager to 'wangle' an easy option. He was concerned that bomber pilots were being used on single-engined aircraft. If he [the bomber pilot] could not accept the responsibility of carrying a crew, he was of no value to a bomber squadron and should be released to fighters, Harris believed, because it was: '...justifiable to give him every chance, by a transfer to single-seater aircraft, to kill as many of the enemy as possible before meeting his inevitable fate through his own ineptitude in flying.'² He would persist with his ruthless attitude to 'weaklings' when he became C-in-C, Bomber Command.

*

The 'W' Memorandum, introduced on 28 September 1940 and continually revised and updated, applied to men who had 'forfeited the confidence of their Commanding Officers'. As we learnt in the previous chapter, decisions on such cases were the joint responsibility of the unit medical officer and commanding officer. The former considered predisposal to nervous breakdown; the latter the airman's efforts to overcome fear. It was the MO's task to distinguish between genuine cases of flying stress and malingerers who were taking advantage of an easy way out. The word chosen by the Air Ministry to define malingering was 'waverer', the letter 'W' to be stamped on the culprit's file in large red lettering. In practice, the terms waverer and LMF were interchangeable.

From the moment the 'W' Memorandum was introduced there was uncertainty and confusion regarding its meaning. 'It has been stated that it does not imply lack of courage but only lack of some special quality of moral fibre necessary for success in flying duties,' wrote the RAF neuropsychiatrists (working with Charles Symonds), and, justifying the existence of the policy, 'Some of those [aircrew] seen by the neuro-psychologists are manifestly lacking in any sense of duty and deserve exemplary treatment.'³ Aircrew had their own interpretation of the term LMF: to them it meant cowardice. An attempt to iron out inconsistencies was made in April 1941. An Air Ministry minute asked for clarification of the term 'Medical "W"'. A 'W' case was a man not suffering a nervous illness, who is fit, but refuses to fly. This would be classed a genuine LMF case; a 'Medical "W"' could be a man who has suffered exceptional strain and whom should not be treated harshly. The minute writer believed the category 'Medical "W"' should be abandoned.⁴

The Air Ministry did not compromise with waverers:

> Though it should be recognised that lack of confidence may persist despite the best will in the world to overcome it, it is of vital importance to morale that unless a man can be proved to have

exercised sufficient determination and perseverance in the attempt to conquer his defect he should be classified as lacking in the quality of moral fibre [margin note: substitute for 'moral fibre' the word 'courage'] expected of aircrews, and in consequence suffer certain penalties. It is also of importance to morale that nervous illness arising from inability to stand up to the strain of flying duties should not be regarded as an honourable or profitable means of escape from these duties, unless there has been exceptional stress.[5]

Making the distinction between genuine and false was not going to be easy. If every man who claimed to have a neurosis brought on by flying stress was removed from duties, the morale of the men who continued to fly would be badly affected. A medical officer pointed out that: 'If they [aircrew] are excused operational duty but retain the privileges and prestige attached to flying status, such action is bound to engender a feeling of resentment among those who have successfully managed to control their own anxiety and fear and continue to face the perils of war.' He continued: 'On the other hand, morale is also affected when men believe that a comrade has been harshly and unjustly treated.'[6] One senior officer believed that: 'You can't have any member of the crew windy – it hazards the whole crew .... LMF cases may be infectious ...... you have a duty to those who stick it .... it is urgent to keep fighting morale high.'[7]

Using the guidelines provided by the RAF neuropsychologists, MOs set about their task, aided by the observations of COs on the character of suspected cases. The CO was in a better position than the MO to judge his men, as already outlined in the chapter on flying stress. His own flying experience would stand him in good stead to opine on cases under his consideration. An Air Ministry comment on the Symonds report was, 'The best of all aids is good squadron morale. When a man shows persistent lack of confidence and on this account cannot be relied upon to perform his duties in the air, it is the duty of the Commanding Officer to have him removed from the unit under his command with the least possible delay, for one man with such lack of confidence may infect others.'[8]

One of a plethora of Air Ministry minutes on the subject of waverers made a distinction between 'Those who shirk but maintain a show of doing their duties' and 'Those who shirk and make no secret of it.'[9] Another minute, including notes of a meeting at which the then Group Captain Symonds was present, reinforced the general attitude that all waverers must be removed but was qualified by a statement that men who had been through traumatic experiences on operations should be treated with sympathy.[10]

Here is an example to illustrate the difficulties confronting both MOs and COs. An air gunner who qualified in January 1941 and had done only twenty-seven hours of non-operational flying, was posted to a squadron and promptly refused to fly. He admitted that he had been afraid of flying since his first flights but had never requested to be taken off flying duties. The station MO declared that the gunner was fit and able to fly. The gunner himself stated, 'I would rather be doing ground duties with complete confidence than flying in mortal fear.' Group Captain Constantine, stationed at Elsham Wolds, asked HQ 1 Group: 'It is requested that immediate disposal action be taken to post this NCO from Elsham as his influence will tend to have a very bad moral effect on the remainder of the aircrew personnel.' The fate of the gunner is unknown.[11]

Other cases were more clear cut. A wop/ag sergeant with 150 Squadron declared that he had 'got the jitters' and that his wife wanted him to stop flying. He had been posted to the squadron on 3 July 1942 but had participated in no operations up to the end of July, when Group Captain Thompson, AOC Snaith, sent his report on the wop/ag to HQ 1 Group. The sergeant had flown six operations in June with his previous squadron, five of them to Essen. He was medically fit. 'Neither the Officer Commanding 150 Squadron nor myself have the least confidence in Sgt. –', wrote Thompson, who continued, 'I consider therefore that he .... be withdrawn from operational flying immediately.'[12] This was a straightforward LMF case.

The AMP chaired a meeting on 23 July 1941, with Sir Charles Symonds, Wing Commander Lawson and Mr. Monk Jones of DPS, Air Ministry present. The subject for discussion was waverers who were engaged on their second tour. It was agreed that if a man broke down on his second tour, he would *not* be classified as a waverer. It was also noted that: 'Groups were of the opinion that an occasional court martial where an individual refused to fly would have the most salutary effect.'[13]

*

Traumatic as being labelled LMF must have been, it was not as serious as facing a court-martial. The charge would contain the following preamble: 'When on active service when under orders to carry out a warlike operation in the air through default failing to use his utmost exertions to carry such orders into effect.'[14]

A rear gunner sergeant of 97 Squadron failed to turn up for an operation in September 1943. He had flown eleven sorties and was a good air gunner, according to his defence counsel, who also informed the court that sitting in a rear turret for hours on end gave ample opportunity for his client to brood about his domestic problems. Unusually, he had been interviewed by an air commodore who took the highly irregular step of telling the sergeant that he was a coward and should be shot. The defence plea was to no avail. The sergeant was reduced to the ranks.[15]

Another air gunner was absent when he should have been on a sortie. His only defence was: 'I am not as keen as I was. My wife is against me flying as it upsets her.' He was sentenced to five years penal servitude and discharged from the RAF.[16] A rear gunner who was accused of sabotaging his turret with an axe was given three years penal servitude.[17] A flying officer whose wife had threatened to commit suicide if he did not stop flying was cashiered. This sentence was repealed in the early post-war years.[18]

*

Periodic attempts were made to remove the 'W' from men's files, as notes from an Air Ministry meeting on 22 February 1943 reveal. The red 'W' was to be retained, with the added wording '.... arising from inability to stand up to the strain of their duties.' At the same meeting it was agreed that the 'W' Memorandum did not apply to men engaged on their second tour, as had been previously agreed in 1941.[19]

When the decision had been made that a man was suffering from flying stress, he then had to be classified as *with moral fibre* or *lacking*. This was revealed in a minute by Sir Charles Symonds, who added, 'There should be no escape for any special group. I do not regard the penalties as too harsh. The policy behind the Memorandum is presumably deterrent.'[20]

Symonds elaborated on disposal in June 1943. Those men who had tried hard to contain their fear and had continued to fly should keep their badges, retain their rank and be transferred to non-flying duties, with no stigma attached. LMF cases would go to the Combined Reselection Centre at Eastchurch, Kent or the Air Crew Disposal Unit, Chessington. RCAF personnel would be sent to the 'R' Depot, Warrington. Symonds emphasised that no man would lose his badge without a hearing from an Air Council Board.[21]

It was rare indeed for LMF policy to be aired outside the walls of the Air Ministry. An accusatory article in the *Daily Mirror* in 1943 was an exception. A journalist who had previously been critical of the inequality of RAF pay scales demanded that the Secretary of State for Air should investigate the indignities suffered by men who, to quote the journalist, 'are debased for no other crime than that their nerves have wobbled under the nightly strain.' Garry Allighan, of the *Mirror*, in his column 'Question Time in the Mess', had received a letter from the wife of a flying officer who had been reduced to general duties, such as sweeping floors. It was immoral to inflict such treatment, she contended, on a man who had served his country. Allighan suggested that, 'Sir Archibald should have this situation independently investigated as it should be no "crime" carrying the punishment of demotion to crack up after several hundred hours on operational flights. Common sense dictates that such men, with exceptional experience, should not be punished by demotion, and wasted on floor sweeping, but allowed to retain their rank and appointed as instructors. Spring is here – and Sir Archibald Sinclair should give his Ministry a good spring clean,' stated Allighan.[22] Such public remonstrations were a rare occurrence but perhaps Sinclair and others took note, because unease over the policy never entirely faded, as volumes of Air Ministry minutes on the subject testify.

Efforts to ameliorate the stigma of LMF were made by the neuropsychiatrists. Sir Harold Whittingham, DGMS, wrote to the AMP, Sir Bertine Sutton, on February 1944, reporting on the neuropsychiatrists' request: asking for 'lack of moral fibre' to be replaced by 'lack of courage'.[23] Whittingham thought that 'lack of courage' was even worse than 'lack of moral fibre' and suggested 'lack of confidence to fly'. His suggestion went unheeded, although others in the Air Ministry supported Mr. Whittingham on the subject: 'I agree with DGMS and SD & R that this term [lack of moral fibre] is not entirely appropriate and would prefer "lack of confidence to fly".²⁴ The terminology might be altered but for aircrew it meant the same thing: an accusation of cowardice.

To complicate matters, step forward Air Marshal Harris. He wrote to Under Secretary of State Balfour on 28 December 1942, with reference to the 'W' Memorandum dated 19 September 1941. A hitherto unfamiliar expression crops up in his missive: 'probably lacking in moral fibre'. He wanted commanding officers to assume extra responsibility:

> Commanding Officers alone are ~~fully~~ [original deletion] competent to assess morale, and to decide if anyone is below standard to an extent which justifies his being labelled 'probably lacking in moral fibre'. They appreciate well the gravity of thus categorising an individual, and they equally realise the importance of maintaining morale, strengthening it, and avoiding any contagion which might weaken it.²⁵

Waverers who had not yet been medically classified should receive the epithet 'apparently lacking in moral fibre' until the final medical assessment was made. Harris did not want LMF suspects anywhere near operational or OTU stations and suggested special units, far from any contact with operational aircrews, to deal with them.²⁶ Air Vice Marshal Robert Oxland, AOC 1 Group, would have agreed wholeheartedly with Harris on the virus which was LMF. He complained about the numbers of airmen falling sick and then loitering around their stations for up to six months. This: '….has a very bad effect on the officers and airmen who are still operating.'²⁷ Oxland took his complaint to H.H. Balfour: 'I consider it is in the interest of the general morale of squadrons that they [waverers] should be withdrawn from the station immediately they are taken off flying, whether at their own request or because they have forfeited the confidence of their Squadron Commander.'²⁸ Any squadron commander who had operational experience was the best man to judge these cases. 'The degree of stress and amount of effort made to overcome fear as compared with average experience and effort,' was the criterion suggested by Symonds.²⁹

This problem had still not been resolved in 1943. The temporary medical category was still being implemented. One year after Harris had requested action Bomber Command HQ pleaded with the Under Secretary of State for Air Balfour for change. 'A very serious position has thus arisen of aircrew personnel who may [be], and in many cases are, ultimately disposed of as lacking in moral fibre, being allowed to remain in close contact with other aircrew personnel where the risk of contamination is a very real one.'[30]

In response, Wing Commander Lawson minuted a month later: 'I disagree entirely with this apparently new category of "Personnel suspected of lack of moral fibre".' Retaining a man on the station, awaiting a final medical assessment was definitely wrong, in his opinion. Lawson had the support of many others who predicted loss of morale as a consequence. Station commanders did not want these men on their stations. Even if they were not eventually classified as LMF the stigma lingered, evident to all on the station. They should be removed to rehabilitation centres or special units to be set up.[31] This idea had its own drawbacks.

Some of those doing the actual flying disagreed with Lawson. A group captain responded to the idea of special units: 'Herding them together at one unit...... the unit would soon gain ...... an unenviable reputation of being a temporary parking ground for "W" cases.' He would prefer men to be retained and to carry out limited flying duties, which would mean contact with their flying comrades, would assist their rehabilitation and prove beneficial to morale for all concerned.[32]

In February 1944 Wing Commander Lawson attempted to effect a change to the 'W' Memorandum. It should be altered to show the difference between the man who tries to overcome fear and the man who does not. At the same time, his belief in the effectiveness of the memorandum was unequivocal: '.... the main object of this procedure must not be overlooked – this is the maintenance of aircrew morale in the true sense of the word; and there can be no doubt that the policy has had and continues to have its effect.'[33]

Sir Archibald Sinclair heard the views of Air Vice Marshal Symonds and Wing Commander Lawson on 'W' cases at a meeting in October 1944. It was Sinclair who had the ultimate responsibility in judging these cases. Referring to men who had commendable operational records but had succumbed to flying stress, Symonds informed Sinclair that many COs were reluctant to 'sign the "death warrant"' of these men. It was certainly an anomaly for a man with a decoration to be classed as lacking in moral fibre. They should definitely be removed from squadrons to protect morale but COs were unhappy that the men would lose their rank and badges. They felt it was unfair and disproportionate. If they were allowed to keep their badges and rank, COs would be content; the offenders would be removed and morale would be protected. Sinclair was satisfied with this arrangement, agreeing that, even though a man had lost the confidence of his commanding officer, he would not have to be stigmatised with the epithet LMF.[34]

At the same meeting it was noted that the Under Secretary of State believed that: 'The symbol "W" had an unfortunate significance in the Service and he felt therefore that the procedure of annotating an airman's 1580 with this symbol in red ink was not altogether free from objection. The form 1580 would be seen by clerks in the Orderly Room and in time this branding of the man would be known among all his colleagues at the station.' An alternative system such as a star or asterisk was suggested, with clerks informed as to its significance.[35]

*

Bomber Command survivors gave their views on LMF. Wing Commander Newman said, 'We were told right at the beginning about the meaning of the initials LMF ..... Anyone who refused to fly on an operation, no matter how many he had already completed, would be branded with that title and would suffer the consequences.......Regrettably, some of the staff, in particular the more senior officers at Lindholme, tended to treat us all as potential deserters.' Newman's flight engineer was 'taken sick'. '...the usual excuse was to tell them [the crew] that he had been taken to hospital and would not be fit for flying for some time.'[36] F/O. Fairhead said, 'The chances of survival were at that time only fifty-fifty and it takes as much courage, perhaps more, to admit being too scared than try and bluff it out.'[37]

F/Lt. Steiner remembered one incident: 'We were made to form three sides of a square. The unfortunate sergeant was marched on the fourth side by the station Warrant Officer, accompanied by Senior Officers. The Adjutant read the sentence and as he got to the words "Reduced to the rank of Aircraftman" the SWO [senior warrant officer] who was standing behind the sergeant, took a pace forward and ripped off his Sergeant's chevrons, which had already been unpicked and lightly tacked on. At the end of the sentencing he was made to double off the square, no doubt to a period of misery. A most humiliating performance for everyone.'[38]

*

As it was so difficult to distinguish between flying stress and LMF it would perhaps be wise to treat the statistics with caution. Little research was carried out on those men who *were* predisposed to breakdown, but who did not break down.[39] Squadron Leader Read wrote: 'Many more cases of LMF might have surfaced if we hadn't been of the generation we were. Disciplined in ourselves, born to respect authority, and obey orders. Above all, regarding any show of fear as an appalling break of the code.'[40] The punitive policy of LMF was introduced as a means of controlling and sustaining morale. Aircrews regarded it as a badge of cowardice. It was a successful deterrent. The number of LMF cases was estimated at 200 per year, an astonishingly low figure.[41]

Chapter 18

Life With the Lions: Nine Months in the Life of 427 (RCAF) Squadron

Most of the factors which determined morale in Bomber Command can be found in the following snapshot of life in one squadron during one phase of the Second World War, encompassing the Battle of the Ruhr. The highs of the successful raids, of the squadron parties, of the revelry in local hostelries, of the squadron's adoption by MGM Studios; the lows of attritional losses, of raid failures, of bad weather stand-downs, of last minute scrubs, of accidents.

....

P/O. Dudley Henderson Burnside eased his lumbering Vickers Valentia biplane transport/bomber off the runway at Lahore; his mission: to bomb tribesmen on the North-West Frontier, in the region known as Waziristan. The fiercely independent Waziris of the Khyber Pass had long been a troublesome thorn in the British side. In an attempt to suppress a fresh revolt in 1937, the RAF was used in a policing role, bombing villages in which the Waziri rebels resided.

Burnside joined the RAF in 1935 and had been posted to 58 Squadron in August 1937. He settled into a routine of ferrying troops, police personnel, politicians and stores. His career as a bomber pilot was very different to that of the men he would later command. Very few, if any, of those had dived down onto remote villages on the North-West Frontier – they were destined for Essen, Dusseldorf, Mannheim and Berlin. 'Bombing of the house of Gul Nawaz', ran one entry in Burnside's logbook; 'Bombing the village of Gulmatti', read another. 'Destructive bombing of Shinethiza village' on

3 December 1940 by six Valentias was yet another of many similar raids Burnside would carry out in attempts to pacify the recalcitrant tribesmen.[1] He was awarded the DFC for his part in the bombing of Waziristan. The unrest on the North-West Frontier died down but occasional sorties in the Valentia were made in 1940 and 1941. His career as a flyer was about to veer off on a very different path. In Europe, a fiercer conflict was raging ....

Dudley Burnside, now a wing commander, was about to exchange the bombing of village huts for the bombing of whole German cities. He took command of 427 (RCAF) Squadron on its formation on 7 November 1942. Burnside, already with seven years of flying experience, demonstrated how, when exceptional leaders were in place, morale was in no danger. He led from the front, flying on operations to known tough targets; he welded a scratch squadron into a formidable team and won the respect of his crews.

The squadron was equipped with Wellingtons and stationed at Croft, Lincolnshire. We pick up its story on New Year's Day 1943, when the squadron, waiting patiently in the freezing cold of an English winter, had yet to carry out its first bombing raid. W/Cmdr. Burnside led six crews on a 'gardening' operation on 3 January but impossible weather conditions prevailed for the next two weeks, with operations cancelled and scrubbed at the last minute. Frustration all round.

The first bombing raid by the squadron took place on 15 January. Dudley Burnside, without his regular crew, led seven aircraft to the U-Boat pens at Lorient. Squadron Leader M. Williams and his crew did not return from this operation. From 16 to 25 January Mother Nature again curtailed any flying activity except for one 'gardening' trip on the 21st by two aircraft, one of which went missing. Exasperatingly, on the 24th ten aircraft were ready to go 'gardening' but were stood down at the last minute.

At last, another bombing mission, on the 29th, again to Lorient. Six aircraft took off. Icing and 10/10^{ths} cloud caused all the squadron aircraft to land at different bases on return. W/Cmdr. Burnside landed safely at Harwell but 'P/O. Taylor crashed into a hillside at Edale near Sheffield .... Miraculously, only P/O. Mortimer was hurt and his injuries were of a slight nature .... Aircraft crashed on the only flat surface within ten miles and although the aircraft was written off the escape of all members of the crew was so fortunate it was therefore the feature story of some Sunday papers.'[2]

On 30 January, it was 427 Squadron's first daylight bombing raid, to Oldenburg, in North-West Germany. The squadron only put up two aircraft, one of which, piloted by P/O. Bennett, failed to return.

Amid days of stand-downs and scrubs at the beginning of February, the squadron again attacked Lorient, on the 4th. W/Cmdr. Burnside led. Nine aircraft took off; eight returned. On the 8th '"B" Flight had a Flight party in Darlington which was very successful.'[3] Four days later, returning from a 'gardening' trip, Sergeant Adlam and his crew crashed into the hills near Thornaby and all were killed.

The adjutant recorded with pride, 'The photograph taken by F/S. Berg of Lorient during the Feb. 4th raid was in all the London papers to demonstrate the destruction caused by the RAF raids.'[4] Two more visits to Lorient, Burnside leading one on the 13th, one to Cologne and two to Wilhelmshaven were interspersed with scrubs and stand-downs. Preparing for take-off on the 25th for a 'gardening' operation, the crew of one Wellington received a nasty shock when a Mustang taxied into it. There were no casualties and only two aircraft set off with their mines. On the 26th it was Cologne again. Five of seven aircraft returned. 'Sgt. Taylor bombed Cologne successfully but on the way home he crashed at RAF station North Luffenham and he and four of his crew were killed and his gunner critically injured. Sgt. Harwood and his crew are missing from this raid.'[5] Another attack on U-Boat pens was made on the 28th, this time St. Nazaire. Five crews took off; four returned.

March 1943 saw 'gardening', stand-downs and scrubs. Six aircraft went to Hamburg on the 3rd; seven to Essen, led by W/Cmdr. Burnside, on the 5th; 'A' Flight party in Darlington were the highlights of the first eleven days of the month. On the next trip to Essen, one week later on the 12th, 'W/Cmdr. Burnside's aircraft was hit by flak before reaching the target; his Navigator (P/O. R.J. Heather) was killed and his Wireless Operator had his foot shot off. [F/Sgt. Geoffrey Keen, Dudley Burnside's wireless operator, was later awarded the Conspicuous Gallantry Medal]. Nevertheless he successfully bombed the target and after many harrowing experiences made a successful forced landing at Stradishall.'[6] *The Reading Standard* reported on 16 April 1943:

> One night in March 1943 Wing Commander Burnside and Pilot Officer [Reginald] Hayhurst were captain and bomb aimer of an

aircraft detailed to attack Essen. When nearing the target area the bomber was hit by anti-aircraft fire. One of the crew was killed and another severely wounded, while the aircraft sustained damage........ Pilot Officer Hayhurst directed his captain to the target, which was successfully bombed and a good photograph obtained. The aircraft was held by searchlights for a few minutes, but Wing Commander Burnside skilfully evaded the defences and set course for home. On the return flight the aircraft encountered enemy fighters, but each time he shook them off..... both these members of the aircraft crew displayed courage and determination of a high order.[7]

Exciting news caused a buzz in the squadron. Dudley Burnside received a telephone call from Wing Commander R.C. Macinnes from RCAF HQ, informing him that the MGM Film Studio wanted to adopt 427 Squadron. There followed more scrubs until the 26th, when thirteen crews set off for Duisburg. On this day 'W/Cmdr. Burnside awarded a bar to his DFC and P/O. R.J. Hayhurst [Burnside's bomb aimer] awarded the DFC for their effort on March 12th over Essen.'[8] Fourteen aircraft took part in another attack on St. Nazaire, on the 28th, followed the next day by a raid on Bochum, from which one aircraft failed to return.

April 1943. Lorient was still suffering a battering and 427 Squadron played its part. It despatched five aircraft there on the 2nd. A much larger force went to Kiel on the 4th, with W/Cmdr. Burnside participating. The unfortunate Heather, killed on 13 March, had been replaced by Sergeant T. Mitcheal and F/Sgt. Keen, minus a foot, was replaced by Sergeant A. Humphries. On the 6th a tragic accident occurred. 'Sgt. Ash swung on take-off, crashed into a tree and the aircraft exploded. Sgt. Ash and Sgt. Dodds were both killed and the other three members of the crew were seriously burned about the face and hands.'[9] The squadron took part in attacks on Duisburg on the 8th and Frankfurt on the 10th; twelve aircraft went to Stuttgart on the 14th. On this op there were more changes in W/Cmdr. Burnside's crew. His navigator on this trip was P/O. J.P. Greening and his Wop/Ag. was Sgt. K.A. Perdue. Fourteen aircraft went to Mannheim on the 16th. At last the squadron was attacking Germany in some strength. A modest boast appeared in the operations record book. 'The 14 aircraft took off in 6 and a half minutes setting a new speed record for the squadron.'[10]

W/Cmdr. Burnside's crew was one of six which departed the squadron on the 19th to train at the HCU at Topcliffe. They would be converting to Halifaxes. '...... instructions were received to "gen" up all personnel on Halifax aircraft as quickly as possible.'[11] More 427 crews would follow. More 'gardening' and a trip to Duisburg on the 27th brought the month to a close. One pilot captain considered Duisburg 'a splendid trip.'[12]

On 2 May 'The Squadron had its official going away party from RCAF Station, Croft. Both the Sergeants and Officers Messes were thrown open to all ranks and a party in true "Lion" style was held.'[13] Two days later the whole squadron departed Croft for its new station in Leeming, North Yorkshire. A pleasant surprise awaited them. 'Facilities for receiving our personnel at Leeming were excellent and the Squadron settled in quickly. The contrast between a Main Station like Leeming and the satellite station at Croft amazed some of the members.'[14] On the 6th W/Cmdr. Burnside addressed the whole squadron and in the evening the squadron had its first party in the officers' mess at Leeming. The CO had become quite a celebrity for his exploits on the Essen raid of 12 March, to the extent that the BBC dramatised the story. He, though, left the squadron for a well-earned leave on the 10th, during which he received his DFC from the King. The squadron crews began to decorate their new 'Halibags', the first depicting a winged lion dropping a bomb. Their aircraft received names too: Z-Zombie, P-Pampers, V-Vicious Victor. After an ENSA concert on the 13th '427 Squadron were very much in evidence, in looking after the female end of the cast.'[15] With squadron strength now at twenty-eight aircraft, the crews enjoyed feeling their way in the Halifaxes and losing the Wellington bias. The 16th saw a fighter affiliation exercise. 'The boys have a great time shaking off the pseudo-enemy fighters (Spitfires).'[16]

On the 21st Dudley Burnside returned from leave but his young crews were probably more interested to know that 'Since the squadron had been informed that each Metro-Goldwyn-Mayer film star was going to adopt an aircraft, a vote was taken today as to which star gets which aircraft. Lana Turner topped the list followed closely by Greer Garson and Hedy Lamarr.'[17] The crews would not have to wait long to find out. On the 24th the whole squadron assembled on the day that 427 (RCAF) Squadron was officially adopted by MGM. Dudley Burnside was presented with a bronze lion, while every member of the squadron would receive privileges at MGM cinemas, much prized by this generation of avid picture-goers. Then the draw for Lana Turner – or rather an *aircraft* named Lana Turner – won by the lucky Sergeant Johnson. The celebration culminated in a party in the sergeants' mess for the whole squadron together with the visitors. Film crews and cameramen recorded the event for posterity.*

Then it was back to the serious business of fighting a war. On the 28th the squadron became operational and the next day thirteen aircraft of the squadron bombed Wuppertal. It was the squadron's first operational task in Halifaxes and it was a fresh target. Wing Commander Burnside set a fine example, flying in this raid with two original members of his Wellington crew.

June 1943. Scrubs for the first five days. The film of the MGM adoption day at Leeming was shown at the Empire, Leicester Square on the 6th. Harrogate superseded Darlington as the mecca of entertainment for squadron personnel and on the 8th various members repaired there for a 'social whirl'. On the 10th there was an ENSA concert and on the 11th seventeen aircraft headed to Dusseldorf in, according to the operations book, 'the greatest raid the RAF ever put on.'[18] All returned. After a raid the next day on Bochum, a sombre note in the ops book announced: 'It was a sad lost [sic] losing P/O. Wellner since he and his crew were original members of the Squadron and were all "gen" men.'[19] W/Cmdr. Burnside returned safely.

The 19th saw 'a special moonlight bombing attack' on the Schneider Works at Le Creusot. All seventeen aircraft which took part returned, including W/Cmdr. Burnside, whose mid-upper gunner F/Lt. Durocher was injured in the heel by a tracer bullet after crossing the French coast on the way home. Danger lurked at every stage of an operation, nerves taut at all times, relaxing only when the props stopped revolving on the runway. This operation was followed by raids on Krefeld and Mülheim, on the 21st and 22nd. W/Cmdr. Burnside was an early return, suffering gyro trouble. Mülheim was particularly grievous for 427 Squadron. Four aircraft were missing, an astonishing 28.5% of the squadron force despatched. 'Their loss

---

* The event was filmed by British Movietone and can be seen in a 4-minute clip on Youtube. Search for *MGM Adopts Lion Bomber Squadron*. W/Cmdr. Burnside makes a speech and Sgt. Johnson is seen chalking the name *Lana Turner* on his aircraft. Many of those smiling at the camera would soon lose their lives.

will be sorely missed in this Squadron since they were an integral part of our Squadron's life.'[20] The crews were those of F/Lt. Webster, P/O. Cadmus, an Argentinian, Sgt. Hamilton and F/O. Reid. A desperate but futile sea search was carried out the next day.

As operations mounted, so did losses. Eleven crews went to Wuppertal on the 24th. One, captained by F/O. Lou Somers did not return. 'Lou was very popular with all Squadron members and will be sorely missed.'[21] Two more crews were lost on the next day's raid to Gelsenkirchen, P/O. Gagnon and F/Sgt. Higgins, who had been awarded the DFM only the month before. 'These two pilots were original members of the Squadron and will both be missed very much.'[22] W/Cmdr. Burnside, scheduled for this raid, crashed on take-off, having no brake pressure. Flight Lieutenant Taylor, no doubt happy still to be in one piece, observed on this raid: 'A/c over target seemed to be coming in all directions and collision only just avoided on several occasions.'[23]

As the month drew to a close there was one more operation, to Cologne, with nine aircraft. One crew, F/Lt. Ganderton's, baled out over England at 03.30. Their aircraft had been badly mauled by cannon fire from a fighter 20 miles east of Bruges. Bombs were jettisoned and the plane crashed near Isleham, Suffolk. Two crew members were injured but all survived. Ganderton was interviewed by the press two day later, his 'superb feat of airmanship' admired by all.

It was Cologne again on 3 July, and it was 'Considered a well concentrated raid…… a very good show,' with the 'Target well pranged and considered a very successful trip.'[24] Six nights later it was a different story. After a raid on Gelsenkirchen there was frustration and despondency, reflected in the debriefing notes: 'PFF scattered and cloud condition caused scattered effort…….. Unable to see damage due to cloud conditions………Results difficult to observe after bombing but believed to have released bombs in target area………. Results not seen due to 10/10^{ths} cloud.'[25]

On 8 July 'In the evening there was a small party in the Officers Mess, when four Canadian girls went through an initiation ceremony – the "Flare Path". They all passed with flying colours.'[26] Intriguing…… The Signals Section threw another party, 'W/Cmdr Burnside and all the section leaders being present. …….. After dinner the mob adjourned to Jock's Dance Hall and proceeded to turn it into a "speakeasy". F/Lt. Izzard "made music" and various verses and songs were sung amid much beer.'[27] The wing commander was in demand, on 20 July turning out in cricket flannels at Bedale. 'W/Cmdr Burnside our CO had a dabble but before we could see what he really was like he was caught by Sgt. Young.'[28]

W/Cmdr. Burnside returned from leave on the 10th and again assumed command of the 'Lions'. Three days later he took part in a raid on Aachen. His debriefing revealed 'Target primary attacked at 01.50 hours from 19,900 ft. Bombed on green TI Markers. Concentrated fires just taking hold and large glow seen after leaving target. PFF markers very well placed.'[29] There was one loss: 'Nothing has been heard of this aircraft since take-off and it therefore must be presumed missing.'[30] This was the crew of Sgt. Sobkowice. There followed days of frustrating scrubs, then a major turning point for the whole Command, the devastating attacks on Hamburg. After the raid on the 24th all crews reported euphorically. 'This was one of the best ops the Squadron has ever done..... Attack seemed pretty well concentrated with ineffective defences.......Considered a very good effort and good show....... Many large fires burning in target area.......Target considered well attacked and a very good trip.......Target was a concentrated collection of fires and very well pranged...... There were no "boomerangs" [early returns] and no losses and according to the crew Hamburg "had it".'[31]

W/Cmdr. Burnside did not participate in this raid, but the next night he led eleven 427 crews in an attack on Essen. He made his views known to the debriefing officer: 'Considered a very good show and PFF technique found to be perfect.' His crews shared his optimism: 'Easy for a Ruhr trip and defences did not have usual punch.......Target well pranged and very little defence for Essen.......A very large explosion seen lasting for about one minute believed to be in area of the Krupp Works. Target well pranged with good concentration of fires........ One explosion seen and about three buildings appeared to be mushroomed into the air. Fires were taking a good hold. Believed to be the best prang of the war.'[32]

There was only one mishap for the squadron on this trip: 'Sgt. Schmitt pranged on landing, having had his undercarriage shot up. It was a very good prang as prangs go.'[33] On the 27th and the 29th it was Hamburg again. A 'gen op' – a success – was the general feeling. On the second of these trips, 'We didn't lose any kites but the boch [sic] suffered one down and one probable, after having attacked P/O. Vandekerckhove and crew. Sgt. McLean the rear gunner deserves credit for this feat, as Jerry's night-fighter boys are generally not so dumb.'[34]

Two nights later the squadron was back over Hamburg, this raid eclipsing Essen of two nights previously as the 'best prang of the war'. More euphoria amongst the crews: 'Believed most successful raid of war......Large fires seen, concentrated and raging......Whole city seemed to be aflame. Much more successful raid than previous one.......Fires seemed to be everywhere and glow could be seen some 225 miles away........Considered very successful prang.......Numerous and fairly concentrated fires were burning in the target area and a column of black smoke rising to 17,000 feet......Terrific blaze. Target could be seen from 100 miles from way in.'[35]

The third Hamburg raid, on 29 July was also considered a success, but without the intensity of the fires from the raid on the 27th. No. 427 Squadron completed the month of July with a raid on Remscheid on the 30th. Again W/Cmdr. Burnside was with his men and, again, he was satisfied with the bombing results: 'Numerous and concentrated fires were burning in centre of town. Glow of fires seen 170 miles away. The raid was an undoubted success.'[36] The squadron suffered its first loss for a while, Sergeant Westerborg and his crew. Westerborg was an Australian on his first trip, perhaps not known to the other crews.

The squadron had lost both experienced and inexperienced crews during July, made bearable by the obvious success of the Hamburg raids. The entry in the operations record book on 1 August was upbeat: 'The satisfaction of knowing they had flattened Hamburg called for a little celebration..... [and] Sgt. Schmitt and his "Happy Valley" crew set off to bust England "wide open" for seven days.'[37]

On the 3rd, 'This evening also saw the crowning achievement of our squadron social life. We held our first real party.... all squadron could attend...... Airmen and airwomen brought their own drinking utensils and the bar soon began to look like Stalingrad at the height of the siege...... Dancing, signing [sic] and thirst quenching went on until 9 p.m. when a stand down was called and everyone settled down to enjoy the cabaret...... The music and lyrics were written by F/L. Izzard ..... Who knows, we may have another Noel Coward on our hands. Anyway, the whole effort turned out into a roaring success, showing the good spirit and moral of the Lions.'[38] Morale appeared to be thriving on 427 Squadron. Jollities continued in a period of stand-downs: on the 13th 'Once more Harrogate and Darlington were severely pranged.' And on the 16th: 'There were no ops scheduled today and the local hideout, the "Willow Tree", famous in the Squadron song, was as usual overflowing.'[39]

The next day the squadron participated in a raid of considerable significance, although at the time, for the crews it was just another trip. To 'a small village on the Baltic coast', as the ops book described it. Peenemunde, site of the German V2 Research Centre. 'Air Marshal Harris, C-in-C Bomber Command, congratulated us on this "prang". There was one loss, Sergeant Brady and crew. Sgt. Schmitt and crew finished their tour, the first to do so on the sqdn.'[40] 'Sgt. Schmitt's parting gift was a Focke Wolf 190 which was shot down by his rear gunner, Sgt. Stubby McNamara.'[41] There were no ops on the 18th, which saw much gaiety in the messes after the success of Peenemunde. Three DFC recipients known as: 'The Gangsters', P/O. Dizzy (Dormand), Davy (P/O. Davy Ross) and P/O. Van (Vandekerckhove) had an alcohol-fuelled get-together in the mess on the 19th. A few days later one would be dead.

There were no losses on the next raid, to Leverkusen, on the 22nd, but the next night over Berlin, 'Unfortunately two of our crews failed to return [the crews of F/O. Baum and Sgt. Cornelius] and although the power "up high" were satisfied with the devastation left behind by our aircraft, the loss of these up and coming crews was a bad blow to the Lions.'[42] An ominous warning in the ops book: 'Apparently the boys are experiencing a lot of opposition from night fighters these days .... This is no doubt an indication that this type of defence will be encountered in future, and to expect heavy losses.'[43]

On 27 August thirteen aircraft joined an attack on Nuremberg. 'Considered a thorough prang,'[44] was P/O. Vandekerckhove's opinion. An interesting observation on LMF appears in the ops book after this raid. 'All crews pranged the target excepting that of "F for Freddie" piloted by Sgt. Buxton, whose Flight Engineer had a case of "cold feet" and only after he fell unconscious did the skipper abandon his task. The flight engineer has been recommended to be removed from flying duties due to the lack of confidence and moral fibre. This is not entirely a fault to be placed on the individual concerned, but rather upon the "production line" methods with which Flight Engineers who have been employed solely on ground duties for a long period of time are within a matter of three or four weeks in some cases from the time of their first flip in an aircraft – placed on operations.'[45] The sympathetic tone may indicate an intervention from the squadron commander - Dudley Burnside, who, it can be sure, knew all of his crews. Sergeant Buxton himself would become one of the missing a few days later.

An unfortunate accident took the life of a pilot and three ground crew on 29 August. 'One of the Lion's crack pilots met with an unfortunate accident this date......... It seems ironic that Sgt. Henry, a very capable pilot who has faced the enemy on 18 raids over enemy territory, totalling 111.21 operational hours, should meet this end.'[46] Munchen-Gladbach was the target on 30 August and W/Cmdr. Burnside flew on this operation. His debriefing notes reveal a hectic night for him and his crew: 'Number of fighters were working in cooperation with S/L cloud reflection. Halifax attacked 5 times by 5 separate enemy aircraft.'[47] Sergeant Buxton and crew did not return this night. P/O. Vandekerckhove took part in this attack. It would prove to be the last from which he would return. The very next night he met his end over Berlin. 'He was one of the best liked members of this Squadron, both with Officers and men alife [sic]. His light-heartedness and cheerful personality was an inspiration to everyone. Only recently did he receive the DFC for "at all times displaying fine airmanship and determination of the very highest order". Had Van been able to complete this sortie he would have completed his first tour of operations...... Incidentally, personnel involved were one of the crack crews of the Lions.'[48] (See also Chapter 4: The Crew)

The time had come for Wing Commander Dudley Burnside to leave 427 (RCAF) Squadron. At the pay parade on 3 September 'all Squadron personnel contributed towards gift for Wing Commander Burnside.'[49] And on the 4th the officers of the squadron took Wing Commander Burnside into Ripon for an informal farewell party. 'Reports indicated that the party was an unqualified success.'[50]

5 September 1943. 'Squadron parade was held and the Adjutant F/Lt. Chasanoff presented gifts of a silver plate a wrist watch and a travelling bag to Wing Commander and Mrs. Burnside as a farewell token of the esteem

in which Wing Commander Burnside was held by the Squadron.'[51] Dudley Burnside took command of the new emergency runway at Woodbridge, in Suffolk, and, eventually, command of 195 Squadron.

....

It was men of the calibre of Dudley Burnside who provide the answer to the question posed at the beginning of this book: how did aircrews face up to their grim task night after night? A high state of morale was maintained by strong, effective leadership. Burnside was undoubtedly a popular and efficient squadron commander. A man who inspired confidence. Bomber Command had many such men, who endured seemingly unbearable losses with unceasing commitment and fortitude, transmitting their qualities to their crews. He survived the war.

*

And what of those young men on his squadron who were deprived of the chance to grow old? Here are 6 of the 55,573: P/O. George Pierre Cornelius Vandekerckhove died on 31 August 1943. P/O.Vandekerckhove hailed from Stony Mountain, Manitoba. His crew, with rank at the time of death, according to the 427 (RCAF) Squadron operations record book for August 1943[52]: F/Sgt. A.K. Young Wop/Ag., aged 23; Sgt. John Amos Albert mid-upper gunner, age 22, from Sandy Lake Manitoba; Sgt. John James McLean, rear gunner, age 27; Sgt. Edward Bartlett, flight engineer, age 19; Sgt. Cyril Campbell Gofton, who was on board as the second pilot, age 20. All are buried in the Reichswald Forest War Cemetery.

Two crew members survived the sortie which claimed their comrades: Sgt. W.A. Williamson, navigator, and Sgt. A.D. Rothwell, bomb aimer. Both became prisoners of war.

Conclusion: A Matter of Life and Death

Flying in Bomber Command truly *was* a matter of life and death. The fantasy film *A Matter of Life and Death*, released one year after the war's end, included scenes depicting row upon row of dead airmen in Heaven. A young airman, played by a very young Richard Attenborough, newly-arrived in Heaven, gazes in awe and exclaims, 'It's Heaven, isn't it?' The sight of so many animated, smiling men, apparently continuing their existence in a better place than the troubled world they had just departed may have given consolation to those who saw this cinematic fantasy and had lost loved ones in the air war. Leaving the cinema, stepping into cold, cruel reality, the members of the families of 55,573 men had to pick up the pieces and face the future their loved ones would not see.

The deeds of Bomber Command were quietly and conveniently forgotten. Admiration of the public for the aircrews, so enthusiastic during the war, mysteriously evaporated. No more praise for gallant airmen in the press. No-one in 1946 was writing poetry about bombing German cities. The scale of destruction in Germany caused unease. With the job done, the war won, bombing could be conveniently forgotten, and with it, the men who had carried out what was now regarded as a distasteful business. No-one wished to dwell on the fact that victory had come partly at the expense of thousands of dead civilians.

The day-to-day existence of a Bomber Command man, wondering if he would still be alive on the morrow, had come to an end. Adapting to his new circumstances was difficult for Pierre Richard: 'For those of us who survived we had to face adjustment to a civilian world and we knew it would not be easy.….It took a long time to adjust to home life but at least you could lie in your bed and no-one could say to you, "You're on ops to Berlin tonight". It was over. Finished.'[1] Lifetime friendships had been established. 'I never regret my five years in the service. It brought me many good friends and we have strong bonds together that can never be broken in life,' said Richard.[2] The intensity of their experiences would never be equalled in peacetime and it is not difficult to understand why every man who survived forged lifetime friendships with fellow crew members. They owed their lives to each other.

*

Even in 1944 it was realised that the crewed bomber was already obsolete. The advent of German rocket-propelled craft, the V1s and V2s, and the dawn of the jet age meant that the last six years would turn out to have been the only time in history that seven men would have to climb aboard a piston-engined bomber to prosecute a bombing offensive. Every time one of those bombers was destroyed, so were the lives of some or all of the crew. Now it would be possible for unmanned craft to do the same onerous work. Alas, it was too late for the 55,573 who would not see the jet age.

*

Measuring morale is difficult. Since no-one knows precisely what it is, it cannot be qualified. If by good, or high, morale, we mean that combatants are motivated to succeed, unfailingly carry out their task and do not weaken in their resolve, then the aircrews of Bomber Command passed the test.

It has been seen that morale in Bomber Command could be assailed by many enemies: the weather, heavy losses with no success, scrubs, delays, 'bullshit' discipline, and (for many) harsh living conditions. These enemies could be overcome, with a combination of astute implementation of Air Ministry policy and the personal qualities of the aircrews themselves. They possessed an innate sense of duty, deference to authority, a feeling of rectitude in their cause, their willingness to accept a measure of discipline as necessary, and, perhaps *the* important factor, the self-esteem and pride in being the member of a crew. A bomber crew was a brotherhood of men, each protective of the others, trusting implicitly in the skill of the others and each knowing that that trust would be mutual.

There was another factor for all operational aircrew which contributed towards individual performance, therefore to the efficiency of each crew, and therefore towards the results of the whole squadron (and on up to Group and Command level). The policy of LMF, designed as a deterrent to prevent the contagion of wavering, exploited the natural desire of men to avoid the ostracism of their comrades. All airmen suffered some degree of fear, but with very few exceptions, they succeeded in controlling it. No-one wanted to 'let the side down'. Fear of being branded LMF was greater than the fear of death. It acted as a very powerful incentive for crews to keep going. There is nothing quite like a measure of fear to encourage good performance.

Effective leadership was the crucial supporting crutch. The crews had absolute faith in Arthur Harris, they respected their immediate superiors and trusted the command structure. Jim Wright had no doubt that morale was sustained by strong and effective leadership through all levels of command from Harris on down. 'He [Harris] was doing a difficult job in a resolute way. Our only hope of winning the war was to follow our leaders and their policies.[3]

Every member of aircrew knew what they had volunteered to do and what their chances of survival were. Some were lucky; others were not. Johnny Johnson recounted the return of Joe McCarthy's crew from the Dams Raid on 16/17 May 1943. 'We eventually landed back at Scampton. In those days Scampton was a grass airfield, it hadn't had a runway laid yet. Landings were always dicey and on this occasion it was very very bumpy. Flak had gone through the undercarriage and burst a tyre. Another foot either way it would have gone into a petrol tank. It would have been goodbye McCarthy's crew .... So we went in for the debriefing and we began to get the tragic story........ We all took off knowing that there was a risk in what we were going to do and we didn't know whether we would come back or not. The crews we lost – they felt the same way. They were less fortunate than we were.[4]

It should never be forgotten that they were all volunteers. No-one had forced them to become airmen. It was truly remarkable self-sacrifice on a mass scale, resulting, for so many, in the sacrifice of their lives. Their comrades who did not perish had every reason to feel pride in the fact that they had answered the call to fight an evil despotism and had done their duty. A desperately small number of them would live to see the memorial to their comrades in Green Park, London, unveiled in 2012.

Conclusion: A Matter of Life and Death

One survivor who did live to see it was Wing Commander A.J. (Jim) Wright DFC, who served with 61 Squadron at Syerston from 10 September to 22 October 1943, then with 630 squadron at East Kirkby from 17 December 1943 to 23 May 1944. He completed 43 operations and, in an aside, he commented, 'Lancaster Aircraft (fortunately) on each operational squadron.' Each time he set off on one of those 43 ops, he wrote to the author, 'I was afraid all the time.'[5] That is a definition of true bravery: the courageous men of Bomber Command *endured*.

Endnotes

Introduction

1. Dr. David Stafford-Clark, 'Morale and Flying Experience: Results of a Wartime Study' in *Journal of Mental Science* Vol. XCV (January 1949) [hereafter Stafford-Clark, *Morale and Flying Experience*], p.23.
2. British Newspaper Archive [hereafter BNA], *Shields Daily News*, 10 October 1939.
3. Public Records Office, [hereafter PRO], AIR 2/4935, Disposal procedure of members of aircrews who forfeit confidence of their commanding officers, Appendix XXXIX 'Flying Stress and Psychoneuroses', Air Ministry confidential letter, 10 May 1940.
4. Paul Fussell, *Wartime: Understanding and Behaviour in the Second World War* (Oxford University Press, 1989) [hereafter Fussell, *Wartime*], p.143.
5. John Baynes, *Morale: A Study of Men and Courage* (Cassell, 1967), pp.94-102.
6. PRO AIR 20/4583, RAF Discipline and Morale, minute regarding morale from D. Colyer, ACAS to DGPS, 19 June 1944.
7. Ibid.
8. Hew Strachan, 'The Soldier's Experience in Two World Wars: Some Historiographical Comparisons' in *Time to Kill: The Soldier's Experience of War in the West, 1939-1945*, (eds) Paul Addison and Angus Calder (Pimlico, 1997), p.374.
9. PRO AIR 6/74, meetings 12/42-18/43, comment by VCAS noted at Air Council meeting on morale and discipline, 14 September 1943.
10. Stafford-Clark, *Morale and Flying Experience*, p.15.
11. PRO AIR14/3512, Air Office Commander-in-Chief correspondence, Secretary of State for Air, 'C-in-C Bomber Command File 3 (1942) Correspondence with the Secretary of State for Air', 29 May 1942.
12. Martin Middlebrook and Chris Everitt, *The Bomber Command War Diaries: An Operational Reference Book, 1939-1945* (Midland, 1996) [hereafter Middlebrook, *Bomber Command War Diaries*], p.11.

Chapter 1: The Zeitgeist

1. Tom Harrison Mass Observation Archive [hereafter MOA], file report fr 568, 4 February 1941.
2. Anthony Kellett, *Combat Motivation* (Kluwer Nijhoff, 1982) [hereafter Kellett, *Combat Motivation*], p.177.
3. Flight Lieutenant Julian Badcock, in an unpublished questionnaire used by Denis Richards in compiling material for *The Hardest Victory: RAF Bomber Command in the Second World War* (Coronet, 1995) [hereafter Richards, *Hardest Victory*] and held by the RAF Museum, Hendon.
4. Richard Overy, *Bomber Command, 1939-1945* (Harper Collins, 1997) [hereafter Overy, *Bomber Command*], p.137.
5. Stafford-Clark, *Morale and Flying Experience*, p.15.
6. BNA, *Bedfordshire Times and Independent*, 24 April 1942.
7. Ibid, *Daily Mirror*, 6 June 1940.
8. Stafford-Clark, *Morale and Flying Experience*, pp.15-16.
9. Angus Calder, *The People's War: Britain 1939-1945* (Pimlico, 1992) [hereafter Calder, *People's War*], p.249.
10. BNA, *Air Eddies* by Oliver Stewart, *The Tatler*, 28 August 1940, p.308.
11. Ibid, *Edinburgh Evening News*, 1 June 1942.
12. Ibid, *Daily Mirror*, 7 February 1940.
13. Ibid, 2 April 1941.
14. Ibid, 28 August 1941.
15. Ibid, *Lincolnshire Echo*, 21 August 1940.
16. Ibid, *Daily News (London)*, 17 April 1942.
17. Ibid, *Western Morning News*, 27 November 1943.
18. Ibid, *Daily Mirror*, 22 December 1943.
19. Ibid, *Aberdeen Evening Express*, 24 November 1943.
20. PRO AIR 6/72, minute of Air Council meeting, 14 October 1941.
21. PRO AIR 14/80, notes of meeting to review press and publicity, 17 November 1939.
22. James Chapman, *The British at War: Cinema, State and Propaganda, 1939-1945* (I.B. Taurus, 1998), p.131.
23. BNA, *Daily Mirror*, 24 July 1941.
24. Terence Rattigan, *Flare Path* (Nick Hern Books, London, 2011), introduction p.xxxvi.
25. BNA, *The Tatler*, 20 June 1945, p.359.

26. Leslie Halliwell, *Halliwell's Film Guide* (Harper Collins Entertainment, 2001), p.882.
27. BNA, *Daily Mirror*, 13 September 1941.
28. Ibid, *Lincolnshire Echo*, 19 October 1940.
29. IWM Sound Archive holds several broadcasts by RAF personnel.
30. PRO AIR 14/2829, transcript of recording titled 'Early Days of RAF Bomber Offensive'.
31. Ibid.
32. PRO AIR 20/2955, Bomber Command Publicity.
33. PRO AIR 14/80, letter from Sir Arthur Harris, C-in-C 5 Group to Bomber Command HQ, 1940.
34. Ibid, letter from Air Ministry to Sir Edgar Ludlow-Hewitt, C-in-C Bomber Command, 15 February 1940.
35. Ibid, notes from conference on the effect of censorship, January 1941.
36. Ibid, Press Censorship: Policy, Memo from Sir Arthur Harris to Sir Charles Portal, CAS, 5 March 1942.
37. MOA fr 895, 26 October 1941, p.1.
38. Ibid, p.3.
39. Kellett, *Combat Motivation*, p.177, See also Martin Middlebrook, *The Battle of Hamburg: Allied Bomber Forces against a German City in 1943* (Penguin, 1984) [hereafter Middlebrook, *Battle of Hamburg*], p.347.
40. PRO AIR 20/3082, letter from Air Ministry to all Commands, 22 March 1944.
41. MOA fr 443, p.1. See also John Costello, *Love, Sex and War: Changing Attitudes 1939-1945* (Pan 1986) [hereafter Costello, *Love, Sex and War*], p.194.
42. Kellett, *Combat Motivation*, p.178.

Chapter 2: Volunteers

1. Flying Officer Pierre Richard, audiotape, 1990.
2. BNA, *Daily Record*, 31 January 1939.
3. Max Hastings, *Bomber Command* (Papermac, 1993) [hereafter Hastings, *Bomber Command*], p.144.
4. Middlebrook, *Battle of Hamburg*, p.347.
5. PRO AIR 20/1369, preliminary aircrew training, Air Ministry report, May 1944.
6. BNA, *Daily Mirror*, 15 June 1940.
7. Ibid, 19 March 1940.
8. Ibid, 16 May 1940.
9. Ibid, 25 June 1940.

10. Ibid.
11. Ibid, 19 March 1940.
12. Ibid, 7 November 1940.
13. Ibid, 21 February 1941.
14. Ibid, 2 October 1941.
15. Ibid, 8 December 1941.
16. Ibid, *Lincolnshire Echo*, 1 June 1942.
17. Ibid, *Daily Mirror*, 11 February 1943.
18. Ibid, 11 February 1943.
19. Vivian Rosewarne, *An Airman's Letter to His Mother* (Putnam, 1940).
20. Sir William Rothenstein, *Men of the RAF* (Oxford University Press, 1942) [hereafter Rothenstein, *Men of the RAF*], p.62.
21. Kellett, *Combat Motivation*, p.62.
22. Chas Bowyer, *Bomber Barons* (William Kimber, 1983) [hereafter Bowyer, *Bomber Barons*], p.197.
23. Hastings, *Bomber Command*, p.21.
24. Russell Braddon, *Cheshire VC* (Arrow, 1972) [hereafter Braddon, *Cheshire VC*], p.42.
25. IWM Sound 2892/02, interview with William Reid VC for the Thames Television series *The World at War*, 1972.
26. Ibid.
27. IWM Documents 19939, D.J. Gill.
28. Wing Commander A.J. Wright, author's questionnaire, June 2000.
29. Overy, *Bomber Command*, p.20 & p.36.
30. Flying Officer Pierre Richard, audiotape, 1990.
31. IWM Documents 14890, Wing Commander K.J. Newman MBE, DFC, 'Left, Left, Steady', unpublished.
32. Roger A. Freeman, *The British Airman* (Arms and Armour, 1989) [hereafter Freeman, *British Airman*], pp.4-6.
33. Ibid.
34. Ibid.
35. Stafford-Clark, *Morale and Flying Experience*, p.18.
36. IWM Sound 13024/2, interview with Harold Nash, 1992.
37. Middlebrook, *Battle of Hamburg*, p.347.

Chapter 3: A Bomber Type: Selection and Training

1. Sir Charles P. Symonds and W/Cmdr. Denis J. Williams, *Psychological Disorders in Flying Personnel of the Royal Air Force Investigated During the*

War, 1939-1945 (HMSO 1947) [hereafter Symonds and Williams, *Psychological Disorders*], p.52.
2. IWM Documents 2030, Flight Lieutenant D. Steiner.
3. Major General F.M. Richardson, *Fighting Spirit: A Study of Psychological Factors in War* (Leo Cooper, 1978), p.94.
4. PRO AIR 14/2821, letter from Medical Officer, 9 Squadron, Honington to Senior Medical Officer, 3 Group Headquarters, Newmarket, 1 February 1942.
5. Ibid.
6. PRO AIR 14/30, anonymous group captain, 12 December 1939.
7. Ibid.
8. Ibid.
9. Ibid, letter from Bomber Command HQ to Sir Victor Richardson, Air Ministry, 18 January 1940.
10. Mark Wells, *Courage and Air Warfare: The Allied Aircrew Experience in the Second World War* (Frank Cassell & Co., 1995) [hereafter Wells, *Courage and Air Warfare*], p.12.
11. Ibid.
12. PRO AIR 2/6345, minutes of meeting of Flying Personnel Research Committee, 5 May 1943.
13. Ibid, Selection by psychological methods, minute by H.E. Whittingham, DGMS.
14. Ibid, meeting of Flying Personnel Research Committee, 29 April 1943.
15. Philip E. Vernon and John B. Parry, *Personnel Selection in the British Forces* (University of London Press, 1949), p.74. See also D.D. Reid, 'The Historical Background to Wartime Research in Psychology in the Royal Air Force' in *Aircrew Stress in Wartime Operations: Papers from the Flying Personnel Research Committee of the Ministry of Defence* (eds) E.J. Dearnaley and P.B. Warr (Academic Press, 1979) [hereafter D.D. Reid, *Historical Background to Wartime Research in Psychology*], p.4.
16. BNA, *The Yorkshire Post and Leeds Intelligencer*, 28 February 1941.
17. PRO AIR 20/1369, preliminary aircrew training, Air Ministry report, May 1944.
18. Overy, *Bomber Command*, p.142.
19. Stafford-Clark, *Morale and Flying Experience*, p.10.
20. PRO AIR 2/4935, letter from Sir Bertine Sutton, AMP to AOC Flying Training Command, 30 March 1943.
21. PRO AIR 10/5034, 'Signs of temperamental unsuitability in aircrew under training' by Symonds and Williams, April 1943.

22. PRO AIR 2/8591, internal minute to Mr. Monk Jones of the DPS, 20 September 1941.
23. Ibid.
24. IWM Documents 2030, Flight Lieutenant D. Steiner.
25. Ibid, Documents 19939, D.J. Gill.
26. Wing Commander A.J. Wright, author's questionnaire, June 2000.
27. PRO AIR 20/981, memorandum from MacNeece Foster, C-in-C 6 Group to HQ Bomber Command, 13 January 1942.
28. Stafford-Clark, *Morale and Flying Experience*, p.10.
29. IWM Documents 20698, Flying Officer R.J. Fairhead.
30. Ibid, Documents 14890, Wing Commander K.J. Newman MBE, DFC, 'Left, Left, Steady', unpublished.
31. Ibid, Documents 2030, Flight Lieutenant D. Steiner.
32. Stafford-Clark, *Morale and Flying Experience*, p.11.
33. Overy, *Bomber Command*, p.142.
34. BNA, *Birmingham Daily Post*, 14 March 1940.
35. Richards, *Hardest Victory*, p.406.
36. IWM Documents 1045, Flying Officer R.J. Fayers, 17 May 1942.
37. Ibid, 2 August 1942.
38. Ibid, Documents 14890, Wing Commander K.J. Newman MBE, DFC, 'Left, Left, Steady', unpublished.
39. Ibid.
40. PRO AIR 20/4106, report by A.G.R. Garrod on his tour of training schools in Canada and the USA, 23 May 1941.
41. George 'Johnny' Johnson, conversation with the author, 11 October 2011.
42. Ibid.
43. PRO AIR 20/4106, letter from Dominions Office to Air Ministry, 3 June 1941.
44. Ibid.
45. PRO AIR 20/3082, minute by Inspector General Sir Philip Joubert to CAS, VCAS, AMP and AMT, 'Discipline and the fighting spirit in the RAF', 14 May 1943.
46. Ibid.
47. Ibid.
48. Wells, *Courage and Air Warfare*, p.19.
49. PRO AIR 20/3082, 'Note by Inspector General II on Discipline and Fighting Spirit in the Royal Air Force', September 1943.
50. IWM Documents 20698, Flying Officer R.J. Fairhead.

51. Ibid.
52. Ibid.
53. PRO AIR 14/2723, minute from A.J. Capel, Air Officer Training, Bomber Command HQ, 12 December 1943.
54. IWM Documents 14890, Wing Commander K.J. Newman MBE, DFC, 'Left, Left, Steady', unpublished.
55. PRO AIR 20/982, letter from Sir Philip Babington, C-in-C Flying Training Command to Under Secretary of State H.H. Balfour, 26 August 1944.
56. PRO AIR 14/2929, 'Bomber Command Monthly Summary of Medical Events', note by Medical Officer at Wyton, December 1942.
57. Symonds and Williams, *Psychological Disorders*, p.41.
58. PRO AIR 10/5034, Symonds and Williams, 'Personal Investigation of Psychological Disorders in Flying Personnel of Bomber Command', p.31.
59. PRO AIR 2/4935, minute from Flying Training Command.
60. PRO AIR 6/72, Conclusions to Air Council Meetings, July-December 1941, 23 December 1941.
61. Symonds and Williams, P*sychological Disorders*, p.41.
62. Martin Middlebrook, *The Nuremberg Raid, 30-31 March 1944* (Penguin, 1986) [hereafter Middlebrook, *Nuremberg Raid*], p.57.
63. PRO AIR 20/982, letter from ACAS Sir Norman Bottomley to VCAS, 17 June 1943.
64. Ibid.
65. Tim Hamilton, *The Life and Times of Pilot Officer Prune* (HMSO, London) [hereafter Hamilton, *P/O. Prune*], 1991.
66. Ibid, p.26.
67. Overy, *Bomber Command*, p.148.
68. Ibid.
69. Mary M. Hill, *The Making of a Pathfinder: Letters from a Navigator* (Merlin 1992), p.69.
70. Flying Officer Pierre Richard, audiotape, 1990.

Chapter 4: The Crew

1. IWM Documents 12886, Pilot Officer J.R. Byrne.
2. AIR 20/10727, 'Report on flying fatigue and stress as observed in the RAF,' undated.
3. Stafford-Clark, *Morale and Flying Experience*, p.15.
4. PRO AIR 10/5034, Symonds and Williams, 'Personal Investigation of Psychological Disorders in Flying Personnel of Bomber Command'.

5. Ibid.
6. IWM Documents 14890, Wing Commander K.J. Newman.
7. PRO AIR 14/1008, letter from Sir Arthur Harris to Air Ministry, 19 February 1943.
8. PRO AIR 8/610, letter from Sir Arthur Harris to H.H. Balfour, Under Secretary of State for Air, 27 February 1942.
9. IWM Documents 20698, Flying Officer R.J. Fairhead.
10. PRO AIR 14/1008, letter from Sir Arthur Harris to Sir Bertine Sutton, AMP, 28 January 1943.
11. Ibid, letter from Sir Arthur Harris to H.H. Balfour, Under Secretary of State for Air, 29 April 1943.
12. PRO AIR 14/1012, 'Captains of aircraft', comments by A.J. Capel, Air Officer Training, Bomber Command HQ on Inspector General's report, 6 March 1943.
13. Wing Commander A.J. Wright, author's questionnaire, June 2000.
14. PRO AIR 20/234, minute of meeting between Sir Charles Portal, CAS, and representatives of all commands on 'Captains of aircraft', 25 August 1943.
15. PRO AIR 14/3544, letter from Ralph Cochrane, AOC 3 Group, to AM Sir Arthur Harris, 19 September 1942.
16. Ibid.
17. Ibid.
18. PRO AIR 14/1008, letter from Sir Arthur Harris to Sir Bertine Sutton, AMP, 19 February 1943.
19. Ibid, letter from Sutton to Harris 17 February 1943.
20. Ibid, letter from Harris to Sutton 19 February 1943.
21. PRO AIR 14/1012, 'Captains of aircraft', letter from Harris to H.H. Balfour, Under Secretary of State for Air, 27 March 1944.
22. PRO AIR 14/2723, letter from Bennett to all PFF Squadrons, 3 April 1943.
23. PRO AIR 14/1762, correlation between success and experience, 16 March 1944.
24. PRO AIR 14/2723, letter from Donald Bennett to all PFF squadrons, 6 August 1943.
25. Ibid, minute to all PFF squadrons from SASO PFF HQ, 27 April 1943.
26. Ibid, letter from Donald Bennett to Sir Arthur Harris, 30 April 1943.
27. Ibid, letter from Donald Bennett to all PFF squadrons, 29 April 1943.
28. Ibid, letter from A.J. Capel, Air Officer Training to PFF HQ, 12 May 1943.
29. Ibid, letter from wing commander, 7 Squadron to PFF HQ, 18 August 1943.
30. Ibid, letter from group captain, 56 Squadron to PFF, HQ, 18 August 1943.
31. Ibid, letter from group captain, 97 (Straits Settlement) Squadron to PFF HQ, 27 August 1943.

32. Ibid.
33. Ibid, letter from A.J. Capel, Air Officer Training to PFF HQ, 12 September 1943.
34. PRO AIR 14/1012, 'Captains of aircraft', minute from Robert Saundby, SASO, to Sir Arthur Harris, 13 March 1944.
35. Ibid, letter from DPS, Air Ministry to all groups, 5 July 1944.
36. PRO AIR 14/1012, Captains of aircraft.
37. Ibid, minute from A.J. Capel, Air Officer Training, 16 July 1944.
38. Ibid, letter from Edward Addison, AOC 100 Group to Bomber Command HQ, 1 November 1944.
39. Ibid, letter from Bomber Command HQ to H.H. Balfour, Under Secretary of State for Air, 13 November 1944.
40. Ibid, letter from DPS, Air Ministry to Bomber Command HQ, 27 September 1945.
41. PRO AIR 14/2380, personal experience reports, minutes from a group captain at 3 Group HQ to Bomber Command HQ, 11 November 1941.
42. PRO AIR 14/49, emergency parachute jumps.
43. PRO AIR 14/2380, experience of P/O. Freberg.
44. Ibid, experience of P/O. Watson.
45. David Garnett, *War in the Air: September 1939-May 1941* (Chatto and Windus, 1941) [hereafter Garnett, *War in the Air*], p.34.
46. IWM Documents 12886, Pilot Officer J.R. Byrne.
47. IWM Documents 14890, Wing Commander K.J. Newman MBE, DFC 'Left, Left, Steady', unpublished.
48. PRO AIR 27/1845/19, No. 427 (RCAF) Squadron Operations Record Book, August 1943, summary.
49. IWM Documents 20698, Flying Officer R.J. Fairhead.
50. Bowyer, *Bomber Barons*, p.197.
51. George 'Johnny' Johnson, conversation with the author, 11 October 2011.

Chapter 5: The Squadron

1. Middlebrook, *Nuremberg Raid*, p.55.
2. Martin Middlebrook, *The Berlin Raids: RAF Bomber Command Winter 1943-44* (Penguin, 1990) [hereafter Middlebrook, *Berlin Raids*], p.318.
3. Richard Holmes, *Firing Line* (Pimlico, 1994), p.307.
4. Ibid, p.315.
5. Kellett, *Combat Motivation*, p.46.

6. John Ellis, *The Sharp End: The Fighting Man in World War Two* (Pimlico, 1993) [hereafter Ellis, *Sharp End*], p.255.
7. PRO AIR 14/2821, report by Squadron Leader Jackson, Senior Medical Officer, Wyton, 9 January 1943.
8. Don Charlwood, *No Moon Tonight* (Goodall, 1995) [hereafter Charlwood, *No Moon Tonight*], p.176.
9. Leonard Cheshire, *Bomber Pilot* (Hutchinson & Co., 1943) [hereafter Cheshire, *Bomber Pilot*], p.96.
10. IWM Sound, 21/85/6/A, Flying Officer Horner, 28 February 1944.
11. Wing Commander A.J. Wright, author's questionnaire, June 2000.
12. Guy Gibson, *Enemy Coast Ahead* (Pan, 1956) [hereafter Gibson, *Enemy Coast Ahead*], p.115.
13. PRO AIR 27/2152/2, No. 630 Squadron Operations Record Book, January 1944.
14. Sir Charles Webster and Noble Frankland, *The Strategic Air Offensive Against Germany, 1939-1945, Vol.1* (HMSO, 1961), p.229, letter from Mr. Dewdney, Bomber Command oil adviser, to Sir Richard Peirse, C-in-C Bomber Command, 1 February 1941.
15. Gibson, *Enemy Coast Ahead*, pp.170-171.
16. Cecil Beaton, *Winged Squadrons* (Hutchinson & Co., 1942) [hereafter Beaton, *Winged Squadrons*], p.18.
17. PRO AIR 27/2152/5, No. 630 Squadron Operations Record Book, January 1944.
18. PRO AIR 27/101/5, No. 7 Squadron Operations Record Book, March 1944.
19. PRO AIR 27/1846/5, No. 427 (RCAF) Squadron Operations Record Book, March 1944.
20. Andrew Brookes, *Bomber Squadron at War* (Ian Allen, 1983) [hereafter Brookes, *Bomber Squadron at War*], p.80.
21. IWM Documents 20698, Flying Officer R.J. Fairhead.
22. PRO AIR 27/1845/21, No. 427 (RCAF) Squadron Operations Record Book, September 1943.
23. PRO AIR 10/5034, 'Casualties'.
24. PRO AIR 27/2152/5, No. 630 Squadron Operations Record Book, January 1944.
25. PRO AIR 27/2152/11, No. 630 Squadron Operations Record Book, April 1944.

Chapter 6: The Bomber Station

1. Flight Lieutenant Henry Treece, 'Lincolnshire Bomber Station' in *Air Force Poetry* (eds) John Pudney and Henry Treece (John Lane: The Bodley Head, 1944) [hereafter *Air Force Poetry*], p.80.

2. Ronald Wilcox, 'Operational Squadron' in *Air Force Poetry*, p.86.
3. John James, *The Paladins* (Futura, 1991) [hereafter James, *Paladins*], p.175.
4. IWM Con Shelf, letters of G.J. Hull, 29 September 1943.
5. PRO AIR 14/2831, 'Bomber Command Monthly Summary of Medical Events', December 1944.
6. IWM 74/93/1, diary of Pilot Officer M.A. Scott, 8 January 1941.
7. John B. Hilling, *Strike Hard: A Bomber Airfield at War: RAF Downham Market and its Squadrons* (Alan Sutton, 1995) [hereafter Hilling, *Strike Hard*], p.16.
8. IWM Documents 14890, Wing Commander K.J. Newman MBE, DFC, 'Left, Left, Steady', unpublished.
9. Ibid, Documents 2030, Flight Lieutenant D. Steiner.
10. Rupert Cooling, unpublished recollections from questionnaire sent by Denis Richards in relation to his book *The Hardest Victory*.
11. IWM Con Shelf, letters of G.J. Hull, 11 January 1944.
12. Beaton, *Winged Squadrons*, p.17.
13. PRO AIR 14/2829, 'Bomber Command Monthly Summary of Medical Events', December 1942.
14. PRO AIR 6/70, 'Air Council Conclusions to Meetings, July–December 1940, 17 September 1940'.
15. IWM 74/93/1, diary of M.A. Scott, 8 January 1941.
16. Ibid, Con Shelf, letters of G.J. Hull, 13 November 1943.
17. PRO AIR 14/2833 and PRO AIR 14/2831.
18. PRO AIR 14/2833, 'Bomber Command Hygiene and Medical Reports, 5 Group Annual Report 1944'.
19. PRO AIR 14/2829, 'Bomber Command Monthly Summary of Medical Events', various reports, June 1942.
20. Ibid.
21. Costello, *Love, Sex and War*, pp.23-25.
22. Major Velyien E. Henderson, *Air Crew in Their Element: Hints for the Maintenance of Fitness and Confidence* (University of Toronto Press, 1942) [hereafter Henderson, *Aircrew in Their Element*], p.34.
23. PRO AIR 20/3082, 'Air Council Committee on morale and discipline,' memo by AMP on aspects of the report by Sir Philip Joubert dated 16 September 1943 on the subject of venereal disease, 1 February 1944.
24. Ibid.
25. Ibid.
26. Ibid.

Endnotes 199

27. Ibid, 'Report on Discipline and Fighting Spirit in the Royal Air Force', Appendix A1: Venereal Disease.
28. Ibid.
29. Ibid.
30. Ibid, minute by AMP, 'Issue of condoms to RAF personnel', report 10 December 1943, 28 February 1944.
31. Ibid.
32. Ibid.
33. PRO AIR 2/4935, lectures on prevention of venereal disease.
34. MOA fr 653, 'Use of Leisure in the RAF', 10 April 1941.
35. Rothenstein, *Men of the RAF*, p.17.
36. Wing Commander Evan Gwyn Jones, unpublished comments on questionnaire sent by Denis Richards in relation to his book *The Hardest Victory*.
37. Flying Officer Pierre Richard, audiotape, 1990.
38. MOA fr 734, 'Morale in the Ranks of the RAF', 12 June 1942, p.7.
39. BNA, *Daily Mirror*, 29 March 1940.
40. IWM Documents 12886, Pilot Officer J.R. Byrne.
41. PRO AIR 14/2829, 'Bomber Command Monthly Summary of Medical Events', report by medical officer at Bottesford, June 1942.
42. PRO AIR 20/4583, 'Report on morale', August 1945.
43. Joanna Bourke, *An Intimate History of Killing: Face to Face Killing in Twentieth Century Warfare* (Granta, 2000) [hereafter Bourke, *An Intimate History of Killing*], p.56.
44. Charlwood, *No Moon Tonight*, pp.46-47.
45. Sir William Rothenstein, *Men of the RAF*, p.74.
46. IWM Con Shelf, letters of G.J, Hull, 1 April 1944.
47. MOA fr 653, pp.4-5.
48. Ibid, p.2.
49. IWM 74/93/1, diary of M.A. Scott, 10 January 1941.
50. Richard Morris, *Guy Gibson* (Penguin, 1995) [hereafter Morris, *Guy Gibson*], p.111.
51. Gibson, *Enemy Coast Ahead*, p.185.
52. Ibid.
53. Henderson, *Air Crew in Their Element*, p.33.
54. An RCAF officer quoted in John Terraine, *The Right of the Line: The Royal Air Force in the European War, 1939-1945* (Hodder and Stoughton, 1985) [hereafter Terraine, *The Right of the Line*], p.464.

55. PRO AIR 20/3082, letter from Sir Charles Portal, CAS, to Sir Philip Babington, AOC Flying Training Command, 3 December 1942.
56. Ibid, letter from G.E.H. Medhurst, VCAS to AMP, 23 November 1942.
57. PRO AIR 20/4583, letter from Sir Philip Joubert, Inspector General, 17 September 1943.
58. PRO AIR 20/3082, letter from Folliott Sandford, Assistant Under Secretary of State for Air to Sir Douglas Evill, VCAS, 3 February 1945.
59. Anthony Aldgate and Jeffrey Richards, *Britain Can Take It: The British Cinema in the Second World War* (Edinburgh University Press, 1994), p.98.
60. RAF Museum Hendon, X001-3600, diary of Sergeant Edward Wiggins, 5 June 1944.
61. Costello, *Love, Sex and War,* pp.101-110.
62. PRO AIR 27/2152/12, No. 630 Squadron Operations Record Book, December 1943.
63. PRO AIR 20/3082, letter from Folliott Sandford, Assistant Under Secretary of State for Air to Sir Douglas Evill, VCAS, 12 May 1944.
64. IWM Con Shelf, Hull Letters, 12 March 1944.
65. PRO AIR 20/3085, letter from Mr. Robert Nichols to F/O. Tomlinson, Officer's Mess, Oakington, 28 November 1942.
66. PRO/AIR 20/4583, 'Report on morale in the RAF for the quarter ending 1 August 1945'.
67. Hilling, *Strike Hard,* p.2.
68. IWM, letters of G.J. Hull, 17 November 1943.
69. Ibid.
70. Flying Officer Pierre Richard, audiotape, 1990.
71. Lord Moran, *The Anatomy of Courage* (Avery, 1987) [hereafter Moran, *Anatomy of Courage*], p.101.
72. Cheshire, *Bomber Pilot,* p.28.
73. Charlwood, *No Moon Tonight,* p.77.
74. Morris, *Guy Gibson,* p.137.
75. Rothenstein, *Men of the RAF,* pp.75-76.

Chapter 7: Collecting a Gong: Incentives

1. Norman Longmate, *The Bombers: The RAF Offensive against Germany, 1939-1945* (Hutchinson, 1983) [hereafter Longmate, *The Bombers*], p.189.
2. MOA fr 569, pp.6-7.
3. Wing Commander A.J. Wright, author's questionnaire, June 2000.

4. BNA, *Daily Mirror*, 8 April 1943.
5. PRO AIR 14/1008, letter from Sir Arthur Harris to Sir Bertine Sutton, 19 February 1943.
6. Ibid, letter from Sir Arthur Harris to Sir Bertine Sutton, Air Ministry, 17 March 1943.
7. Ibid.
8. Ibid.
9. Private papers of Sergeant W.D. Morrison, 1 February 1940.
10. Wells, *Courage and Air Warfare*, p.122.
11. MOA fr 569, pp.3-4.
12. Wells, *Courage and Air Warfare*, p.124.
13. PRO AIR 14/1012, 'Captains of aircraft', letter from Mr. Monk Jones, Air Ministry to AM Sir Arthur Harris, 23 February 1944.
14. PRO AIR 14/1008, minute from Sir Arthur Harris to H.H. Balfour, Under Secretary of State for Air, 20 December 1942.
15. PRO AIR 14/1011, Air Staff Paper, 'The Status of the air gunner in relation to his duties.', July 1944.
16. PRO AIR 14/1008, letter from Sir Arthur Harris to Sir Bertine Sutton, AMP, 17 March 1943.
17. PRO AIR 14/1012, 'Captains of aircraft', letter from Ralph Cochrane, AOC 5 Group to Bomber Command HQ.
18. PRO AIR 14/1008, letter from Sir Bertine Sutton to Sir Arthur Harris, 13 March 1943.
19. Ibid, letter from Sir Arthur Harris to Sir Bertine Sutton, AMP, 17 March 1943.
20. Ibid, letter from Sir Arthur Harris to H.H. Balfour, Under Secretary of State for Air, 'commissioning of aircrews', 9 July 1943.
21. PRO AIR 14/1012, 'Captains of aircraft', letter from 3 Group HQ to Bomber Command HQ, 18 March 1945.
22. Wing Commander A.J. Wright, author's questionnaire, June 2000.
23. Symonds and Williams, *Psychological Disorders*, p.56.
24. Ibid.
25. PRO AIR 10/5034.
26. BNA, Oliver Stewart, *Air Eddies* in *The Tatler*, 1 October 1941.
27. Ibid, 29 July 1942.
28. Jack Currie, *Lancaster Target: The Story of a Crew Who Flew From Wickenby* (Goodall, 1997) [hereafter Currie, *Lancaster Target*], p.92.
29. Wing Commander A.J. Wright, author's questionnaire, June 2000.

30. Middlebrook, *The Berlin Raids*, p.237.
31. Brookes, *Bomber Squadron at War*, p.72.
32. Symonds and Williams, *Psychological Disorders*, p.55.

Chapter 8: Ringmasters: Leadership

1. Nevil Shute, *Pastoral* (William Heinemann, 1944) [hereafter Shute, *Pastoral*], p.147.
2. Hastings, *Bomber Command*, pp.216-217.
3. BNA, *The Tatler*, 18 March 1942.
4. IWM Sound, 2893/03.
5. BNA, *Edinburgh Evening News*, 5 May 1942.
6. Ibid, *Belfast Newsletter*, 3 June 1942.
7. IWM Sound, 2897/03.
8. BNA, *Daily Mirror*, 29 July 1942.
9. Ibid, *Sunday Post*, 21 November 1943.
10. Ibid, *The Scotsman*, 31 July 1942.
11. Wing Commander A.J. Wright, author's questionnaire, June 2000.
12. IWM Sound, 2893/03.
13. PRO AIR 20/2780, minute from Sir Arthur Harris, when DCAS, to Sir Charles Portal, CAS, 26 January 1941.
14. PRO AIR 20/3082, 'Agreed note of a meeting held in the Air Council Room at 3 p.m. on Thursday 6 January 1944, to consider Training Measures to improve Morale and Discipline'. Present CAS, AMP, AMSO, AMT, VCAS, Sir Harold Howitt plus all Command Cs-in-C, including Harris.
15. Richards, *Hardest Victory*, p.435.
16. Beaton, *Winged Squadrons*, p.18.
17. PRO AIR 10/5034, *Factors Affecting the Man's Ability to Carry the Load* in 'Personal Investigation of Psychological Disorders in Flying Personnel of Bomber Command' by Air Vice Marshal Sir Charles P. Symonds KBE, CB, MD, FRCP and Wing Commander Denis J. Williams DSC, MD, FRCP, August 1942.
18. PRO AIR 20/3082, report by Sir Philip Joubert on Morale and Discipline, 17 September 1943.
19. N. Kinser Stewart, 'Military Cohesion' in *War*, (ed) Lawrence Freedman (Oxford University Press, 1994), p.147.
20. Moran, *Anatomy of Courage*, p.98.
21. Wells, *Courage and Air Warfare*, p.138.

22. Bourke, *An Intimate History of Killing*, p.56.
23. Kellett, *Combat Motivation*, pp.152-154.
24. Miles Tripp, *The Eighth Passenger* (Macmillan, 1969) [hereafter Tripp, *The Eighth Passenger*], p.6.
25. IWM Documents 14890, Wing Commander K.J. Newman MBE. DFC, 'Left, Left, Steady', unpublished.
26. Richards, *Hardest Victory*, p.435.
27. PRO AIR 20/8038, minute from Sir Arthur Harris, when ACAS, to CAS Sir Charles Portal, 5 February 1941.
28. Ibid.
29. Wells, *Courage and Air Warfare*, p.146.

Chapter 9: Bags of Bull: Discipline

1. *Tee Emm*, Volume 1, No. 6, September 1941.
2. PRO AIR 20/4583, notes of a meeting chaired by Sir Charles Portal, CAS, in the Air Council room on 11 August 1942 to discuss discipline in the RAF.
3. PRO AIR 20/3082, 'Discipline in the RAF'.
4. MOA fr 569, pp.3-5.
5. Hastings, *Bomber Command*, p.214.
6. Moran, *Anatomy of Courage*, p.166.
7. Ellis, *Sharp End*, p.191.
8. PRO AIR 20/3082, note by Sir Philip Joubert, Inspector General of the RAF on 'Discipline and Fighting Spirit in the Royal Air Force, 1943.
9. Ibid, Air Council Committee on morale and discipline, memo by AMP on aspects of the report by Sir Philip Joubert dated 16 September 1943 on the subject of VD, 1 February 1944.
10. PRO AIR 10/5034, Symonds and Williams, *Psychological Disorders*, p.57.
11. Stafford-Clark, *Morale and Flying Experience*, p.17.
12. PRO AIR 10/5034, Symonds and Williams, *Psychological Disorders*, p.58.
13. PRO AIR 20/4583, minute from Sir Norman Bottomley, ACAS to Sir Wilfred Freeman, VCAS, 26 July 1942.
14. Ibid.
15. Stafford-Clark, *Morale and Flying Experience*, p.17.
16. Ibid.
17. Ibid.
18. PRO AIR 14/1000, 'Avoidable flying accidents', Air Ministry minute, 27 March 1942.

19. Ibid.
20. Ibid, report on aircrew refresher school, Brighton, December 1942.
21. Ibid.
22. PRO AIR 20/2859, notes by Inspector General Sir Edgar Ludlow-Hewitt of visits to 'Suspendair' disposal centres at Blackpool, Uxbridge and Brighton, all in December 1942.
23. PRO AIR 14/1000, course for aircrew personnel involved in flying accidents, report of Sgt. Stevens, 487 Squadron, sent by HQ 2 Group to HQ Bomber Command, 8 December 1942.
24. Ibid, minute from 91 Group HQ to HQ Bomber Command HQ relating to aircrew refresher school, Brighton, 29 November 1942.
25. PRO AIR 20/3082, extract from draft conclusions of Air Council meeting, 14 September 1943.
26. Ibid, 'Discipline in the RAF'.
27. Ibid.
28. Ibid.
29. Ibid, letter from R.C. Richards, Air Ministry to Bomber Command HQ, 13 August 1943.
30. Ibid, notes for talks to personnel, September 1944.

Chapter 10: Are You Happy in Your Work?: Humour

1. Denis Clark, *Tail End Charlie* (Lutterworth Press, 1946), p.91.
2. Richards, *Hardest Victory*, p.439.
3. Moran, *Anatomy of Courage*, p.144.
4. Freeman, *British Airman*, p.68.
5. Eric Partridge, *A Dictionary of RAF Slang* (Michael Joseph Ltd., 1945) [hereafter Partridge, *Dictionary of RAF Slang*], p.6.
6. T.T. Paterson MA, Phd, RAF (Ret'd), *Morale in War and Work: An Experiment in the Management of Men* (Max Parrish, London 1955), p.62.
7. Partridge, *Dictionary of RAF Slang*, various examples.
8. BNA, 'RAF Have Their Own Slanguage', *Daily Mirror*, 26 January 1940.
9. Ibid, *Lincolnshire Echo*, 19 August 1942.
10. Partridge, *Dictionary of RAF Slang*, p.23.
11. Hamilton, *P/O. Prune*, p.119.
12. Richards, *Hardest Victory*, unpublished comments from Richards' questionnaire.
13. Eric Partridge (ed), *A Dictionary of Forces Slang 1939-1945* (Secker & Warburg, 1948), p.200.

Endnotes 205

Chapter 11: Bus Drivers: The Tour

1. Overy, *Bomber Command*, p.149.
2. PRO AIR 20/2861, memorandum on second operational tours by AMT, 20 November 1944.
3. Symonds and Williams, *Psychological Disorders*, p.38.
4. Moran, *Anatomy of Courage*, p.71.
5. PRO AIR 20/982, minute from Sydney Bufton for DB, Ops to ACAS, 6 February 1943.
6. Ibid, minute from T.M. Williams, 27 September 1944.
7. Stafford-Clark, *Morale and Flying Experience*, pp.19-20.
8. IWM Documents 19939, D.J. Gill.
9. Ibid, Documents 7811, Flight Lieutenant T.W. Fox, RAFVR.
10. Stafford-Clark, *Morale and Flying Experience*, pp.19-20.
11. PRO AIR 20/2860, note on operational tours policy, for attention of Sir Charles Portal, CAS, undated.
12. PRO AIR 8/733, Air Ministry minute, 16 November 1942.
13. Wells, *Courage and Air Warfare*, p.127.
14. PRO AIR 8/733, letter from Garrod, AMT to CAS, 21 December 1942.
15. PRO AIR 20/2859, minute from M.S. Laing to AMT, 13 November 1942.
16. PRO AIR 8/733, letter from Garrod, AMT to CAS, 21 December 1942.
17. PRO AIR 20/2860, letter from CAS Sir Charles Portal to Sir Alfred Garrod, 24 December 1942 and PRO AIR 8/733, letter from Portal to Sir Christopher Courtney AMSO, Air Ministry, 24 December 1942, the same day he replied to Harris.
18. PRO AIR 20/2859, agenda for a meeting on 7 January 1943 concerning length of operational tours, chaired by CAS.
19. Noella Lang, *'The Rest of My Life With 50 Squadron: The Letters and Diaries of Flying Officer P. Rowling* (published privately and held at the R.A.F. Museum, Hendon) [hereafter Lang, *Letters and Diaries of Flying Officer P. Rowling*], 8 October 1942.
20. IWM, letters of G.J. Hull, 16 February 1944.
21. PRO AIR 10/5034, 'Spacing of operations'.
22. PRO AIR 20/982, minute from Sir Norman Bottomley, ACAS, to Sir Charles Portal, CAS, through Sir Wilfred Freeman, VCAS, 7 February 1943.
23. PRO AIR 14/1016, 'Duration of operational tours'.
24. Ibid, letter from Air Ministry regarding length of tours, 8 May 1943.
25. PRO AIR 20/2860, notes of meeting, 7 January 1943.

26. PRO AIR 20/2859, letter from D.G. Simmons, SO to Sir Wilfred Freeman, VCAS, 14 November 1942.
27. Ibid, letter from SO to Sir Wilfred Freeman, VCAS, concerning impending meeting on 7 January, 4 January 1943.
28. PRO AIR 8/739, minute from Sir Arthur Harris to Sir Charles Portal, CAS, 26 January 1943.
29. PRO AIR 20/10727, comments by Air Commodore C.P. Symonds on 'A study of gunners returned from combat', (Office of the Air Surgeon, American Air Force HQ), March 1945.
30. PRO AIR 20/982, most secret memo from Harris, 'Second Tour of Operations: Note by C-in-C Bomber Command'.
31. PRO AIR 2/8039, 'Comments on Air Staff Paper, operational employment of aircrews, note by Sir Arthur Harris', 14 November 1942.
32. PRO AIR 20/982, 'most secret' letter from Harris to CAS Portal, 26 January 1943.
33. Ibid, letter from Sir Edgar Ludlow-Hewitt to Sir Norman Bottomley, ACAS, 27 January 1943.
34. PRO AIR 20/982, memorandum, 14 April 1943.
35. Ibid.
36. PRO AIR 20/2861, letter from Folliott Sandford, Assistant Under Secretary of State, Air Council, to all commands, 'Operational Tours of Aircrews', 17 November 1944.
37. Ibid.
38. PRO AIR 14/1016, duration of operational tours, minute from Roderick Carr, AOC 4 Group to Bomber Command HQ, 18 May 1943.
39. PRO AIR 20/2861, minute from Sir Bertine Sutton, AMP to Sir Robert Saundby, SASO, through Sir Charles Portal, CAS, 11 December 1944.
40. Ibid, minute from Sir Charles Portal, CAS, to Secretary of State for Air, Sir Archibald Sinclair.
41. Ibid.
42. PRO AIR 14/1016, duration of operational tours, letter from Air Ministry to Sir Arthur Harris, May 1943.
43. Ibid, duration of operational tours for Mosquito crews, letter from Sir Robert Saundby, SASO, to H.H. Balfour, Under Secretary of State for Air, 5 March 1944.
44. PRO AIR 20/982.
45. PRO AIR 14/1016, duration of operational tours for 138 and 161 Special Operations Squadrons, letter from Sir Robert Saundby to H.H. Balfour, Under Secretary of State for Air, 30 July 1943.

46. Ibid, duration of operational tours, letter from Sir Arthur Harris to Secretary of State for Air, Sir Archibald Sinclair, 8 March 1944.
47. Ibid.
48. PRO AIR 14/1762, review of policy on length of tours.
49. PRO AIR 14/1016, duration of operational tours, letter from Bomber Command HQ to all groups, reply to query from 5 Group HQ, 17 February 1944.
50. Ibid, duration of operational tours, minute from Bomber Command HQ to PFF 8 Group HQ, 10 September 1943.
51. PRO AIR 20/2861, minute from AHMS to Sir Charles Portal, CAS, 15 March 1945.
52. Ibid, minute from T.M. Williams, ACAS to Sir Wilfred Freeman, VCAS, 8 March 1945.
53. PRO AIR 20/982, extension of operational tours in Bomber Command, minute from Sir Bertine Sutton, AMP, to Secretary of State for Air Sir Archibald Sinclair, via AMT and VCAS, 6 March 1945.
54. Ibid, letter from Sir Robert Saundby, SASO, writing for Harris to H.H. Balfour, Under Secretary of State for Air, 1 February 1945.
55. PRO AIR 20/2861, minutes from and to AHMS and AMP, 14 February 1945.
56. Ibid, letter from Sir Arthur Harris to Sir Bertine Sutton, AMP, 12 March 1945.
57. Ibid.
58. Ibid, minute from T.M. Williams, ACAS (Ops) to Secretary of State for Air Sir Archibald Sinclair.
59. PRO AIR 2/8039, minute from Sir Archibald Sinclair to Sir Bertine Sutton, AMP, 12 June 1944.
60. Ibid.
61. IWM Documents 20698, Flying Officer R.J. Fairhead.
62. Ibid, letters of G.J. Hull, 16 February 1944.
63. Ibid, 94/37/1, diary of J. Bormann, 10 May 1944.
64. Ibid, 24 June 1944.
65. Ibid, Documents 7811, Flight Lieutenant T.W. Fox, RAFVR.
66. Ibid, Documents 12886, Pilot Officer J.R. Byrne.
67. Ibid.
68. Ibid.
69. MOA fr 569, observer's comments, 25 June 1941, pp.9-10.
70. IWM Documents 7811, Flight Lieutenant T.W. Fox, RAFVR.

Chapter 12: There's No Future in it: Combat

1. Cheshire, *Bomber Pilot*, p.28.
2. IWM 94/37/1, diary of J. Bormann, 24 February 1944.
3. *Winged Words: Our Airmen Speak for Themselves* (Wm. Heinemann, 1941), p.128.
4. PRO AIR 20/981, memorandum from ACAS to VCAS Sir Douglas Evill, 13 February 1944.
5. PRO AIR 14/2380, personal experience reports, minute from a group captain at 3 Group HQ to Bomber Command HQ, 11 November 1941.
6. WO 208/3319, Reginald Lewis, evasion and escape.
7. PRO AIR 50/182/50, 15 Squadron combat report.
8. AIR 14/2380, aircrew report on personal experiences.
9. Ibid, report on statement made by Sergeant W. McLean, only survivor of a Stirling of 7 Squadron, Oakington, 20 OTU, 6 December 1942.
10. Ibid, experience of P/O. Freberg, navigator, 7 Squadron, Oakington, Stirling lost on 10 September 1942.
11. PRO AIR 50/178/50, combat report, 23/24 October 1942.
12. PRO AIR 50/213/50, combat report, 29/30 May 1943.
13. PRO AIR 50/191/50, combat report, 11/12 June 1943.
14. PRO AIR 50/180/50, combat report, 25/26 June 1943.
15. PRO AIR 27/538/36, No. 57 Squadron Operations Record Book, July 1943.
16. PRO AIR 27/970/38, No. 141 Squadron Operations Record Book, July 1943.
17. PRO AIR 27/578/22, No. 61 Squadron Operations Record Book, November 1943.
18. PRO AIR 27/815/24, No. 103 Squadron Operations Record Book, December 1943.
19. PRO AIR 50/200/140, combat report, 4 September 1943.
20. PRO AIR 50/191/199, combat report, 30/31 March 1944.
21. Ibid.
22. PRO AIR 50/191/206, combat report, 30/31 March 1944.
23. PRO AIR 27/579/5, No. 61 Squadron Operations Record Book, March 1944.
24. PRO AIR 27/1846/5, No. 427 (RCAF) Squadron Operations Record Book, March 1944.
25. BNA, *Bradford Observer*, 1 April 1944.
26. Middlebrook, *Berlin Raids*, p.223.
27. IWM Documents 14890, Wing Commander K.J. Newman MBE, DFC, 'Left, Left, Steady', unpublished.

28. William Anderson, *Pathfinders* (Jarrold's, 1946), p.43.
29. Currie, *Lancaster Target*, p.43.
30. Ibid.
31. PRO AIR 14/2076, 'A Note on recent enemy pyrotechnic activity over Germany', report 53 by RAF Operational Research Section, 25 September 1942.
32. PRO AIR 14/1886, letter from RAF Operational Research Section to 4 Group HQ, 30 December 1943.
33. Ibid.
34. Longmate, *Bombers*, p.184.
35. IWM Documents 20698, Flying Officer R.J. Fairhead.
36. Wells, *Courage and Air Warfare*, p.131.
37. D.C.T. Bennett, *Pathfinder* (Sphere, 1972) [hereafter Bennett, *Pathfinder*], p.211.
38. PRO AIR 14/1803, 'Casualties among air crew personnel directly due to enemy action on night operations', secret, 17 February 1943.
39. Ibid, relation between aircraft wastage and crew wastage, letter from Operational Research Section to AMP, 7 July 1943.
40. PRO AIR 14/3230, 'The effect of experience on operational efficiency', 2 May 1944.
41. Lang, *The Rest of My Life With 50 Squadron*, p.88.
42. George 'Johnny' Johnson, conversation with the author, 11 October 2011.
43. Wing Commander A.J. Wright, author's questionnaire, June 2000.
44. Symonds and Williams, *Psychological Disorders*, p.50.
45. IWM 85/6/1, diary of Bernard Dye, 7 May 1944.
46. Charlwood, *No Moon Tonight*, p.99.
47. IWM 85/6/1, diary of Bernard Dye, 24 March 1944.
48. Middlebrook, *Bomber Command War Diaries*, p.449.
49. BNA, *Midlothian Advertiser*, 3 September 1943.
50. Ibid, *Ballymena Weekly Telegraph*, 25 February 1944.
51. Ibid, *Daily News (London)*, 19 July 1944.
52. PRO AIR 27/1164/40, No. 195 Squadron Operations Record Book, February 1945.

Chapter 13: Newton Got Him: Occupational Hazards

1. Stafford-Clark, *Morale and Flying Experience*, p.13.
2. Hamilton, *P/O. Prune*, the final verse of 'Ten Little Bomber Boys' p.61.

3. James, *Paladins*, p.207.
4. Wells, *Courage and Air Warfare*, p.29.
5. PRO AIR 81/13440, accident report.
6. PRO AIR 81/21756, accident report.
7. IWM Documents 14890, Wing Commander K.J. Newman MBE, DFC, 'Left, Left, Steady', unpublished.
8. IWM Documents 2030, Flight Lieutenant D. Steiner.
9. IWM Documents 12886, Pilot Officer J.R. Byrne, accident at OTU, 10 June 1944.
10. Ibid, accident at OTU, 15 July 1944.
11. Currie, *Lancaster Target*, pp.89-90.
12. IWM Documents 14890, Wing Commander K.J. Newman MBE, DFC, 'Left, Left, Steady', unpublished.
13. PRO AIR 6/72, Air Council meeting, 9 September 1941.
14. Ibid, and PRO AIR 6/74, 3 November 1942.
15. PRO AIR 14/2160, memorandum from Sir Arthur Harris to all groups, 10 March 1942.
16. Ibid.
17. Ibid.
18. Ibid, letter from 5 Group HQ to all 5 Group pilots.
19. Ibid.
20. PRO AIR 81/3565, Blenheim, 30 September 1940.
21. PRO AIR 27/2152/7, No. 630 Squadron Operations Record Book, February 1944.
22. Bowman, Martin W., *RAF Bomber Stories: Dramatic First-Hand Accounts of British and Commonwealth Airmen in World War 2* (Patrick Stevens Ltd.) [hereafter Bowman, *RAF Bomber Stories*], pp.35-36.
23. PRO AIR 81/5114, accident report.
24. PRO AIR 81/11499, accident report.
25. Ibid.
26. PRO AIR 81/12427, accident report.
27. PRO AIR 81/9778, accident report.
28. PRO AIR 81/3195, accident report.
29. PRO AIR 14/125, 'Flying restrictions at OTUs', letter from F. MacNeece Foster, AOC 6 Group to Bomber Command HQ, 21 June 1941.
30. Ibid.
31. PRO AIR 14/341, collision of aircraft with balloon barrage cables.

32. Ibid, letter from 3 Group to Bomber Command HQ, 26 January 1941.
33. Ibid.
34. PRO AIR 20/2780, letter from VCAS Freeman to Peirse, 4 September 1941.
35. Alastair Revie, *The Lost Command* (Corgi, 1972), pp.93-94.
36. James, *Paladins*, p.208.
37. PRO AIR 81/12554, accident report.
38. PRO AIR 27/815/24, No. 103 Squadron Operations Record Book, December 1943.
39. IWM Documents 19939, D.J. Gill.
40. PRO AIR 81/14229, accident report.
41. PRO AIR 27/815/24, No. 103 Squadron Operations Record Book, December 1943.
42. Hastings, *Bomber Command*, p.151.
43. Middlebrook, *Bomber Command War Diaries*, p.273.
44. Currie, *Lancaster Target*, p.102.
45. Middlebrook, *The Berlin Raids*, p.203.
46. Bowman, *RAF Bomber Stories*, p.139.
47. Ibid, p.140.
48. Tripp, *The Eighth Passenger*, pp.23-24.
49. Mike Garbett and Brian Goulding, *The Lancaster at War* (PRC Publishing Ltd., 1991) [hereafter Garbett and Goulding, *The Lancaster at War*], p.271.
50. Tripp, *The Eighth Passenger*, p.34.
51. Bowman, *RAF Bomber Stories*, p.95.
52. PRO AIR 14/1876, various correspondence, including Harris to Portal.
53. Ibid.
54. IWM 94/37/1, log book of Flight Lieutenant J.S.A. Marshall, 6 June 1944.
55. Tripp, *The Eighth Passenger*, p.13.
56. Letters of Sergeant Morrison, 5 November 1940.
57. Gibson, *Enemy Coast Ahead*, p.115.
58. Tripp, *The Eighth Passenger*, pp.27-28.
59. Bennett, *Pathfinder*, p.215.
60. AIR 20/4241, minute from Sir Richard Peck to ACAS, 13 January 1944.
61. Ibid, letter from Radcliffe, Ministry of Information, to Sir Richard Peck, Air Ministry, 25 January 1944.
62. Ibid.
63. Ibid, minute pertaining to Goebbels article in *Völkischer Beobachter*, May 1944.

64. Ibid, German threats of reprisals against Allied aircrews.
65. IWM Documents 12886, P/O. J.R. Byrne.
66. PRO AIR 20/4241, minute from ACAS to Under Secretary of State, 6 June 1944.
67. Richards, *Hardest Victory*, p.413.
68. Symonds and Williams, *Psychological Disorders*, p.56.
69. Ibid.
70. BNA, 'Air Eddies by Oliver Stewart', *The Tatler*, 29 July 1942.
71. Edward Smithies, *War in the Air: The Men and Women Who Built, Serviced and Flew Warplanes Remember the Second World War* (Penguin Books, 1992) [hereafter Smithies, *War in the Air*], p.48.
72. Middlebrook, *The Battle of Hamburg*, pp.42-43.
73. Smithies, *War in the Air*, p.66.
74. IWM, letters of G.J. Hull, 6 January 1944.
75. PRO AIR 20/2780, minute from Sir Wilfred Freeman, VCAS to Portal, CAS, 10 May 1942.
76. Ibid, letter from Sir Arthur Harris to Freeman, 1 June 1942.
77. Ibid, letter from Freeman to Harris, 3 June 1942, reply to Harris's letter of 1 June 1942.
78. Ibid, letter from Harris to Freeman, VCAS, 8 October 1942.
79. Ibid.
80. IWM Documents 7811, Flight Lieutenant T.W. Fox, RAFVR.
81. PRO AIR 20/2780, letter from Harris to Freeman, 10 April 1942.
82. Ibid, letter from Freeman to Harris, 12 April 1942.
83. PRO AIR 27/2044/16, No. 571 Squadron Operations Record Book, November 1944.
84. IWM Documents 1489, Wing Commander K.J. Newman MBE, DFC, 'Left, Left, Steady', unpublished.
85. Middlebrook, *Battle of Hamburg*, pp.309-311.
86. IWM 94/37/1, log book of Flight Lieutenant J.S.A. Marshall, 31 May 1944.
87. George 'Johnny' Johnson, conversation with the author, 11 October 2011.
88. IWM 94/37/1, log book of Flight Lieutenant J.S.A. Marshall, 31 May 1944.
89. PRO AIR 27/204/5, No. 15 Squadron Operations Record Book, March 1944.
90. Garbett and Goulding, *The Lancaster at War*, p.107.
91. IWM Documents 20698, F/O. Fairhead.
92. PRO AIR 27/815/24, No. 103 Squadron Operations Record Book, December 1943.

93. PRO AIR 27/2152/5, No. 630 Squadron Operations Record Book, January 1944.
94. Overy, *Bomber Command*, p.164.
95. Tripp, *The Eighth Passenger*, p.41.
96. Symonds and Williams, *Psychological Disorders*, p.45.
97. PRO AIR 27/203/61, No. 15 Squadron Operations Record Book, July 1943.
98. Symonds and Williams, *Psychological Disorders*, p.45.
99. PRO AIR 14/1452, Meteorology in Bomber Command during the European War 1939-1945.
100. PRO AIR 10/5034, reliability of aircraft.
101. Hamilton, *P/O. Prune*, p.68.
102. IWM Documents 1045, R.J. Fayers, 1 August 1942.
103. Flying Officer Pierre Richard, audiotape, 1990.
104. Ellis, *Sharp End*, p.105.
105. Fussell, *Wartime*, p.50.
106. Stafford-Clark, *Morale and Flying Experience*, p.16.
107. Ibid.
108. IWM Documents 12812, J. Walsh.
109. Ellis, *Sharp End*, p.106.
110. Tripp, *The Eighth Passenger*, p.30.

Chapter 14: Bang On!: Bombing Results

1. Kellett, *Combat Motivation*, p.172.
2. Hamilton, *P/O. Prune*, p.67.
3. PRO AIR 27/815/24, No. 103 Squadron Operations Record Book, December 1943.
4. PRO AIR 10/5034, bombing results.
5. MOA fr 569, 25 June 1941, pp.9-10.
6. Symonds and Williams, *Psychological Disorders*, p.50.
7. Ibid.
8. Moran, *Anatomy of Courage*, p.71.
9. PRO AIR 20/2780, letter from Charles Portal, then C-in-C Bomber Command to Sir Cyril Newall, then CAS, 8 May 1940.
10. Ibid, letter from Portal to Sir Richard Peirse, 17 May 1940.
11. Ibid, letter from Portal as C-in-C Bomber Command to Peirse, 15 May 1940.
12. Garnett, *War in the Air*, p.67.
13. Letters of Sergeant Morrison, 18 December 1940.

14. PRO AIR 20/2780, reply from Peirse to Winston Churchill, 24 December 1940.
15. PRO AIR 14/92, reply letter from Peirse as C-in-C BC to Ludlow-Hewitt, 20 March 1941.
16. Ibid, letter from Peirse to Robb, AOC 2 Group.
17. Ibid, letter from AOC 3 Group to Bomber Command HQ, 'Information regarding operations', 26 March 1941.
18. PRO AIR 20/3085, minute from A.B. Elwood, DDB Ops to DB Ops, 13 November 1941.
19. PRO AIR 14/92, letter from Sir Edgar Ludlow-Hewitt, RAF Inspector General, to Sir Richard Peirse, C-in-C Bomber Command, 18 March 1941.
20. Ibid.
21. Ibid, memorandum by Jack Baldwin, AOC 3 Group.
22. PRO AIR 20/3085, minute from A.B. Elwood, DDB Ops to DB Ops, 13 November 1941.
23. Constance Babbington Smith, quoted in Gavin Lyall, *The War in the Air 1939-1945: An Anthology of Personal Experience* (Pimlico 1994) [hereafter Lyall, *War in the Air*], p.99.
24. Terraine, *The Right of the Line*, p.272.
25. Lyall, *War in the Air*, p.99.
26. John Keegan, *The Second World War* (Pimlico, 1997), p.351.
27. Calder, *People's War*, p.230.
28. Lang, Letters and Diaries of F/O. P. Rowling.
29. Ibid.
30. PRO AIR 14/1243, letter from C.G. Caines. Air Ministry to C-in-C Bomber Command (Peirse), 17 September 1941.
31. BNA, *Daily Mirror*, 3 August 1940.
32. PRO AIR 20/2780, letter from Portal to Peirse, 23 November 1941.
33. Ibid, letter from Sir Wilfred Freeman, Vice Chief of Air Staff to Sir Arthur Harris, C-in-C Bomber Command, 1 April 1942.
34. Ibid, minute by D.A. Parry, Parliamentary Secretary to VCAS, regarding exaggerated reports of bombing success, 1 April 1942.
35. Ibid, letter from Freeman to Harris, 6 April 1942.
36. PRO AIR 20/3082, memorandum from Air Ministry to all commands, 22 March 1944.
37. Beaton, *Winged Squadrons*, p.45.
38. MOA fr 734, p.4.
39. Sir Arthur Harris, *Bomber Offensive: The Memoirs of One of the Greatest – and Most Controversial – Commanders of World War II* (Greenhill, 1998), pp.107-108.

40. PRO AIR 20/2780, letter from Harris to Freeman, VCAS, 29 April 1942.
41. Middlebrook, *Bomber Command War Diaries*, p.271.
42. Ibid, p.300.
43. PRO AIR 14/1243, memorandum on night photographs.
44. PRO AIR 27/2148/10, No. 630 Squadron Operations Record Book, March 1944.
45. PRO AIR 14/1243, minute from H.V. Satterley, SASO 5 Group, 19 July 1942.
46. Ibid, minute from unknown wing commander to Deputy SASO, 4 May 1942.
47. PRO AIR 14/3544, letter from Jack Baldwin, AOC HQ 3 Group to Harris, 16 May 1942.
48. Ibid, letter from Harris in reply to Baldwin, 3 June 1942.
49. Ibid, minute headed 'Bomber Command', 9 June 1942.
50. Ibid, memo 'The Night Bomber Problem', 9 June 1942.
51. PRO AIR 14/2723, aircrew qualifications and employment policy.
52. Ibid.
53. Middlebrook, *Bomber Command War Diaries*, p.301.
54. PRO AIR 20/3085, minute from Baker DB Ops to VCAS regarding Nichols, 14 September 1942.
55. Middlebrook, *Bomber Command War Diaries*, p.363.
56. Middlebrook, *Battle of Hamburg*, p.42.
57. PRO AIR 27/687, No. 83 Squadron Operations Record Book, 28 July 1943.
58. Middlebrook, *Battle of Hamburg*, p.251.
59. BNA, *Daily Mirror*, 18 August 1943.
60. Ibid, *Daily Mirror*, 25 May 1943.
61. Ibid, *Lincolnshire Echo*, 23 November 1943.
62. Ibid, 3 December 1943.
63. Ibid, *Daily Mirror*, 29 January 1944.
64. Middlebrook, *Bomber Command War Diaries*, p.448.
65. Ibid, p.487.
66. Ibid, p.449.
67. Middlebrook, *Berlin Raids*, p.315.
68. PRO AIR 27/1164/40, No. 195 Squadron Operations Record Book, February 1945.
69. Ibid.

Chapter 15: Sex-Appeal Bombing: Ethics

1. Middlebrook, *Battle of Hamburg*, p.349.
2. Richard Overy, *Why the Allies Won* (Pimlico, 1996), p.295.

3. R.A.C. Parker, *The Second World War: A Short History* (Oxford University Press, 1997), p.163.
4. *Tee Emm*, Volume 1, No. 1, April 1941.
5. Stephen Garrett, *Ethics and Air Power in World War 2: The British Bombing of German Cities* (St. Martins, 1997), pp.77-79.
6. MOA fr 668, p.1, 22 April 1941.
7. Ibid.
8. Ibid.
9. Ibid.
10. Norman Longmate, *How We Lived Then* (Arrow, 1971), p.383.
11. MOA fr 668, p.1, 22 April 1941.
12. BNA, Live Letters [readers' letters] *Daily Mirror*, 9 February 1944.
13. J.M. Spaight, *Bombing Vindicated* (Robert Maclehose & Co., 1944), p.105.
14. 'A Wing Commander', *Bomber's Battle: Bomber Command's Three Years of War* (Riverside Press, 1943), p.207.
15. Beaton, *Winged Squadrons*, p.32.
16. IWM, letters of George Hull, 16 February 1944.
17. Ibid, 85/6/1, diary of Bernard Dye.
18. Ibid, Documents 12886, Pilot Officer J.R. Byrne.
19. Ibid, 80/46/1, letters of F.H.B. Lackman, October 1942.
20. Bowyer, *Bomber Barons*, p.48.
21. IWM, letters of George Hull, 26 February 1944.
22. Robert Raymond, *A Yank in Bomber Command* (David and Charles, 1977), p.103.
23. Charlwood, *No Moon Tonight*, p.171.
24. Braddon, *Cheshire VC*, p.115.
25. MOA fr 569, pp.9-10.
26. Bourke, *An Intimate History of Killing*, p.6.
27. RAF Museum, Hendon, facsimile of the log book of Guy Gibson, 17 January 1943.
28. Letters of Sergeant Morrison, 18 December 1940.
29. MOA fr 569, 25 June 1941.
30. Flying Officer Pierre Richard, audiotape, 1990.

Chapter 16: Teased Out: Flying Stress

1. Stafford-Clark, *Morale and Flying Experience*, p.22.
2. PRO AIR 2/4935, Appendix XXXIX 'Flying Stress and Psychoneuroses' Air Ministry confidential letter, 10 May 1940.

3. PRO AIR 20/2041, report on flying stress, letter from Iredell to senior medical officer 24 Group, 18 November 1940.
4. D.D. Reid, 'Historical Background to Wartime Research in Psychology in the RAF', p.1.
5. PRO AIR 14/2829, memorandum 'Medical Welfare of Aircrews'.
6. PRO AIR 10/5034, 'Personal Investigation of Psychological Disorders in Flying Personnel of Bomber Command' by Air Vice Marshal Sir Charles P. Symonds and Wing Commander Denis J. Williams, August 1942.
7. BNA, *Portsmouth Evening News*, 19 November 1941.
8. PRO AIR 6/73, Air Council minutes of meetings 10 March 1942 and 3 November 1942.
9. Air Vice Marshal Sir Charles Symonds and Wing Commander Denis J. Williams, 'Clinical and Statistical Study of Neurosis Precipitated by Flying Duties' in *Aircrew Stress in Wartime Operations: Papers of the Flying Personnel Research Committee of the Ministry of Defence* (eds) Dearnaly and Warr (Academic Press, 1979), p.17.
10. Symonds and Williams, *Psychological Disorders*, p.60.
11. Shute, *Pastoral*, p.134.
12. Hastings, *Bomber Command*, pp.221-222.
13. PRO AIR 20/10727, letter from Sir H.E. Whittingham to Prof. F.C. Bartlett, Psychological Lab, Cambridge, 20 March 1944. Whittingham is quoting Symonds report on USAAF study of 14 March 1944.
14. PRO AIR 10/5034, 'Personal Investigation of Psychological Disorders in Flying Personnel of Bomber Command' by Air Vice Marshal Sir Charles P. Symonds and Wing Commander Denis J. Williams, August 1942.
15. Ibid.
16. Symonds and Williams, *Psychological Disorders*, p.43.
17. Ibid, p.9.
18. Moran, *Anatomy of Courage*, p.160.
19. Symonds and Williams, *Psychological Disorders*, p.43.
20. Ibid.
21. Ibid.
22. PRO AIR 10/5034.
23. Ibid.
24. PRO AIR 14/2821, 'Notes for Medical Officers on the Psychological Care of Flying Personnel', official pamphlet, May 1939.
25. PRO AIR 2/4935, minute from DGPS to AMP, 1 March 1944.

26. Ibid, 'Notes for the guidance of Medical Officers on the differentiation between personnel unfit for flying for medical and temperamental reasons'.
27. Ibid.
28. Stafford-Clark, *Morale and Flying Experience*, p.10.
29. Ibid, p.13.
30. Ibid, p.14.
31. Ibid.
32. Ibid, p.30.
33. Ibid, p.27.
34. Ibid, p.29.
35. Ibid, p.23.
36. PRO AIR 20/10727, Symonds, then a group captain consultant in neurology, comments on Stafford-Clark.

Chapter 17: Frozen on the Stick: Waverers

1. Allan D. English, 'A Predisposition to Cowardice?' Aviation Psychology and the Genesis of 'Lack of Moral Fibre' in *Motivating Soldiers: Morale or Mutiny*, (ed) Peter Karsten (Garland, 1998) [hereafter English, 'A Predisposition to Cowardice?'], pp.229-249.
2. PRO AIR 2/8591, letter from Sir Arthur Harris as AOC 5 Group to Under Secretary of State for Air, 10 October 1940.
3. PRO AIR 2/4935, 'Comments on the Memorandum on the disposal of members of aircrews who forfeit the confidence of their Commanding Officers by the Consultants in Neuro-psychology', 1 June 1943.
4. PRO AIR 2/8591, minute sheet meeting about disposal of 'W' cases, 17 April 1941.
5. PRO AIR 2/4935, 'Comments on the Memorandum on the disposal of members of aircrews who forfeit the confidence of their Commanding Officers by the Consultants in Neuro-psychology', 1 June 1943.
6. D.D. Reid, 'Historical Background to Wartime Research in Psychology in the RAF', p.4.
7. PRO AIR 2/4935, notes on the 'W' [Waverers] Memorandum, unsigned and undated.
8. Ibid, 'Comments on the Memorandum on the disposal of members of aircrews who forfeit the confidence of their Commanding Officers by the Consultants in Neuro-psychology', 1 June 1943.
9. PRO AIR 2/8591, minute August 1940, referring to 'W' Memo.

Endnotes 219

10. Ibid, minutes of conference on 'W' 16 July 1940.
11. Ibid, minute from W.A. Constantine, group captain commanding Elsham Wolds to 1 Group HQ, 7 June 1942.
12. Ibid, minute from Group Captain D.L. Thompson, AOC Snaith, to 1 Group HQ, 31 July 1942.
13. Ibid, minutes of a meeting on 23 July 1941. AMP in chair, Symonds, W/Cmdr. Lawson of DPS and Mr. Monk Jones of DPS all present. Subject: waverers doing a second operational tour.
14. PRO AIR 18/19.
15. Ibid.
16. PRO AIR 18/10.
17. PRO AIR 18/21.
18. PRO AIR 18/23.
19. PRO AIR 2/4935, notes on the preliminary meeting, 22 February 1943.
20. Ibid, appendix to above by C.P. Symonds, Air Commodore Consultant in Neuro-Psychology, 16 February 1943.
21. Ibid, 'Comments on the Memorandum on the disposal of members of aircrews who forfeit the confidence of their Commanding Officers by the Consultants in Neuro-psychology', 1 June 1943.
22. BNA, *Daily Mirror,* 8 April 1943.
23. PRO AIR 2/4935, minute sheet to AMP from H.E. Whittingham, DGMS, 21 February 1944.
24. Ibid, minute from DGPS to AMP, 1 March 1944.
25. Ibid, letter from Sir Arthur Harris to Under Secretary of State for Air, 28 December 1942.
26. Ibid.
27. PRO AIR 2/8591, letter from AVM Oxland, AOC 1 Group, 18 June 1942.
28. Ibid, letter from AVM Oxland to Under Secretary of State for Air H.H. Balfour, 20 May 1942.
29. PRO AIR 2/4935, 'Comments on the Memorandum on the disposal of members of aircrews who forfeit the confidence of their Commanding Officers by the Consultants in Neuro-psychology', 1 June 1943.
30. PRO AIR 2/8592, letter from Bomber Command HQ to Under Secretary of State for Air H.H. Balfour, 20 December 1943.
31. Ibid, minute from W/Cmdr. Lawson to DGPS, January 1944.
32. Ibid, minute from unknown group captain, 5 January 1944.
33. PRO AIR 2/4935, further minute from W/Cmdr. Lawson, 24 February 1944.

34. PRO AIR 19/632, notes of a meeting to consider 'W' cases, 20 October 1944. Secretary of State for Air Archibald Sinclair, Symonds and W/Cmdr. Lawson present.
35. PRO AIR 2/8592, meeting on "W" issue, October 1944.
36. IWM Documents 14890, Wing Commander K.J. Newman MBE, DFC, 'Left, Left, Steady', unpublished.
37. Ibid, Documents 20698, Flying Officer R.J. Fairhead.
38. Ibid, Documents 2030, Flight Lieutenant D. Steiner.
39. English, 'A Predisposition to Cowardice?', pp.240-242.
40. Richards, *Hardest Victory*, p.446.
41. Wells, *Courage and Air Warfare*, p.205.

Chapter 18: Life With the Lions: Nine Months in the Life of 427 (RCAF) Squadron

1. RAF Museum, Hendon, MF 10086/13, Group Captain Dudley Burnside, pilot's flying log book, 1937-1941.
2. PRO AIR 27/1845/5-6, No. 427 (RCAF) Squadron Operations Record Book, January 1943.
3. PRO AIR 27/1845/7-8, No. 427 (RCAF) Squadron Operations Record Book, February 1943.
4. Ibid.
5. Ibid.
6. PRO AIR 27/1845/9-10, No. 427 (RCAF) Squadron Operations Record Book, March 1943.
7. BNA, *Reading Standard*, 16 April 1943.
8. PRO AIR 27/1845/9-10, No. 427 (RCAF) Squadron Operations Record Book, March 1943.
9. PRO AIR 27/1845/11-12, No. 427 (RCAF) Squadron Operations Record Book, April 1943.
10. Ibid.
11. Ibid.
12. Ibid.
13. PRO AIR 27/1845/13-14, No. 427 (RCAF) Squadron Operations Record Book, May 1943.
14. Ibid.
15. Ibid.
16. Ibid.

17. Ibid.
18. PRO AIR 27/1845/15-16, No. 427 (RCAF) Squadron Operations Record Book, June 1943.
19. Ibid.
20. Ibid.
21. Ibid.
22. Ibid.
23. Ibid.
24. PRO AIR 27/1845/17-18, No. 427 (RCAF) Squadron Operations Record Book, July 1943.
25. Ibid.
26. Ibid.
27. Ibid.
28. Ibid.
29. Ibid.
30. Ibid.
31. Ibid.
32. Ibid.
33. Ibid.
34. Ibid.
35. Ibid.
36. Ibid.
37. PRO AIR 27/1845/19-20, No. 427 (RCAF) Squadron Operations Record Book, August 1943.
38. Ibid.
39. Ibid.
40. Ibid.
41. Ibid.
42. Ibid.
43. Ibid.
44. Ibid.
45. Ibid.
46. Ibid.
47. Ibid.
48. Ibid.
49. Ibid.
50. Ibid.

51. PRO AIR 27/1845/21-22, No. 427 (RCAF) Squadron Operations Record Book, September 1943.
52. PRO AIR 27/1845/19-20, No. 427 (RCAF) Squadron Operations Record Book, August 1943.

Conclusion: A Matter of Life and Death

1. Flying Officer Pierre Richard, audiotape, 1990.
2. Ibid.
3. Wing Commander A.J. Wright, authors questionnaire, June 2000.
4. George 'Johnny' Johnson, conversation with author, 11 October 2011.
5. Wing Commander A.J. Wright, authors questionnaire, June 2000.

Bibliography

Unpublished Sources

BNA = British Newspaper Archive
IWM = Imperial War Museum
PRO = Public Records Office/The National Archive

Imperial War Museum

IWM 94/37/1, (Now Documents 2708), J. Bormann, private papers.
IWM Documents 12886, Pilot Officer J.R. Byrne, private papers.
IWM 85/6/1, (Now Documents 3512), Bernard Dye, private papers.
IWM Documents 20698, Flying Officer R.J. Fairhead, private papers.
IWM Documents 1045, Flying Officer R.J. Fayers, private papers.
IWM Documents 7811, Flight Lieutenant T.W. Fox, RAFVR, private papers.
IWM Documents 19939, D.J. Gill, private papers.
IWM Con Shelf, (Now Documents 141), G.J. Hull, private papers.
IWM 80/46/1, letters of F.H.B. Lackman, private papers.
IWM Now Documents 2826, Flight Lieutenant J.S.A. Marshall, private papers.
IWM Documents 14890, Wing Commander K.J. Newman MBE, DFC, private papers.
IWM 74/93/1 (Now Documents 431), Pilot Officer M.A. Scott, private papers.
IWM Documents 2030, Flight Lieutenant D. Steiner, private papers.
IWM Documents 12812, J. Walsh, private papers.

Imperial War Museum Sound Archives

IWM Sound, 21/85/6/A, Flying Officer Horner.
IWM Sound 2892/02, interview with William Reid VC for the Thames Television series *The World at War*, 1972.
IWM/2893/03 Sound.
IWM Sound 2897/03, interview with Hamish Mahaddie for the Thames Television series *The World at War*, 1972.
IWM Sound 13024/2, interview with Harold Nash, 1992.

The National Archives

Note: The original research for my dissertation was conducted at the Public Records Office, as it then was so named. I used the initialism PRO for reference in the bibliography and in the endnotes. For my recent research I have continued using this initialism for all National Archives Documents referenced in this bibliography and endnotes.

PRO AIR 2/4935: Disposal Procedure of members of aircrews who forfeit confidence of their commanding officers.
PRO AIR 2/6345: Medical (Code B48) and Royal Air Force Personnel (Code B68) Proposal for selection of candidates for aircrew by combined psychiatric and psychological method.
PRO AIR 2/8039: Aircrews: length of operational tours.
PRO AIR 2/8591: Aircrew who refuse or are unfit to fly: disposal policy.
PRO AIR 2/8592: Aircrew who refuse or are unfit to fly: disposal policy.

PRO AIR 6/70: Air Council: conclusions to 1st-11th meetings, July-December 1940.
PRO AIR 6/72: Air Council: conclusions to 13th-24th meetings, July-December 1941.
PRO AIR 6/73: Air Board and Air Ministry, Air Council: minutes and memoranda. Air Council minutes meetings 1-11.
PRO AIR 6/74: Air Council: conclusions to meetings, 1 July- 31 December 1941.

PRO AIR 8/610: Aircrew training.
PRO AIR 8/730: Discipline at RAF Stations: report by Inspector General, December 1942-October 1943: discipline at RAF Stations: reports by Inspector General.
PRO AIR 8/733: 'Chances of survival of aircrews': Safeguarding of information.
PRO AIR 8/739: RAF Aircrew: length of operational tour.

PRO AIR 10/5034: Psychological disorders in flying personnel of the Royal Air Force investigated during the War 1939-1945.

PRO AIR 14/30: Vocational selection of pilots.
PRO AIR 14/49: Emergency parachute jumps.
PRO AIR 14/80: Press censorship: policy.
PRO AIR 14/92: Preparation of crews for operations.
PRO AIR 14/125: Balloon barrages: measures to counter danger to friendly aircraft.
PRO AIR 14/341: Collisions of aircraft with balloon barrage cables: reports on damage.
PRO AIR 14/1000: Course for aircrew personnel involved in flying accidents.
PRO AIR 14/1008: Commissioning of aircrew: policy.

Bibliography 225

PRO AIR 14/1011: Composition of aircrews: Duties and rates of pay.
PRO AIR 14/1012: Captains of aircraft: commissioning and selection.
PRO AIR 14/1016: Duration of operational tours.
PRO AIR 14/1243: Interrogation of bomber crews.
PRO AIR 14/1451: Press and Publicity: policy.
PRO AIR 14/1452: Meteorology in Bomber Command 1939-1945.
PRO AIR 14/1762: Effect of experience of aircrews on success in target information.
PRO AIR 14/1803: Research into bomber losses.
PRO AIR 14/1876: Investigations into the Risk of Destruction of Aircraft by Bombs from Friendly Aircraft: Investigation.
PRO AIR 14/1886: Investigations into causes of abortive sorties.
PRO AIR 14/2076: Enemy Defences: phenomena.
PRO AIR 14/2160: Flying Accidents: correspondence about causes and preventive measures.
PRO AIR 14/2380: Aircrew reports on personal experiences.
PRO AIR 14/2723: Aircrew qualifications and employment policy.
PRO AIR 14/2821: Medical History of the War: collection of material.
PRO AIR 14/2829: Monthly summary of medical events.
PRO AIR 14/2830: Monthly summary of medical events.
PRO AIR 14/2831: Monthly summary of medical events.
PRO AIR 14/2833: Hygiene and medical reports.
PRO AIR 14/2929: No. 192 Squadron flight reports.
PRO AIR 14/3230: No. 4 Group: effect of operational experience on aircrew loss rate.
PRO AIR 14/3512: Air Office Commander-in-Chief correspondence: Secretary of State for Air.
PRO AIR 14/3544: Air Office Commander-in-Chief correspondence: Air Officer commanding No. 3 Group.

PRO AIR 18/10: Failure to carry out a warlike operation.
PRO AIR 18/19: Failure to carry out a warlike operation.
PRO AIR 18/21: Failure to carry out a warlike operation.
PRO AIR 18/23: Failure to carry out a warlike operation.

PRO AIR 19/632: LMF (lack of moral fibre) and W (waverers): disposal of members of aircrew who forfeit the confidence of their Commanding officers.

PRO AIR 20/234: Aircrews.
PRO AIR 20/981: Aircraft Crews: Composition.

PRO AIR 20/982: Aircrew: length of operational tours.
PRO AIR 20/1369: Preliminary aircrew training: report.
PRO AIR 20/2041: Bomber OTUs: flying hours and accidents.
PRO AIR 20/2780: Bomber Command: correspondence.
PRO AIR 20/2859: Aircrew: operational tours.
PRO AIR 20/2860: Aircrew: extension of operational tours.
PRO AIR 20/2861: Aircrew: extension of operational tours.
PRO AIR 20/2955: Bomber Command: publicity.
PRO AIR 20/3082: RAF: morale and discipline.
PRO AIR 20/3085: Bomber crews: memoranda by Mr. Robert Nichols.
PRO AIR 20/4106: Empire Air Training Scheme Committee papers.
PRO AIR 20/4241: German threats of reprisals against Allied aircrews.
PRO AIR 20/4583: RAF: discipline and morale.
PRO AIR 20/8038: Operations Miscellaneous.
PRO AIR 20/10727: Flying Stress: DGMS (RAF)'s correspondence.

PRO AIR 27/101: Operations Record Book, No. 7 Squadron.
PRO AIR 27/203: Operations Record Book, No. 15 Squadron.
PRO AIR 27/204: Operations Record Book, No. 15 Squadron.
PRO AIR 27/538: Operations Record Book, No. 57 Squadron.
PRO AIR 27/578: Operations Record Book, No. 61 Squadron.
PRO AIR 27/579: Operations Record Book, No. 61 Squadron.
PRO AIR 27/687: Operations Record Book, No. 83 Squadron.
PRO AIR 27/815: Operations Record Book, No. 103 Squadron.
PRO AIR 27/970: Operations Record Book, No. 141 Squadron.
PRO AIR 27/1164: Operations Record Book, No. 195 Squadron.
PRO AIR 27/1845/5-20 inclusive: Operations Record Book, No. 427 (RCAF) Squadron.
PRO AIR 27/1846: Operations Record Book, No. 427 (RCAF) Squadron.
PRO AIR 27/2044: Operations Record Book, No. 571 Squadron.
PRO AIR 27/2152: Operations Record Book, No. 630 Squadron.

PRO AIR 50/178/50: Combat report, Sergeant Pointer, 7 Squadron, 23 October 1942.
PRO AIR 50/180/50: Combat report, Sergeant Wooward, 10 Squadron, 27 June 1943.
PRO AIR 50/191/50: Combat report, Sergeant Grant, 61 Squadron, 11 June 1943.
PRO AIR 50/191/199: Combat report, Pilot Officer Paul, 61 Squadron, 30 March 1944.

PRO AIR 50/191/206: Combat report, Pilot Officer Freeman, 61 Squadron, 30 March 1944.
PRO AIR 50/200/140: Combat report, Second Lieutenant Wright, 97 (Straits Settlement) Squadron, 3 September 1943.
PRO AIR 50/213/50: Combat report, Flying Officer Andrews, 115 Squadron, 29 May 1943.

Accident reports:
PRO AIR 81/14229.
PRO AIR 81/3195.
PRO AIR 81/3565.
PRO AIR 81/5114.
PRO AIR 81/9778.
PRO AIR 81/11499.
PRO AIR 81/12427.
PRO AIR 81/12554.
PRO AIR 81/13440.
PRO AIR 81/21756.

WO 208/3319: escape of Reginald Lewis.

RAF Museum, Hendon

Group Captain Dudley Burnside, pilot's flying log book, 1937-1941, MF 10086/13.
Group Captain Dudley Burnside, pilot's flying log book, 1941-1954, MF 10086/14.
Guy Gibson, log book facsimile, X00-2371/071.
Noella Lang, *The Rest of My Life with 50 Squadron: Letters and Diaries of F/O P. Rowling,* (Private publication), X001-0463.
Denis Richards, original completed questionnaires from ex-Bomber Command personnel, used in *The Hardest Victory,* (Coronet, 1995), X003-9931.
Tee Emm, Volume 1, Nos. 1-6, April-September 1941, Volume 2, No. 11, February 1943, X001-3777.
Edward Wiggins, diary, X001-3600.

Tom Harrison Mass Observation Archive

File report 443: *Attitude and access to news amongst servicemen.*
File report 462: *Morale.*
File report 568: *Morale in 1941.*

File report 569: *Morale in the RAF.*
File report 653: *Use of leisure in the RAF.*
File report 668: *Untitled.*
File report 734: *Morale in the ranks of the RAF.*
File report 895: *Public attitudes to RAF news.*
File report 1290: *Morale in May 1942.*
File report 1401: *Miscellaneous material regarding morale in July 1942.*
File report 1829: *Morale in May 1943.*
File report 2000: *Reprisals.*

Author's Questionnaire

Wing Commander A.J. (Jim) Wright DFC.

Conversations With the Author

Johnson, George Leonard (Johnny) MBE, DFM.
Reid, William VC.

Private Collections

Letters of Sergeant W.D. Morrison.
Audiotape of Pierre Richard, recorded in 1990.

Published Sources

British Newspaper Archive

Aberdeen Evening Express
Ballymena Weekly Telegraph
Bedfordshire Times and Independent
Belfast Newletter
Birmingham Daily Post
Bradford Observer
Daily Mirror
Daily News (London)
Daily Record
Edinburgh Evening News
Lincolnshire Echo
Midlothian Advertiser

Portsmouth Evening News
Reading Standard
The Scotsman
Shields Daily News
Sunday Post
The Tatler
Western Morning News
The Yorkshire Post and Leeds Intelligencer

Official Publications

Bomber Command: The Air Ministry Account of Bomber Command's Offensive Against the Axis, September 1939-July 1941 (HMSO, 1941).

Bomber Command Continues: The Air Ministry Account of the Rising Offensive Against Germany, July 1941-June 1942 (HMSO, 1942).

Symonds, Air Vice Marshal Sir Charles P. and Williams, Wing Commander Denis J., *Psychological Disorders in Flying Personnel in the Royal Air Force 1939-1945* (HMSO, 1947).

Webster, Sir Charles and Frankland, Noble, *The Strategic Air Offensive Against Germany, Vol.1* (HMSO, 1961).

Articles

English, Allan D., 'A Predisposition to Cowardice? Aviation Psychology and the Genesis of Lack of Moral Fibre', *Motivating Soldiers: Morale or Mutiny*, (ed) Peter Karsten (Garland, 1998), pp.229-249.

Kinzer, Stewart N., 'Military Cohesion', *War*, (ed) Lawrence Freedman (Oxford University Press, 1994), pp.144-149.

Reid, D.D., 'The Historical Background to Wartime Research in Psychology in the Royal Air Force', *Aircrew Stress in Wartime Operations: Papers From the Flying Personnel Research Committee of the Ministry of Defence*, (eds) Dearnaley, E.J. and Warr, P.B. (Academic Press, 1979), pp.1-8.

Stafford-Clark, Dr. David, 'Morale and Flying Experience: Results of a Wartime Study', *Journal of Mental Science* Vol. XCV (January 1949) pp.10-50.

Strachan, Hew, 'The Soldier's Experience in Two World Wars: Some Historiographical Comparisons', *Time to Kill: The Soldier's Experience of War in the West 1939-1945*, (eds) Addison, Paul and Calder, Angus (Pimlico, 1997), pp.369-378.

Symonds, Air Vice Marshal Sir Charles P. and Williams, Wing Commander Denis J., 'Clinical and Statistical Study of Neurosis Precipitated by Flying Duties', *Aircrew Stress in Wartime Operations: Papers From the Flying Personnel Research Committee of the Ministry of Defence,* (eds) Dearnaley, E.J. and Warr, P.B. (Academic Press, 1979), pp.9-40.

Books

Aldgate, Anthony and Richards, Jeffrey, *Britain Can Take It: The British Cinema in the Second World War* (Edinburgh University Press, 1994).
Anderson, Wing Commander William, *Pathfinders* (Jarrold, 1946).
Anonymous, *Winged Words: Our Airmen Speak for Themselves* (Wm. Heinemann, 1941).
Baynes, John, *Morale: A Study of Men and Courage* (Cassell, 1967).
Beaton, Cecil, *Winged Squadrons* (Hutchinson & Co., 1942).
Bennett, D.C.T., *Pathfinder* (Sphere, 1972).
Bourke, Joanna, *An Intimate History of Killing: Face to Face Killing in Twentieth Century Warfare* (Granta, 2000).
Bowman, Martin W., *RAF Bomber Stories: Dramatic First-Hand Accounts of British and Commonwealth Airmen in World War 2* (Patrick Stevens Ltd., 1998).
Bowyer, Chas, *Bomber Barons* (Wm. Kimber, 1983).
Braddon, Russell, *Cheshire, VC* (Arrow, 1972).
Brookes, Andrew, *Bomber Squadron at War* (Ian Allen, 1983).
Calder, Angus, *The People's War: Britain 1939-1945* (Pimlico, 1992).
Chapman, James, *The British at War: Cinema, State and Propaganda 1939-1945* (I.B. Taurus, 1998).
Charlwood, Don, *No Moon Tonight* (Goodall, 1995).
Cheshire, Leonard, *Bomber Pilot* (Hutchinson, 1943).
Clark, Denis, *Tail End Charlie* (Lutterworth Press, 1946).
Costello, John, *Love, Sex and War: Changing Values 1939-1945* (Pan, 1986).
Currie, Jack, *Lancaster Target* (Goodall, 1997).
Dearnaley, E.J. and Warr, P.B., (eds), *Aircrew Stress in Wartime Operations: Papers From the Flying Personnel Research Committee of the Ministry of Defence* (Academic Press, 1979).
Ellis, John, *The Sharp End: The Fighting Man in World War Two* (Pimlico, 1993).
Freeman, Roger, *The British Airman* (Arms and Armour, 1989).
Fussell, Paul, *Wartime: Understanding and Behaviour in the Second World War* (Oxford University Press, 1989).

Garbett, Mike and Goulding, Brian, *The Lancaster at War* (PRC Publishing Ltd, 1991).

Garnett, David, *War in the Air: September 1939 to May 1941* (Chatto and Windus, 1941).

Garrett, Stephen, *Ethics and Air Power in World War Two: The British Bombing of German Cities* (St. Martins, 1997).

Gibson, Guy, *Enemy Coast Ahead* (Pan, 1956).

Halliwell, Leslie, *Halliwell's Film and Video Guide 2001* (Harper Collins Entertainment, 2000).

Hamilton, Tim, *The Life and Times of P/O Prune* (HMSO, 1991).

Harris, Sir Arthur, *Bomber Offensive* (Greenhill, 1998).

Hastings, Max, *Bomber Command* (Papermac, 1993).

Henderson, Major Velyien E., *Air Crew in Their Element: Hints for the Maintenance of Fitness and Confidence* (University of Toronto Press, 1942).

Hill, Mary M., *The Making of a Pathfinder: Letters From a Navigator: F/O Douglas Knight Williams* (Merlin, 1992).

Hilling, John B., *Strike Hard: A Bomber Airfield at War: RAF Downham Market and Its Squadrons 1942-1946* (Alan Sutton, 1995).

Holmes, Richard, *Firing Line* (Pimlico, 1994).

James, John, *The Paladins* (Futura, 1991).

Keegan, John, *The Second World War* (Pimlico, 1997).

Kellett, Anthony, *Combat Motivation: The Behaviour of Soldiers in Battle* (Kluwer Nijhoff, 1982).

Longmate, Norman, *The Bombers: The RAF Offensive Against Germany 1939-1945* (Hutchinson, 1983).

Longmate, Norman, *How We Lived Then* (Arrow, 1971).

Lyall, Gavin, *The War in the Air 1939-1945: An Anthology of Personal Experience* (Pimlico, 1994).

Middlebrook, Martin, *The Nuremberg Raid 30-31 March 1944* (Penguin, 1986).

Middlebrook, Martin, *The Battle of Hamburg: Allied Bomber Forces Against a German City in 1943* (Penguin, 1984).

Middlebrook, Martin, *The Berlin Raids: RAF Bomber Command's Winter 1943-1944* (Penguin, 1990).

Middlebrook, Martin and Everitt, Chris, *The Bomber Command War Diaries: An Operational Reference Book 1939-1945* (Midland, 1996).

Morris, Richard, *Guy Gibson* (Penguin, 1995).

Moran, Lord, *The Anatomy of Courage* (Avery, 1987).

Overy, Richard, *Bomber Command 1939-1945* (Harper Collins, 1997).
Overy, Richard, *Why the Allies Won* (Pimlico, 1996).
Parker, R.A.C., *The Second World War: A Short History* (Oxford University Press, 1997).
Partridge, Eric, *A Dictionary of Forces Slang 1939-1945* (Secker and Warburg, 1948).
Partridge, Eric, *A Dictionary of RAF Slang,* (Michael Joseph Ltd., 1945).
Paterson, T.T., MA, Phd, RAF (Ret'd), *Morale in War and Work: An Experiment in the Management of Men* (Max Parrish, London 1955).
Pudney, John and Treece, Henry, (eds), *Air Force Poetry* (John Lane: The Bodley Head, 1944).
Rattigan, *Flare Path* (Nick Hern Books, 2011).
Raymond, Robert, *A Yank in Bomber Command* (David and Charles, 1977).
Revie, Alastair, *The Lost Command* (Corgi, 1972).
Richards, Denis, *The Hardest Victory: RAF Bomber Command in the Second World War* (Coronet, 1995).
Richardson, Major General F.M., *Fighting Spirit: A Study of Psychological Factors in War* (Leo Cooper, 1978).
Rosewarne, Vivian, *An Airman's Letter to His Mother* (Putnam and Co., 1940).
Rothenstein, Sir William, *Men of the RAF* (Oxford University Press, 1942).
Shute, Nevil, *Pastoral,* (Wm. Heinemann, 1944).
Smithies, Edward, *War in the Air: The Men Who Built, Serviced and Flew Warplanes Remember the Second World War* (Penguin, 1992).
Spaight, J.M., *Bombing Vindicated* (Robert Maclehose and Co., 1944).
Terraine, John, *The Right of the Line: The Royal Air Force in the European War 1939-1945* (Hodder and Stoughton, 1985).
Tripp, Miles, *The Eighth Passenger* (Macmillan, 1969).
Vernon, P.E. and Parry, J.B., *Personnel Selection in the British Forces* (University of London Press, 1949).
Wells, Mark K., *Courage and Air Warfare: The Allied Aircrew Experience in the Second World War* (Frank Cassell and Co., 1995).
'A Wing Commander', *Bomber's Battle: Bomber Command's Three Years of War* (Riverside Press, 1943).

Index

3 Squadron, xix
7 Squadron, xix, 36, 38, 42, 102–103
9 Squadron, 15
10 Squadron, xix, 104
15 Squadron, xviii, 101, 120, 131–2
29 (Fighter) Squadron, xvii
37 Squadron, xix
42 Squadron, 122
50 Squadron, 120, 123
56 Squadron, 36
57 Squadron, xviii, 41, 104
58 Squadron, 172
61 Squadron, xviii, xix, 103, 105–107
76 Squadron, 123
77 Squadron, 120, 145
83 Squadron, 121, 145
97 Squadron, xviii–xix, 36–7, 105, 166
103 Squadron, xix, 105, 119, 122, 131, 135
107 Squadron, 119
115 Squadron, xix, 103
138 (Special Duties) Squadron, xviii, 92, 100–101
141 Squadron, xvii, 104
144 Squadron, 120
149 Squadron, xix, 119
150 Squadron, xix, 165
161 (Special Duties) Squadron, 92
193 Squadron, 122
195 Squadron, xviii, 114, 147, 183
207 Squadron, 24
214 Squadron, xviii
408 (RCAF) Squadron, 121
419 Squadron, 38
427 (RCAF) Squadron, xviii, 39, 42–3, 107, 172–83

571 Squadron, xviii, 129
576 Squadron, 123
617 (Dambusters) Squadron, xix, 124
627 Squadron, xviii
630 Squadron, xviii, xix, 41–3, 54, 119, 143

1 Group, 144, 165, 168
2 Group, 138
3 Group, 33, 38, 62, 94, 100, 120, 138
4 Group, 91
5 Group, 62, 69, 72, 118, 125, 144, 162
6 Group, 120
8 Group (Pathfinders), 34, 69, 94, 144
91 Group, 78
92 Group, 116
100 Group, 38

Aachen (Germany), 132, 179
accidents, in training, 27–8, 115–17
Addison, Edward, AOC 100 Group,
 wearing of armlets by captains, 38
Adlam, Sergeant,
 fatal accident, 174
administration, of bomber stations, 53–4
Air Cadets,
 at summer camp, 11,
 local education classes, 17
Air Council,
 propaganda, 4
 need for true statements of bombing effectiveness, 6
 poor quality of OTU instructors, 26
 station welfare, 46
 group commanders, 69

discipline, 73
discipline, 78
survival rates, 87
accidents, 118
Air Council Board, 167
Air Ministry,
   secret minute, subject: chances of survival, xxi
   definition of morale, xxiii
   disciplinc and morale, xxv
   assistance in production of *The Lion has Wings*, 4
   information to be divulged to the public, 6
   public access to news, 6
   'vague' press communiques, 6–7
   adequate information to be available to aircrews, 8
   appeal for volunteer aircrew, 10
   selection, 15
   the 'right type', 16
   screening of recruits at selection, 16–17
   importance of crew spirit fostered at OTUs, 20
   EATS, 22
   importance of captains of aircraft, 30
   acting captains, 34
   wearing of armlets by captains, 37–8
   crews, 38
   disruption of crew cohesion, 39
   venereal disease, 47
   issue of condoms, 49
   lectures on venereal disease, 49
   tolerance among aircrew, 52
   officer/men relations, 52
   all ranks dances, 55
   ENSA, 55
   RAF dissatisfaction, 60
   mixed rank crews, 61
   commissioning, 61–2
   discipline, 73
   discipline and morale, 74
   refresher courses, 77
   directives on behaviour and discipline, 78–9
   unacceptable behaviour of aircrew at personnel despatch centres, 79
   tour length, 85
   survival rates, 86
   the weather and tour length, 88
   tour length, 89
   abolition of second tour, 90
   tour-expired instructors at OTU, 91
   request from Harris for extension of PFF tour, 92
   minute to Portal regarding half and third sorties, 93
   tour extension, 94
   letter from Harris regarding 'alienisation' of the RAF, 94–5
   effect of combat on morale, 100
   personal experience reports, 101
   losses not caused by enemy action, 121
   no action on 'friendly' bombs, 124
   German reprisal action against aircrews, 125–6
   industrial smoke, 132
   aircrew ignorance of their purpose, 138
   minute to Peirse regarding misleading raid reports, 140
   Commando Bombing Force, 144
   aircrew awareness of policy, 144
   retaliation bombing, 150
   flying stress guidelines, 155
   waverers, 163–5
   medical "W" cases, 163
   meeting notes on "W" cases, 166
   Daily Mirror criticism of LMF policy, 167
   use of the term 'lack of courage', 167–8
aircraft, numbers destroyed, xxvi
aircraft types, 127–30

Index

Aircrew State Committee,
  tour extension, 94
Albert, Sergeant John,
  lost on operations, 183
Alkemade, Nicholas, 100
Allen, Michael, xvii–xviii
  combat, 104–105
Allighan, Garry,
  Daily Mirror article on LMF, 167
Amiens Prison Raid, 5
Andrews, Flying Officer, 103
anticipatory anxiety, 158–9
Appointment in London, 52
Arcadia, Florida, 23
area bombing, xxv
argot, 80–84
armlets, wearing of by captains, 37–8
Armstrong, Flying Officer, 148
Armstrong-Whitworth Whitley, 24, 120, 127
Army Air Corps (USA), 23
Arras (France),
  combat report, 104
Ash, Sergeant,
  fatal accident, 175
Attenborough, Richard, 184
Ault (France),
  combat report, 104
Australia,
  EATS, 21
  EATS trainees arrival in Britain, 23, 29, 152
Avro Lancaster, xxv, 18, 12, 25, 31, 93, 103, 105–106, 109, 112, 116, 119, 123–5, 127–30, 144, 146–7, 149, 152, 187
Avro Manchester, 130

Babington, Sir Philip,
  letter to H.H. Balfour regarding OTU instructor grievances, 25
  station chain of command, 53

Badcock, Flight Lieutenant Julian, 1
Baldwin, Flight Sergeant, 105
Baldwin, Jack, AOC 3 Group, aircrew ignorance of their purpose, 138
  aircrew ignorance of purpose, 139
  letter to Harris regarding the Target Finding Force, 143–4
Balfour, H.H., letter from Sir Philip Babington regarding OTU instructor grievances, 25
  letter from
  Sir Arthur Harris regarding second pilots, 31
  letter from Harris regarding NCO pilots, 32
  wearing of armlets, 38
  letter from Harris regarding commissions, 61
  letter from Sir Robert Saundby regarding Mosquito tour length, 92
  letter from Saundby regarding special duties squadrons tour length, 92
  extended tours, 94
  removal of stressed crews, 94
  letter from ACAS regarding German executions of Great Escape participants and effect on morale, 126
  letter from Harris regarding LMF, 168
  letter from Robert Oxland regarding LMF, 168
  letter from Harris regarding LMF, 169
Ball, Sergeant,
  fatal accident, 121–2
Ballymena Weekly Telegraph,
  crew morale, 113–14
Barnetby, Yorkshire, 57
barrage balloons, 120–21

Bartlett, Sergeant Edward,
    lost on operations, 183
Barton, North Lincolnshire, 122
Battle of Britain, The, 1, 147
Baum, Flying Officer,
    lost on operations, 181
BBC, broadcast of *Bomber Over
    Berlin: an impression of the work of
    Bomber Command*, 6
    raid information, 142
    Burnside raid success, 176
Beachy Head, East Sussex, 105
Beaton, Cecil,
    squadron spirit, 42
    station morale, 46
    leadership, 70
    raid information on radio, 141
    aircrew attitudes to bombing, 151–2
Beattie, Flying Officer R.L., 100–101
Bedale, Yorkshire, 179
Belfast Newsletter, 'The Harris Touch',
    67
Belgium, xix 124, 136
Bell, Pilot Officer Ernest, 100–101
Bennett, Donald, AOC 8 Group,
    'odd bods', 34
    attempts to split PFF crews, 35–7
    correspondence with all 8 Group
        AOCs, 35
    disagreement with Capel on splitting
        crews, 36
    letter from Capel regarding splitting
        of crews, 37
    leadership, 69
    fringe merchants, 110
Bennett, Pilot Officer,
    lost on operations, 174
benzedrine, 47
Berg, Flight Sergeant, 174
Berlin (Germany),
    early raid on, 3, 6, 39, 42
    Battle of, 54
    Battle of, 86, 93
    Battle of, 94
    Battle of, 109
    Battle of, 111
    Battle of, 113
    Battle of, 119
    Battle of, 122
    Battle of, 123
    Battle of, 130
    Battle of, 131
    Battle of, 135
    Battle of, 146
    Battle of, 147
    Battle of, 152–4, 172, 181
Betteridge, Jim,
    reason for volunteering, 13
Biggs, Pilot Officer,
    lost on operations, 43
Billington, Sergeant, 106
Bishop of Wakefield, The, 151
Bissett, Pilot Officer. J.M.,
    lost on operations, 42
Black Thursday, 130
Blackpool refresher course, 77
Blida (Algeria), xix
Blitzkrieg, 136
Bochum (Germany), 175, 177
Bomber Command, 1941 pamphlet, 4
Bomber Command Memorial,
    Green Park, London, 186
Bomber Over Berlin,
    BBC radio programme, 6
bomber station, the, 44–58
    conditions on, 45–6
    welfare on, 45–51
    the Mess, 51–3
    administration, 53–4
    entertainment on, 54–5
    the camp cinema and dances, 54–5
    the local community and, 56
bombing results,
    inaccuracy, xxv
    costly daylight raids, xxv
    innovations in navigational aids, xxv

introduction of the 'heavies', xxv
concentration raids, xxv
area bombing, xxv, 135–48
exaggerated reports of effectiveness of, 140
concentration raids, 145
Bormann, J., loss of friends, 96
  perception of survival chances, 99
Boston, Lincolnshire, 119
Boston Park, Doncaster, poor morale, 25
Bottomley, Sir Norman,
  proposed second instructing tour at OTUs, 26
  NCOs, 55
  disparaging remarks about NCOs, 75–6
  suggested penal battalions for recalcitrant NCOs, 76
  minute to Portal regarding sortie definition, 88
  letter from Ludlow-Hewitt regarding 2nd tour policy, 90
Bourn, Cambridgeshire,
  RAF Station, xviii, xix
Bournemouth Aircrew Reception Centre,
  delays and effect on morale, 23-4
Brady, Sergeant,
  lost on operations, 181
Brampton, Cumberland, 120
Bray, Sergeant William,
  fatal accident at OTU, 116
Brazzier, Sergeant,
  combat report, 106
Bremen (Germany),
  first sortie by F/O. Fairhead, 95
  1,000 Raid, 143
Brighton, East Sussex, 19
  refresher course, 77–8
Bristol, xx
Bristol Beaufighter, xvii, 104, 116
Bristol Beaufort, 122
Bristol Blenheim, 119, 127
Broadbent, Sergeant Arthur,
  fatal accident at OTU, 116

Brookes, Andrew,
  squadron losses, 42
Brown, Flight Sergeant James,
  decorations, 64
Bruges (Belgium), 178
Bufton, Sidney,
  tour length, 85
Burger, Sergeant O.E.,
  successful bombing, 145
Burnside, Dudley (Pilot Officer/Wing Commander/Group Captain), xviii, 172–83
Butt Report, The, 139
Buxton, Sergeant,
  lost on operations, 181–2
Byrne, Pilot Officer J.R.,
  thoughts of a wop/ag, 29–30
  unhappy crew, 39
  the Mess, 51
  losses, 96
  OTU accidents, 116–17
  thoughts on being shot down, 126
  revenge bombing, 152

Cadmus, Pilot Officer,
  lost on operations, 178
Caen (France), 54
Cambridge, 16
Canada, 18–19
  EATS, 21, 24, 28–9
  tour-expired instructors, 91, 95
Canadian aircrew,
  exemption from extended tours, 94
Capel, Arthur John, Air Officer Training,
  crew readiness for HCU, 25
  agreement with Harris on NCO captains, 32–3
  disagreement with Donald Bennett on splitting crews, 36
  letter to Bennett regarding splitting crews, 37
  wearing of armlets by captains, 37
captains of aircraft, 30

Carr, Roderick, AOC 4 Group,
    retention of non-flying
    commanders, 91
casualties, xxii
CEMA, 55
Charlwood, Don,
    squadron spirit, 40–41
    the Mess, 51
    unreality, 57
    combat, 112
    ethics, 153
Chasanoff, Flight Lieutenant J., 182
Chateauneuf d'Isere (France), 101
Chateauneuf-de-Galoure (France), 101
Chedburgh, Suffolk, RAF Station, xix
Cheshire, Leonard, xxii
    reason for volunteering, 12
    squadron spirit, 41
    unreality, 57
    leadership, 72
    combat, 99
    attitude to bombing, 153
Chessington Aircrew Disposal Unit,
    Surrey, 167
Chivers, Maxwell, xviii
Churchill, Sir Winston, 6
    leadership, 68
    letter to Peirse asking for bombing
        policy, 138
    aircrew ignorance of raid policy, 138
Clermont-Ferrand (France), 143
Coastal Command,
    air gunner Terence Rattigan with, 5
    venereal disease, 48
Cochrane, Sir Ralph, AOC 3 Group,
    then 5 Group, mixed NCO/officer
    crews, 33
    commissioning at OTU, 62
    leadership, 69
collisions, 122–3
Cologne (Germany),
    the 1,000 Raid, 67
    combat report, 104
    collisions over, 123

15 Squadron operations book, 132
    the 1,000 Raid, 138
    the 1,000 Raid, 142
    the 1,000 Raid, 143
    the 1,000 Raid, 151, 174, 178
colorado beetle plan, 137
Colyer, Douglas,
    quoting Ludlow-Hewitt on morale,
    xxiv
combat, 99–114
combat reports, 101
Combined Recruiting Centre, 11
Commando Bombing Force, 144
commissions, 61–2
concentration raids, xxv, 145
conditions of bomber stations, 45–6
Coningsby, Lincolnshire,
    RAF Station, xviii, 46, 51
Constantine, Group Captain, 165
Cooke, Squadron Leader, 100–101
Cooling, Flight Lieutenant Rupert,
    station conditions, 46
corkscrewing, 103, 105–106
Cornelius, Sergeant,
    lost on operations, 181
Counsell, Sergeant S.,
    fatal accident, 122
Courage and Air Warfare, 71
courts-martial, 166
Coventry, 120
Coward, Noel, 181
Cranswick, Alec, ethics, 152–3
creepback, 110
crew, the,
    'crewing up', xxv
    'crewing up', 19–21
    reasons for choosing crewmates,
        19–21, 29–39
    NCO or officer captains, 32–3
    mixed NCO/officer crews, 32–3
    acting captains, 34
    splitting of crews, 34–7
    medical treatment of, 47
Crieff, Perthshire, xix

Croft, Lincolnshire,
  RAF Station, xviii, 173, 176
Crosby, Bing, 57
Crown Film Unit, 5
Currie, Jack,
  scarecrows, 108
  accident, 117–18
  collisions, 123
cut-off point, 18

Daily Mirror,
  poem, 1–2
  praise for *Target for Tonight*, 4–5
  Jane cartoon, 8
  volunteer article, 11
  inter-station rivalry, 50–51
  Jane, 52
  quotes Sir Archibald Sinclair, 59
  RAF slang, 82
  raid on Hamburg, 140
  retaliation bombing, 151
  LMF, 167
Daily News,
  quality of aircrews, 114
Dambusters, The, xx, 186
Darlington, County Durham, 174, 177, 181
datum line, 85, 92
D-Day, 54
de Havilland Mosquito, 85, 88, 92, 129, 146, 154
decorations, 63–5
delays,
  for volunteers, 10
  for volunteers, 11
  of Dominion aircrews, 23
  in posting between units, 23
  in movement from OTUs and HCUs, 23–4
Denmark, 144
deserters, 57
Diamond, Frank, xviii
Dimbleby, Richard,
  describes raid, 58, 153

discipline, 73–9
Dixon, Ron,
  praise for the Short Stirling, 127–8
Dodds, Sergeant,
  fatal accident, 175
Dormand, Pilot Officer 'Dizzy', 181
Dortmund (Germany), 96
Dresden (Germany), 147–8
Dreux (France),
  combat report, 105
Duisburg (Germany), 124, 175–6
Duncan, Pilot Officer D.A.,
  successful bombing, 145
Durocher, Flight Lieutenant, 177
Dusseldorf (Germany), xix–xx
  combat report, 103
  William Reid's VC, 105, 123
  J.R. Byrne, revenge bombing, 152, 172, 177
Dye, Bernard,
  combat, 112–13, 152

early returns, 109
Early, Sergeant,
  fatal accident, 119–20
Earnshaw, Sergeant,
  fatal accident, 120
East Kirkby, Lincolnshire,
  RAF Station, xviii, xix, 41–3, 54, 119, 187
Eastchurch Combined Reselection Centre, Kent, 167
EATS, 19, 21–4
  inauguration of, 21
  discipline problem on USA EATS courses, 22–3
  European weather conditions, difficulties for trainees from EATS, 24, 28, 79
Edale, Derbyshire, 173
Eden, Sir Anthony, EATS, 21
Edinburgh Evening News,
  praise for Bomber Command, 3
  praise for Arthur Harris, 66–7

Elsham Wolds, North Lincolnshire,
    RAF Station, xix, 45, 122, 165
Elwood, Mr., Bombing Operations,
    raid secrecy, 139
Emerson, Flight Sergeant, 105
Empire Cinema, Leicester Square,
    London, 177
Enemy Coast Ahead, 50
ENSA, 55, 176–7
entertainment at bomber stations, 54–5
Essen (Germany), 101
    scarecrows over, 108
    1,000 Raid, 143, 165, 172, 174–6,
    179–80
ethics, 149–54
Evill, Sir Douglas, morale and
    discipline, xxiv–xxv

Fairey Battle, 129, 136
Fairhead, Flying Officer R.J.,
    'crewing up', 20
    training experiences, 24
    emergency replacement for pilots,
    31–2
    survival of experienced crews, 39
    squadron losses, 42–3
    first sortie, 95
    early returns, 109–10
    LMF, 170
Farben, I.G., 4
Farquarson, Squadron Leader, 147–8
Fayers, Flying Officer R.J.,
    training on EATS course, 21–2
    gremlins, 132–3
Felixstowe, Suffolk, 120
FIDO (Fog Investigation and Dispersal
    Operation), 132
Fieldson, Flying Officer Elwyn,
    collision, 123
Fighter Command, xvii, 1, 41, 125
Filstead, Pilot Officer,
    lost on operations, 96
Firth of Forth, The, 122

Fiskerton, Lincolnshire,
    RAF Station, 45
flak, 107–109
Flare Path, 5
Flensburg (Germany), 144
flying stress, 155–61
Flying Training Command, 18, 25–6
Foot, Dingle, 68
Ford, Sergeant C.S.,
    lost on operations, 114
Ford, West Sussex,
    RAF Station, xvii
form 700, 121
form 1580, 170
Formby, George, 13
Foster, William Foster MacNeece,
    120
Foulsham, Norfolk,
    RAF Station, xviii
Fox, Flight Lieutenant T.W.,
    tour survival, 86
    losses, 96
    survival of his tour, 97–8
    praise for the Handley-Page Halifax,
    129
France, xix, 100, 136
Frankfurt (Germany), 42, 137, 146
    George Hull, revenge bombing, 152,
    175
Freberg, Pilot Officer, 38
    combat report, 102
Freeman, Flying Officer,
    combat report, 106
Freeman, Sir Wilfred,
    letter from Norman Bottomley,
    ACAS, regarding undisciplined
    NCOs, 75–6
    tour length, 89
    first tour extension, 93
    accident inquiry, 121
    correspondence with Harris
    regarding extra armour for Avro
    Lancasters, 128

Index

correspondence with Harris regarding the Handley-Page Halifax, 129
correspondence with Harris regarding the de Havilland Mosquito, 129
letter to Peirse regarding aircrew ignorance of their purpose, 138
correspondence with Harris regarding misleading raid results, 140–41
raid publicity, 141
'friendly' bombs, 124
'friendly' fire, 124–5
fringe merchants, 110
Frost, Warrant Officer, 105

Gagnon, Pilot Officer, lost on operations, 178
Gale, Flight Sergeant Charles, 80
Ganderton, Flight Lieutenant, 178
'gardening' (mine laying), 93, 121, 132, 173–4, 176
Garrod, Sir A.G.R.,
  discipline on USA EATS courses, 22
  letter to Portal regarding survival rates, 86–7
Garson, Greer, 176
Gelsenkirchen (Germany), 104, 178
Genoa (Italy), 102
Germany, xxvi, 4, 6, 8, 24, 57–8, 67, 78, 93, 104, 111, 113, 125, 137, 141–2, 146, 152, 174, 184
Gestapo, 126
Ghent (Belgium), 101
Gibraltar, xix, 101
Gibson, Guy, xxii
  rivalry between Bomber and Fighter Command, 41
  photography and squadron competitiveness, 41
  drinking culture, 50
  comments on John Wooldridge, 52
  unreality, 58
  leadership, 72
  barrage balloon collision, 121
  'friendly' fire, 125
  as Mosquito pilot, 129
  bombing, 153
Gill, D.J.,
  reason for volunteering, 12
  criticism of training, 19
  tour survival, 86
  fear of collisions, 122
Glazzard, Sergeant,
  combat report, 103
Goebbels, Joseph, xxv
  threat of reprisals, 126
Goering, Hermann, 146
Gofton, Sergeant Cyril, lost on operations, 183
Gordon, Johnnie, 153
Gornall, Flying Officer, 100–101
G.P., Miss, of Salisbury, criticism of airmen, 3
Great Escape, The, 126
Greening, Pilot Officer J.P., 175
Greig, Flight Lieutenant, 104
gremlins, 127, 132–3
Gul Nawaz, 172
Gulmatti (Waziristan, Pakistan India before partition in 1947), 172
gunnery officers, 101

Hall, Eddie, 20–21
Hamburg (Germany), Gibson barrage balloon collision, 121, 130
  false press reports of destruction of, 140
  July 1943 Raids, 145
  March 1943 raid, 174
  July 1943 Raids, 179
  July 1943 Raids, 179–80
  July 1943 Raids, 180
Hamilton, Sergeant,
  lost on operations, 178

Handley-Page, 129
Handley-Page Halifax, xxv, 18, 25, 93, 96, 100, 104, 123, 128–9, 146–7, 149, 176–7, 182
Handley-Page Hampden, 120–1, 127, 141
Happy Valley, 39
Harris, Brian Edward Barton, xviii
Harris, Sir Arthur Travers, xxii
  becomes C-in-C Bomber Command, xxv
  letter to Sir Archibald Sinclair, subject: safeguarding of Bomber Command, xxv
  as "Bomber", 4
  at premiere of *The Way to the Stars*, 5
  the gutter press, 6
  letter to Portal regarding the gutter press, 7
  keeping crews together, 31
  letter to H.H. Balfour regarding second pilots, 31
  letter to Bertine Sutton regarding NCO captains, 32
  further letter to Bertine Sutton regarding commissions for NCO captains, 33
  'headless' crews, 33–4
  frustration with Air Ministry regarding acting captains, 34
  correspondence with Donald Bennett regarding the splitting of crews, 35
  wearing of armlets by captains, 37
  living-in policy, 52
  letter to Bertine Sutton comparing RAF and civilian rates of pay, 60
  letter to H.H. Balfour regarding commissions, 61
  'useless' selection boards, 62
  commissioning at OTU, 62
  leadership, 66–8
  'broadcast' to Germany, 67
  German Radio, 68
  letter to Portal regarding commanders, 69
  correspondence with Portal regarding non-flying commanders, 72
  leadership, 72
  discipline, 73
  tour length, 89
  letter to Portal regarding scrapping of second tour, 90
  extension of PFF tour, 92
  letter to Sinclair regarding the datum line, 92–3
  definition of a sortie, 93
  extended tours, 94
  removal of stressed crews, 94
  possible disobedience, 94
  letter to Bertine Sutton regarding Canadian aircrew and extended tours, 94
  'alienisation' of the RAF, 94
  avoidable accidents, 118
  letter to Portal, subject: no action on 'friendly' bombs, 124
  correspondence with Sir Wilfred Freeman regarding extra armour for Avro Lancasters, 128
  correspondence with Freeman regarding the Handley-Page Halifax, 129
  correspondence with Freeman regarding the de Havilland Mosquito, 129
  letter from Freeman regarding misleading raid results, 140–41
  assurances from Freeman regarding raid publicity, 141
  raid publicity, 142
  introduction of heavies, 142
  thoughts on Lubeck and Rostock raids, 142
  letter from Baldwin regarding Target Finding Force, 143–4

message to crews, 146
'Butch' Harris criticised by crews
 during the Battle of Berlin, 147,
 152, 154
waverers, 162–3
letter to H.H. Balfour regarding the
 "W" Memorandum, 168
letter to Balfour regarding LMF, 169
congratulating 427 (RCAF) Squadron
 on Peenemunde raid, 181
his leadership, 186
Harrogate, North Yorkshire, 177, 181
Harwell, Oxfordshire, RAF station, 46
Harwell, Nottinghamshire, 173
Harwich, Essex, 120
Harwood, Sergeant,
 lost on operations, 174
Hastings, Max
 leadership, 66
 collisions, 123
Hawarden, Flintshire,
 RAF Station, No.57 OTU, 24
Hawker, Flight Lieutenant D.,
 line shooting, 83–4
Hayhurst, Pilot Officer Reginald, 174–5
hazards, 115–34
HCU,
 No.1657 HCU, xviii, 18, 21, 23
 No.1656 HCU Lindholme, 25
 commissioning at, 33
 P/O. Byrne at, 39
 tour expired instructors at, 91
 accidents at, 115–17
 Lindholme, 116
 Topcliffe, 176
Heather, Pilot Officer R.J.,
 lost on operations, 174–5
Heaton Park Aircrew Holding Unit, 19
Hemswell, Lincolnshire,
 RAF Station, 45–6, 116
Hendon Air Pageant, 13
Henry, Sergeant,
 fatal accident, 182

Higgins, Flight Sergeant,
 lost on operations, 178
Hinton-in-the-Hedges,
 Oxfordshire, RAF Station,
 92 Group OTU, 116
Hislop, Pilot Officer,
 lost on operations, 96
Hitler, Adolf, 1, 151
Hixon, Staffordshire,
 RAF Station, No.30 OTU, 22
Hodges, Sir Lewis,
 training accidents, 28
Hokey-Cokey, 54
holding units, 11,
 Heaton Park, 14
Holland, 124, 136, 141
Honington, Suffolk,
 RAF Station, 46
Hope, Bob, 54
Horner, Flying Officer,
 pride in squadron, 41
Howard-Williams, E.L.,
 crew morale, 113
Hull, George,
 station conditions, 45–7
 the Mess, 51–2
 mixed-rank dances, 55
 reactions to aircrew behaviour in
  Lincoln, 56
 leave, 56–7
 chance of survival, 87–8
 losses, 95–6
 praise for the Avro Lancaster, 128
 revenge, 152
 ethics, 152–3
humour, 80–84
Humphries, Sergeant A., 175
Hunter, D.,
 accident, 122

icing, 131
I.G. Farben, 4
India, xviii

Initial Training Wing, Cambridge, 16–18
  Hastings, 19
  Usworth, 24
  Brighton, 77
instructors, tour-expired, at OTUs, 25–6
  Harris's view on tour-expired instructors, 90
Isle of May, 122
Isleham, Suffolk, 178
Italy, xxvi, 138
Izzard, Flight Lieutenant, 179–81

Jackson, Sergeant Norman, 100
Jacksonville, Florida, 21
Jane,
  cartoon character in the *Daily Mirror*, 8
  reading in the Mess, 52
  jargon, 80–4
Jefferies, Flight Sergeant, 105
Jenner, Alfred,
  reason for volunteering, 13
Johnson, George 'Johnny', xx
  experiences on EATS course, USA, 22–3
  trust in his pilot, 39
  combat, 112
  St. Elmo's Fire, 130
  the Dams Raid, 186
Johnson, Sergeant, 177
Jones, Wing Commander Evan Gwynn,
  drinking culture, 50
Joubert, Sir Philip,
  as Inspector-General, xxiv
  cause of delays, 23
  letter to Portal regarding discipline, 23
  venereal disease, 48
  discipline on bomber stations, 53
  importance of group captains, 70
  discipline, 74, 77

Juvincourt (France), combat report, 104

Keen, Flight Sergeant Geoffrey, 174–5
Kellett, Anthony,
  combat motivation, 1
  combatant/civilian interaction, 8
Kenley, Croydon, xix
Kharkov (Ukraine), war crimes trials, 125
Kiel (Germany), 175
King George VI, 176
Kirmington, Lincolnshire, RAF Station, xix
Krefeld (Germany), 177
Krupp Works, Essen, 4, 179

'lacking moral fibre', xxv, 18, 116, 162–71
  possible LMF case in 427 (RCAF) Squadron, 181–2
  deterrent value of, 185–6
Lackman, Flying Officer F.H.B., 152
Lahore (Pakistan; India before partition in 1947), 172
Laing, M.S.,
  secret minute regarding aircrew survival, xxi
Laird, G.J.,
  lost on operations, 42
Lakenheath, Suffolk, RAF Station, xix
Lamarr, Hedy, 176
Lambeth Walk, 54
Lamour, Dorothy, 54
Lawson, Wing Commander,
  LMF, 165
  LMF, 169
  meeting with Sir Archibald Sinclair, 169–70
Le Creusot (France), 177
leadership, 66–72
leave, 56–7

Leeming, North Yorkshire,
    RAF Station, xviii, 176
Leipzig (Germany), 96, 152
LeMarchant, Harry, xviii
Leuchars, Fife,
    RAF Station, 122
Leverkusen (Germany), 181
Lewis, Reginald, xviii-xix
    evasion and escape, 100–101
Lincoln, 56
Lincolnshire Echo,
    RAF slang, 82
Lindholme, South Yorkshire,
    RAF Station, No.1656 HCU, 25, 116, 170
line shooting, 83–4
Linton-on-Ouse, North Yorkshire,
    RAF Station, 120
Lion has Wings, The, 4
living-in policy, 52, 156
LMF, xxv, 18, 116, 162–71
    possible LMF case in 427 (RCAF) Squadron, 181–2
    deterrent value of, 185–6
'load, the', 157
local communities and bomber stations, 56
Lofthouse, Charles, xix
London, 150, 152, 174
    Green Park Memorial, 186
Longmate, Norman, 59
Lorient (France), 173–5
Lubeck (Germany), 142, 146
Ludlow-Hewitt, Sir Edgar, healthy state of morale, xxiv
    visits to refresher schools, 77
    morale and discipline, 78
    scrapping of second tour, 90
    aircrew ignorance of their purpose, 138–9
Ludwigshafen (Germany), 96
lynching, 19, 125–6
Lyneham, Wiltshire,
    RAF Station, 101

MacDonald, Sergeant Douglas,
    fatal accident, 122
McCalla, talismans, 134
McCarthy, Joe,
    pilot ability, 39, 130, 186
McGibney, Sergeant,
    combat report, 106
McKinnon, Sergeant,
    fatal accident, 121
McLean, Sergeant,
    combat report, 102
McLean, Sergeant John, 180
    lost on operations, 183
McNamara, Sergeant 'Stubby', 181
McPhee, Pilot Officer,
    lost on operations, 42
Maastrict (The Netherlands), xix
Macinnes, Wing Commander R.C., 175
Mahaddie, Hamish,
    Harris's leadership, 67
    loss of second tour aircrew, 89
Main Force, The, 37, 88, 92, 94, 110, 144, 153
Manchester, 152
Mann, Flight Sergeant, 105
Mannheim (Germany), combat report, 102, 137
    first area raid, 138, 153, 172, 175
Manston, Kent,
    RAF Station, 104
marcolins, 132–3
Marconi Wireless Telegraphy, 132
Marham, Norfolk,
    RAF Station, xix
Marshall, J.S.A.,
    'friendly' fire, 124
    weather, 130
Mass Observation,
    attitudes of the public to the RAF, 8
    leisure pursuits in the RAF, 50
    drinking culture, 50
    'bullshit' discipline, 74
    aircrew perception of survival, 97

retaliation bombing, 150
  ethics, 151
  ethics of bombing, 153
  reprisal bombing, 153-4
Matter of Life and Death, A, 184
Medhurst, C.E.H.,
  station chain of command, 53
medical reports, 47
Meiktila (Myanmar, formerly Burma), xix
Melbourne, Yorkshire,
  RAF Station, xix
Mellor, Gordon Herbert, xix
Merritt, Sergeant Jack,
  fatal accident, 118
Merseburg (Germany), 96
Mess, The, 51-3
  need for tolerance, 52
  NCO/officer segregation, 53
Metro-Goldwyn-Mayer, 172, 176-7
Metropole Hotel, Brighton, 19
Middlebrook, Martin,
  the squadron, 40
  morale, 143
  Battle of the Ruhr and morale, 144
  Battle of Berlin and morale, 147
Midlothian Advertiser, crew morale, 113
Miami, Florida, 22
Milan (Italy), raid on, 3
Mildenhall, Suffolk,
  RAF Station, xviii-xix, 5, 119-20
Ministry of Economic Warfare, 68
Ministry of Information, 5
  squadron spirit, 42
  German reprisals, 126
  lynching, 126
Ministry of Labour, pay rates, 60
Mitcheal, Sergeant T., 175
Moncton (Canada), 19
Monk Jones, Mr.,
  second tour waverers, 165
Montgomery, Alabama, 21
Montorgueil (France), 96

morale, definition, xxiii
Moran, Lord,
  unreality, 57
  leadership, 71
  discipline, 74
  the power of humour, 80
  tour limit, 85
  courage, 158
  courage, 162
Morris, Sergeant W.,
  fatal accident, 121
Morrison, Sergeant W.D.,
  satisfaction with pay rates, 61
  'friendly' fire, 124-5
  Mannheim raid, 137
Mannheim, 153
Mortimer, Pilot Officer, 173
Mosquito squadrons,
  tour length, 88
  crews, risk on operations relative to Main Force, 92
  tour length, 92
  versatility and negligible losses, 129
Mrs. Miniver, 22
Mulheim (Germany), 177
Munchen-Gladbach (Germany), 182
Munich (Germany), 43
Murray, 2nd Lieutenant L.B.,
  fatal accident, 120

navigational aids, xxv
  Oboe, Gee, H2S, 144
New Zealand, EATS, 21, 29
Newall, Sir Cyril,
  letter from Portal regarding morale, 136
Newham, Douglas, xix
Newman, Wing Commander K.J.,
  reason for volunteering, 13
  'crewing up', 20-21
  experiences while training on EATS, 22
  class differences in aircrews, 22

training experiences, 25
captain's responsibility, 31
unhappy crew member, 39
station conditions, 45–6
leadership, 71
scarecrows, 107–108
OTU accidents, 116
accident, 118
LMF, 170
Nichols, Robert,
correspondence regarding station entertainment, 55
nickelling, 93, 137
No Moon Tonight, 153
Norris, Sergeant, 105
North Luffenham, Rutland, RAF Station, 121, 174
Norway, 100
Nuremberg (Germany), 42
March 1944 Raid combat report, 106
March 1944 Raid 427 (RCAF) Squadron operations book comments, 107
March 1944 Raid, 146–7
427 (RCAF) Squadron raid August 1944, 181
Nutt, Flight Sergeant,
lost on operations, 104

Oakington, Cambridgeshire, RAF Station, xviii, xix, 55, 102
Oldenburg (Germany), 174
Operational Research Section,
scarecrows, 108–109
investigation of casualties caused by enemy action, 110
operations record books, 101
OTU, No.26 OTU, xviii, 18
Wymeswold, 19
'crewing up' at, 19–21
No.30 OTU Hixon, 22–3
No.57 OTU, 24
progression to HCUs, 25

instructors, 25
unpopularity of, among tour-expired instructors, 25–6
fatal accidents at, 27
pilots of OTU crews, 32
commissioning at, 62
3 Group OTUs, 62
instructors from PFF crews suffering fatigue, 88
tour expired instructors, 90
tour expired instructors, 91
accidents at, 115–17
No.2 OTU, 116
92 Group OTU, 116
Lindholme, 116
barrage balloon hazards at, 120
collisions, 123
on the 1,000 Raid to Cologne, 143
good quality of crews, 144
best crews to PFF, 144
Ouistreham (France), combat report, 105
Oxland, Robert, AOC 1 Group, LMF, 168

PACT Wing, 18
Paige, Sergeant, 29
Paris, combat report, 102
Partridge, Eric,
RAF argot, 81
line shooting, 84
Pastoral, 156–7
Pathfinder Force, 34
splitting crews, 35–7
tour length, 88
tour extension, 92
definition of a sortie, 93–4
scarecrows, 108
formation of 8 Group, 110
collision, 123
Tee-Emm poem, 135
formation of, 144
Paul, Flying Officer,
combat report, 106

pay, 10, 59–61
Peck, Sir Richard,
  German reprisals, 125–6
Peenemunde (Germany), 181
Peirse, Sir Richard,
  succeeded by Harris, 66
  senior officers from outside Bomber Command, 69
  accident inquiry, 121
  letter from Portal asking for bombing policy, 137
  letter from Churchill asking for bombing policy, 138
  letter from Freeman regarding aircrew ignorance of their purpose, 138
  misleading raid reports, 140
  admonished and dismissed by Portal, 140
Perdue, Sergeant K.A., 175
personal experience reports, as morale boosters, 38, 101
personnel despatch centres, unacceptable behaviour of aircrew, 79
Pery-Knox-Gore, Flying Officer, lost on operations, 43
Phoney War, 137
photography, Guy Gibson and, 41
  and bombing accuracy, 143
Pickard, Percy 'Pick',
  death on Amiens Raid, 5
  as Mosquito pilot, 129
pilots, suitability for bombers or fighters, 16
Portal, Sir Charles,
  secret letter regarding aircrew survival, xxi
  in audience for *Flare Path*, 5
  letter from Harris regarding the gutter press, 7
  endorsement of *Tee-Emm*, 27
  NCO captains, 33
  letter from Harris regarding commanders, 69
  note regarding group commanders, 69
  correspondence with Harris regarding non-flying commanders, 72
  letter from Garrod regarding survival rates, 86-7
  letter to Garrod regarding survival rates, 87
  minute from Bottomley regarding bombing results, 88
  loss of second tour aircrew, 89
  letter from Harris regarding scrapping of second tour, 90
  second tours, 92
  minute from Air Ministry regarding half and third sorties, 93
  letter from Harris, no action on 'friendly' bombs, 124
  extra armour for Avro Lancasters, 128
  casualties and effect on morale during Blitzkrieg in France and the Low Countries, 136
  letter to Peirse asking for his bombing policy, 137
  misleading bombing results, 140
  admonishes and dismisses Peirse, 140
Portsmouth Evening News, flying stress, 155–6
Powell, Squadron Leader, lost on operations, 96
'probably lacking in moral fibre', 168–9
promotion, 62–3
Prune, P/O. Percy, 27
psychological and psychiatric methods, used in aircrew selection process, 17
Pursuit through Darkened Skies, xviii

RAF,
  in public esteem, 2–3
  propaganda and truth, 4

Film Unit, 5–6
  public response to RAF news, 8
  class barrier to enlistment in, 9
  remuneration, 10
  appeal for volunteers, 10–11
  St. Johns Wood Reception Centre, 15
  incidence of venereal disease, 47
  venereal disease rates, 49
  living-in policy, 52
  deserters, 57
  discipline and morale, 59
  class barriers, 61
  disciplinary structure, 73
  differences of rank, 74
  behaviour and deportment in public, 78–9
  Air Ministry memorandum to encourage pride in all ranks, 141
  press praise, 145–6
  pamphlet addressing flying stress, 159
Rampling, Group Captain J.K.,
  lost on operations, 42
Rathbone, Flight Sergeant, 131
Rattigan, Terence, 5
Rawlins, C.G.C.,
  leadership, 70–2
Raymond, Robert,
  ethics, 153
RCAF, venereal disease rates, 49
  tolerance of different personalities in aircrew, 52–3
  separate messes and effect on morale, 53
  tour-expired instructors, 91
  exemption from tour extension, 94
  LMF cases, 167
  MGM adoption of 427 (RCAF) Squadron, 175
  427 (RCAF) Squadron departure from Croft, 176
Read, Squadron Leader, LMF, 171
Reading Standard, 174–5

Reed, Flying Officer J.S., 100–101
refresher courses ('Suspendair), 76–7
Reichswald Forest War Cemetery (Germany), 183
Reid, Flying Officer,
  lost on operations, 178
Reid, William VC, xix–xx
  reason for volunteering, 12
  combat report, 105
  hit by 'friendly' bombs, 124
Remscheid (Germany), 180
remuneration, 10, 59–61
Rheims (France), combat report, 104, 124
Rhine, The, 132
Rhodesia, EATS, 21
Richard, Pilot Officer Pierre,
  Chapter 2 introductory quote, 9
  reason for volunteering, 13
  training, 28
  drinking culture, 50
  unreality, 57
  faith, 133
  justification of bombing, 154
  aftermath, 184–5
Richards, Mr,
  punishments for unacceptable behaviour of aircrew in public places, 79
Richter, Flight Sergeant,
  fatal accident, 122
Rilly-La-Montagne (France), xx, 124
Ripon, North Yorkshire, 182
River Orwell, 120
Robb, James,
  AOC 2 Group, 138
Rollinson, Wing Commander J.D.,
  lost on operations, 42–3
Rolton, Sergeant, 105
Roosevelt, Eleanor,
  in audience for *Flare Path*, 5
Rosewarne, Flying Officer Vivian, 11–12
Ross, Pilot Officer Davy, 181
Rostock (Germany), 142, 146

Rothenstein, Sir William, 12
  leisure pursuits in the RAF, 50
  unreality, 58
Rothwell, Sergeant A.D., 183
Rowling, Flying Officer P.,
  survival, 87
  combat, 111–12
  bombing results optimism, 140
Ruhr, The, 4, 39
  Battle of the, 111, 131
  Battle of the, 135, 143–4
  Battle of the, 145
  Battle of the, 146
  Battle of the, 172, 179
Russell-Fry, Flying Officer, 122
Rye, East Sussex, 104

S. Marcel (France), 101
St. Athan, Vale of Glamorgan, Wales, 24
St. Elmo's Fire, 130
St. John's Wood, London,
  RAF Reception Centre, 15
St. Nazaire (France), 174–5
San Sebastian Hotel, Jacksonville,
  Florida, 22
Sandford, Folliott,
  mixed-rank dances, 55
  second tours, 91
Sandy Lake, Manitoba, Canada, 183
Saundby, Sir Robert,
  wearing of armlets by captains, 37
  letter to H.H. Balfour regarding
    length of
  Mosquito tour, 92
  letter to H.H. Balfour regarding
    length of special duties tours, 92
  removal of stressed crews, 94
  extended tours, 94
Scampton, Lincolnshire,
  RAF Station, xviii, 186
scarecrows, 107–109
Schiphol (The Netherlands), 103
Schmitt, Sergeant, 179–81
Schneider Works, Le Creusot, 177

Scholven (Germany), 114
Schweinfurt (Germany), 147
Scott, Pilot Officer M.A.,
  station conditions, 45
  inactivity on station, 46–7
  the Mess, 52
scrubs, 88, 131–2, 158
Searle, Sergeant C.N.,
  praise for the Short Stirling, 127
Seighford, Staffordshire,
  RAF Station, 45
selection, 15-17
  role of psychiatry in, 15
  'wrong' reasons for volunteering,
    15–16
  the 'right' type, 16
  appraisal of skills, 16
  recognition of unsuitable candidates,
    16
Shallufa (Egypt), xix
Shawbury Advanced Training Unit
  No.1, Shropshire, 22
Sheffield, South Yorkshire, 173
Shinethiza (Waziristan, Pakistan;
  India before partition in 1947),
  172–3
Shipdham, Norfolk, RAF Station, 105
Short Stirling, xxv, 18, 25, 38, 93,
  101–103, 120, 127–8, 144, 149
Shute, Neville, Chapter 8 opening
  quote, 66, 156–7
Simmons, D.G., tour length, 89
Sinclair, Sir Archibald,
  letter from Harris regarding
    the safeguarding of Bomber
    Command, xxv
  appeal for volunteers, 10–11
  RAF dissatisfaction, 59
  second tours, 92
  letter from Harris regarding the
    datum line, 92–3
  definition of a sortie, 93
  Canadian aircrew, 95
  fluctuating tour lengths, 95

criticism by *Daily Mirror* regarding
    LMF, 167
meeting with Sir Charles Symonds
    and Wing Commander Lawson,
    subject: "W" cases, 169–70
Skegness, Lincolnshire, 119
slang, 80–4
Smith, Graham King, xix
Smith, Squadron Leader,
    lost on operations, 96
Snaith, Yorkshire,
    RAF Station, 165
Sobkowice, Sergeant,
    lost on operations, 179
social class a bar to entry into RAF, 9
SOE, xix, 92, 100
Solingen (Germany), 124
Somers, Flying Officer Lou,
    lost on operations, 178
South Africa, EATS, 21
    EATS trainee K.J. Newman, 22, 24
Spaight, J.M., 151
Spain, xix
squadron, the, 40–3
    inter-squadron rivalry, 41
    flying and non-flying commanders, 42
Stafford-Clark, Dr. David,
    casualty rate, xxii
    aircrew reaction to public adulation, 2
    value of crewing up, 20
    crew spirit, 30
    poor discipline of air gunners, 75
    lack of discipline and effect on
        morale, 76
    aircrew resistance to traditional
        discipline, 76
    tour length and morale, 86
    tour length and survival, 87
    talismans and superstition, 133
    praise for Sir Charles Symonds, 159
    flying stress, 159–60
    effect of flying stress on morale, 160
    waverers, 160–1

praise from Symonds, 161
Stalingrad, 180
Steiner, Flight Lieutenant Denis,
    experience at recruiting centre, 15
    passage through training, 19
    'crewing up', 21
    station conditions, 45–6
    OTU accident, 116
    LMF, 170–71
Stevens, Sergeant,
    Brighton Refresher Course, 77–8
Stewart, Oliver,
    praise for Bomber Command, 2–3
    decorations, 64
    praise for the Avro Lancaster, 127
Stony Mountain,
    Manitoba, Canada, 183
Strachan, Hew,
    punishment as deterrent in combat
        motivation, xxiv
Stradishall, Suffolk,
    RAF Station, 174
Stratford-upon-Avon,
    Warwickshire, 124
Strong, Patience,
    poem by, 1–2
Stuttgart (Germany), 119, 148, 175
Summers, Pilot Officer, 96
'Suspendair' Disposal Centres, 77
Sutton, Sir Bertine,
    duties of trainees, 18
    letter from Arthur Harris regarding
        NCO captains, 32
    further letter from Harris regarding
        commissions for NCO captains, 33
    venereal disease, 48
    correspondence with Arthur Harris
        comparing RAF and civilian rates
        of pay, 60
    commissioning at OTU, 62
    commenting on discipline report by
        Joubert, 74–5
    morale and discipline, 78

second tours, 92
first tour extension, 93
possible disobedience of Harris, 94
letter from Harris regarding
    Canadian tour, 94
crew wastage, 111
LMF, 167
Swanton Morley, Norfolk,
    RAF Station, xviii
Syerston, Nottinghamshire,
    RAF Station, xviii–xix, 187
Sylt (Germany), 50–1
Symonds, Sir Charles,
    tour of EATS OTUs, 18
    recognition of unsuitable trainees, 18
    the crew, 31
    effect of praise on morale, 65
    self-imposed crew discipline when in
        the air, 75
    second tour crews, 89-90
    faith in aircraft type, 127
    effect of scrubs on morale, 131
    domestic troubles and flying stress, 156
    flying stress study and report, 157
    flying stress, 158
    praise from Stafford-Clark, 159
    praise for Stafford-Clark, 161
    waverers, 163
    squadron morale, 164
    sympathetic treatment of potential
        waverers, 165
    second tour waverers, 165
    deterrence value of "W"
        Memorandum, 166
    judgement of flying stress cases, 167
    criterion for judging LMF, 168
    meeting with Sir Archibald Sinclair,
        169–70

Tait, 'Willie',
    loss of second tour aircrew on
        operations, 89
    tour length, 89

talismans, 133–4
Tangmere, West Sussex,
    RAF Station, xvii, 24
Target Finding Force, 143–4
Target for Tonight, 4
Tatler, The, Air Eddies column, 2, 64, 66
Taylor, Flight Lieutenant, 178
Taylor, Pilot Officer, 173
Taylor, Sergeant,
    fatal accident at OTU, 116
Taylor, Sergeant,
    fatal accident, 174
Tee-Emm,
    first issue, 27
    accident poem, 27
    crew poem, 29
    MHDOIF, 83
    bombing poem, 135
    bombing justification, 150
Tempsford, Bedfordshire,
    RAF Station, xix, 100
Thompson, Group Captain, 165
Thornaby, Yorkshire,
    RAF Station, 174
Thorney Bay, Canvey Island,
    Essex, 121
Times, The, 12
Topcliffe, North Yorkshire,
    RAF Station, HCU, 176
Torquay, Devon, xx
tour, the, 85–98
training, 17–28
    10-hour cut-off point, 18
    EATS, 21–4
    tour-expired instructors, 25–6
Transport Command, 91
Treece, Flight Lieutenant Henry,
    poem, 44
Tripp, Miles,
    'wingless wonders', 71
    'friendly' bombs, 124
    'friendly' fire, 124–5
    talismans, 134

Turin (Italy),
  raid on, 3
  combat report, 102
Turner, Lana, 176–7

U-Boat patrols, 93
Ulceby, North Lincolnshire, 122
USA, 4, 18
  EATS, 21
  Johnny Johnson on EATS course, 22, 24
USAAF, venereal disease rates, 49
Usworth, Sunderland,
  RAF Station, 24
Uxbridge Receiving Centre, London Borough of Hillingdon, 24
  refresher course, 77

V-1 and V-2, 184
Vandekerckhove, Pilot Officer George, 39, 180–1
  lost on operations, 182–3
venereal disease, 47–9
  rates of infection, 48
  rates of infection, 49
  issue of prophylactics, 49
Vickers Valentia, 172–3
Vickers Wellington, 16, 38, 110
  (Wimpey) 116, 119, 127, 141, 144, 173–4, 176–7
Volkischer Beobachter, 126
volunteers, public adulation, 1, 9–14
  calibre of, 9
  recruiting advertisements, 10–11
  appeal for volunteers by Sir Archibald Sinclair, 10–11
  glut of, 11
  at holding units, 11
  reasons for volunteering, 11–14

"W" Memorandum, The, 163, 168
Walsh, J., 'chop girls', 133
Walters, Sergeant Sidney,
  fatal accident, 118

Warren, R., 120
Warrington "R" Depot, Cheshire, 167
Waterkloof (South Africa), 22
Watson, Pilot Officer, 38
Wattisham, Suffolk,
  RAF Station, 119
waverers, 18, 77, 161–71
Way to the Stars, The, 4–5
Waziristan (Pakistan; India before partition in 1947), 172–3
weather, the, difficult conditions for trainees from EATS, 24, 130–32
Webster, Flight Lieutenant,
  lost on operations, 178
Weicker, Pilot Officer, 107
welfare, 46–51
Wellner, Pilot Officer,
  lost on operations, 177
Wells, Mark, leadership, 71
West Malling, Kent,
  RAF Station, xvii, 104
West Raynham, Norfolk,
  RAF Station, xviii
Westerborg, Sergeant,
  lost on operations, 180
Wheeler, Eddie,
  reason for volunteering, 13
White, Harry, xviii, 104
Whittingham, Sir Harold, LMF, 167
Wiesbaden (Germany), 130
Wiggins, Sergeant,
  the cinema, 54
Wigsley, Nottinghamshire,
  RAF Station, 45–7, 51
Wilcox, Ronald, poem, 44
Wilhelmshaven (Germany), 174
Williams, Douglas Knight,
  training accidents, 28
Williams, Sergeant,
  fatal accident, 120
Williams, Squadron leader M.,
  lost on operations, 173

Williams, Thomas,
  first tour extension, 93–4
  Canadian aircrew, 95
Williams, Wing Commander Dennis,
  the crew, 31
  effect of scrubs on morale, 131
  domestic troubles and flying stress, 156
  flying stress study and report, 157
  flying stress, 158
Williamson, Sergeant W.A., 183
Wingham, Flight Lieutenant, 80
Withicombe, Flying Officer, 100–101
Wittering, Cambridgeshire,
  RAF Station, xvii, 105
Wood, Sir Kingsley, xxiii–xxiv
Woodbridge, Suffolk,
  RAF Station, 105, 183
Woodhall Spa, Lincolnshire,
  RAF Station, xviii
Wooldridge, John, 52
World at War, The, xx
Wratting Common, Suffolk,
  RAF Station, xviii
Wright, Flying Officer M.C.,
  praise for EATS, 21

Wright, Wing Commander A.J. (Jim)
  Wright, xvii, xix
  reason for volunteering, 12–13
  praise for EATS, 19
  captains of aircraft, 32
  pride in squadron, 41
  satisfaction with pay rates, 59
  promotion, 63
  decorations, 64
  assessment of Arthur Harris's
    leadership, 68
  combat, 112
  Harris's leadership, 186–7
Wuppertal (Germany), 103, 177–8
Wymeswold, Leicestershire,
  RAF Station, xviii, 19
Wyton, Cambridgeshire,
  RAF station, 26

Yatesbury, Wiltshire, Electrical
  Wireless School, 21
Yorkshire Post, Air Cadets article, 17
Young, Flight Sergeant, A.K.,
  lost on operations, 183
Young, Sergeant, 179